THE CHARLTON STANDARD

Lilliput Lane™

SECOND EDITION

By Annette Power

W.K. Cross
Publisher

The Charlton Press

Birmingham, Michigan ● Toronto, Ontario

Canadian Cataloguing In Publication Data

Power, Annette
            The Charlton standard catalogue of Lilliput Lane
2nd ed.
First ed. published under title: The collector's handbook
of Lilliput Lane cottages.
Includes index.
ISBN 0-88969-194-5

1. Lilliput Lane Limited - Catalogues.   2. Pottery, English -
Catalogs. 3. Miniature pottery - England - Catalogs.
I. Title.

NK4210.L5P68 1997   738.8'2   C97-930496-2

**Printed in Canada
in the Province of Ontario**

EDITORIAL

Editor	Nicola Leedham
Editorial Assistant	Jean Dale
Graphic Technician	Davina Rowan

ACKNOWLEDGEMENTS

I would like to offer my thanks to the many Lilliput Lane enthusiasts - both collectors and dealers - for their advice, help and support regarding the content of this book; my thanks also to Lilliput Lane Limited for an interesting tour of the Collectors Centre at Skirsgill, particularly the production process, which formed the basis for the section entitled "Discovering Lilliput Lane Cottages."

CONTRIBUTORS TO THE SECOND EDITION

Thanks must go to Stuart and Janette Allatt, Julian Best, Mrs. Brown, Mrs. Dalton, Bob Douglas, Mrs. Girling, Louise Irvine, Tony Klucking, Isabel Pearson, Eileen Walder and Stan Worrey for their assistance with the photographs and for their suggestions on the draft.

Special thanks to Graham Weeks for all his assistance in helping me obtain photographs and information.

Without the help of my father (Tom) these books would not have been possible. I would like to dedicate this edition to him with a big thank you.

PHOTOGRAPHY

Stuart and Janette Allatt, Mrs. Brown, Elaine David Studios (Isle of Wight), Donna Morgan, David Nairn Byers (Oak Lodge),Tom Power, Graham Weeks and Stan Worrey.

A SPECIAL NOTE TO COLLECTORS

The Charlton Press has an ongoing commitment to excellence and completeness in the production of all its reference works. We will consider editorial additions or corrections regarding colourways, varieties, or dating of patterns. Your help in providing new or previously unobtainable data on any aspect of Lilliput Lane collecting will be considered for inclusion in subsequent editions. Those providing information will be acknowledged in the contributor's section of this catalogue.

Please send your contributions together with your name, address and phone number to our editorial offices in Toronto:

The Charlton Press

Editorial Office
2040 Yonge Street, Suite 208
Toronto, ON M4S 1Z9
Phone: 1-800-442-6042   Fax: 1-800-442-1542

HOW TO USE THIS BOOK

The book gives individual details of the wide range of models produced by Lilliput Lane since the company began in 1982. The "cottage" models are in alphabetical sequence and for each model, details are given of the name, the collection it belongs to, a brief history and architectural details of the building upon which the model is based (if applicable), information about the Lilliput Lane model, the year that the model was introduced and the year it was retired (if the model is no longer current), the height, the number of versions produced, the backstamps carried by the model during its production period, and the current value in pounds sterling and Canadian and US dollars of the model. Following the cottages, there are seperate sections which contain the clowns, mugs, plates, plaques, signs and vans produced by Lilliput Lane, as well as a Land of Legends section.

STYLES AND VERSIONS

STYLE: A change in style occurs when a major element of the design is altered or modified as a result of a deliberate mould change. An example of this is Country Church Style One and Two.

VERSIONS: Versions are modifications in a minor style element, such as the chimney becoming shorter, as in Holly Cottage.

VARIATIONS: A change in colour, for example Bermuda Cottage or San Francisco House, is referred to as a variation.

PRICES

If the cottage is still in primary distribution then the prices listed are Lilliput Lane suggested retail prices in the three market areas. When the cottage is discontinued then the prices are those of the secondary market. The pound sterling and dollar prices are not straight conversions at currency rates; the prices are different because various factors can affect the secondary market values. For instance, a model which was only available in the USA may not command as high a value in the USA as it does in the UK (Seven Dwarfs Cottage is an example of this).

One final comment about secondary market values. A wide variety of sources have been used to establish the prices given in this handbook, and all of the prices given are for perfect examples which are not damaged; for damaged or restored models the price should be reduced accordingly. All of the prices are intended purely as a guide to collectors as to what they should expect to pay for a particular model. You will find models priced higher, you will find models priced lower; remember that a secondary market is just that, a market, and a market price must be determined by a buyer and a seller.

DATES

Regarding the production dates for Lilliput Lane Collectors Club models, it should be remembered that the dates of the Club year differ between the UK and the USA; the UK Club year runs from March to the following February, whereas the USA Club year runs from May to the following April. Whenever the months of introduction and retirement are mentioned for Collectors Club models the UK Club year has been used, for USA Club members the introduction and retirement will be two months later.

TABLE OF CONTENTS

PREFACE

Towards the end of 1985 I purchased my first Lilliput Lane cottage; it was Tuck Shop from the English Collection - Northern and it took pride of place in my display cabinet at home. I was fascinated by the detail and accuracy of the model and by the attractive colouring. Little did I realise when I made this purchase that I had just been bitten by the collecting bug, and after Tuck Shop, Castle Street soon followed, and then Scroll on the Wall, and then . . .

And so it continued; the collection grew and grew. I considered limiting it to buildings from one particular region, however that approach failed as soon as another model was introduced which I liked, but which came from another region. In short, I had become an avid collector.

Since that first purchase in 1985 I have gathered together a considerable amount of information about the cottages: the mould and colour changes to the models; special commissions; limited editions; and so on. Having discovered these various facts, I began to wonder whether the thousands of other Lilliput Lane collectors were aware of the fascinating and intriguing insights into the models that Lilliput Lane have produced. Did they know that possibly only two versions of Sussex Mill existed? Were they aware of the ladders and crosses on Adobe Village? Had they ever seen Penny Lanes? And how many of them had the series of clowns in their collection?

The more I thought about this, the more convinced I became of the need for me to broaden and amplify the information I had, with a view to publishing it. However, having decided to go ahead with the book it was then that the hard work really began, as I needed to obtain the information that was missing and verify the information that I already had.

To achieve these objectives I had meetings with numerous Lilliput Lane enthusiasts and collectors and we had many lengthy chats and discussions about the models, the versions available, and the related items which are now becoming collectable such as brochures and other promotional material. Those meetings also confirmed my belief that the wealth of material would be beneficial to other collectors.

I have endeavoured to make the information in the book as accurate as possible, and I hope that it will be of interest and benefit to both new and established collectors. However, there are some models where either I have not been able to obtain a photograph or where the information is not as detailed as I would have liked. If any Lilliput Lane collectors have any information, photographs or comments which can help to make this book even more comprehensive, thenplease do not hesitate to contact me at: The Collector, 9 Church Street, Marylebone, London, England, NW8 8DT.

Annette Power

INTRODUCTION

Discovering Lilliput Lane Cottages

One of the best ways to learn about Lilliput Lane past and present is to visit their Collectors Centre at Skirsgill, near Penrith, Cumbria. The lure of the company museum, showroom and studio tour, set in spectacular Lake District scenery, draws collectors from all over the world and they return home even more knowledgeable and enthusiastic about their chosen hobby. The centre is only open to members of the Lilliput Lane Collectors Club and advance booking is required for the studio tour.

Vernacular Architecture

The journey north from London passes through many of the areas celebrated in the Lilliput Lane collection and, if time allows, it is worth a detour to explore the charming Cotswold villages, with cottages built of the local honey-coloured stone, or the black and white timber-framed buildings of the Midlands, aptly described as 'Magpie' style.

Comparing the original buildings with the authentically detailed Lilliput Lane models helps illustrate how the different character of towns and villages have been shaped by the availability of building materials and the development of specialist local crafts, such as thatching or pargeting. Indeed, part of the fun of collecting Lilliput Lane Cottages is having a greater appreciation of vernacular architecture, described by company founder David Tate as "buildings built by the people for the people with the materials that lay around them."

Starting the Company

Travelling north-west into the Lake District, the landscape changes dramatically and hill farms, hewn from local stone, cling to exposed mountain slopes. Thousands of visitors come to this area every year to marvel at the majesty of the scenery and enjoy the climbing and water-sports, and it was here that David Tate decided to base his new cottage company in 1982.

Workshops were found at Skirsgill, near Penrith, in the converted stables of an old mansion house and somewhat basic accommodation was provided at Rose Cottage for David, his wife and two teenage daughters.

The old coach house at Skirsgill, now Gulliver's Pantry

The Collectors Centre

It is hard to imagine the Tate family's spartan existence arriving at the Lilliput Lane workshops today. When the new Collectors Centre was created in 1991, Rose Cottage was converted into a charming little museum and showroom set in a cobbled courtyard, complete with Victorian lamp-posts and a traditional red telephone box, which was rescued from certain destruction. The old coach house for the Skirsgill estate now forms Gulliver's Pantry, which provides welcome refreshments after a tour of the studios. Having started with 800 square feet of workshop space and six staff, the company now dominates the stable block and has expanded to several different sites in Cumbria with some 700 employees.

David Tate

Some collectors may be fortunate enough to meet David Tate during their visit as he is still actively involved in the running of the company, that is when he is not travelling the world with his audio-visual show, presenting the Lilliput Lane cottages to an ever-growing international audience. It was his energy and determination that got the company off the ground and he sustained its growth with a combination of talents, including a strong visual memory and exceptional engineering skills acquired in SRP industry.

His speciality was fibreglass moulding and he developed a new technique for moulding small, intricately detailed cottages in one piece, unlike traditional production methods in the ceramic industry which require sculptures to be assembled from several parts. He was so convinced of the potential of his new cottage models that he sold his house to get started and, despite constant cash-flow problems in the early years, he has succeeded in building up a company which has won the highly-coveted Queen's Award for Export and Achievement and the lion's share of awards at the international collectables shows.

In 1988 he was honoured personally with the MBE and since November 1993 the company has been publicly quoted on the London Stock Exchange - a remarkable catalogue of achievements in just 12 years.

Honeysuckle Cottage Museum

The results of his endeavours can be seen in the Honeysuckle Cottage Museum, which displays a wide range of Lilliput Lane Cottages past and present. The collection began in 1982 with fourteen cottages modelled by David himself. Many were inspired by the vernacular buildings which he had grown to love in the Lake District and his native Yorkshire, for example, Lakeside House and Dale Farm. Rural Hampshire, where he had lived for some years, suggested Honeysuckle Cottage and April Cottage.

A few models from the launch collection are now extremely rare as they were not made for very long, notably Old Mine, which was discontinued after ten months with only 200 pieces produced, and Drapers which was withdrawn at the same time with only 360 pieces made in two different colour treatments.

Technical Developments

Many modelling and colour changes were made to the cottages in the early years as David gradually improved production techniques as well as the body and paint formulations.

The first important development in 1983 was the use of glass-reinforced plastic moulds instead of the traditional plaster type and this enabled much more complex sculptures to be reproduced. Originally a basic Crystacel plaster was used for the body of the cottages, but this was too light weight and brittle and in 1984 he perfected Amorphite, a much harder and stronger material suitable for reproducing more intricate detail.

The paints also needed to be improved as the original colours were liable to fade in bright sunlight. After much experimentation, in 1984 David introduced new earth-based pigments which could be applied in colour washes, enhancing all the different textures of the model, and these were reformulated in 1990 to make them even more transparent and brighter.

Not one to rest on his laurels, David is constantly looking for new ways to improve processes and techniques and his Research and Development department is a hive of activity. For obvious reasons this building is not part of the studio tour nor is the Modelling department where the artists work on the future cottage introductions. However, the Lilliput Lane tour guides explain the nature of all the 'behind the scenes' stages before conducting visitors around the various production processes.

Behind the Scenes

David Tate and his team of artists travel many thousands of miles each year searching out suitable subject matter for the Lilliput Lane collection and they have built up an extensive library of reference books and photographs of vernacular architecture.

Once a specific building has been chosen for reproduction the detailed research begins. It is photographed from every angle and sketches are made on location to capture the unique atmosphere of the property and its surroundings. Back in the studio, the sculptor produces lots of interpretative sketches, emphasizing certain features, before preparing the final working drawing. The scale they work to for the finished sculpture is generally 1/76th of the original building, but that can change.

The sculptors work with a specially formulated wax and they manipulate this warm, malleable material into the basic shape of the building before carving the detail with an assortment of tools.

Dental instruments have proved very useful for achieving the right texture for tiny details, such as bricks or window panes, which are carefully cut into the walls. If the building requires roofing slates or tiles, these are cut from a thin sheet of wax and individually applied - a very time-consuming task.

Many pieces have elaborate gardens which will be 'planted' painstakingly with intricately sculpted bushes and flowers. The artists all study the different flower seasons to ensure their gardens are accurately interpreted.

Generally it takes the sculptors a minimum of two weeks to create a finished wax for the general range, complex prestige or limited edition pieces take much longer.

Touring Production

The wax original is destroyed in the mould-making process so there is no margin for error in the skilled tooling department. First of all a solid block mould is produced in silicone rubber and several resin copies or 'masters' of the original are cast. The master is then coated with a thin layer of plastic, and fibreglass is carefully laid on top of this to form a multi-part case.

Smoothing the base

After hardening the fibreglass case is removed in sections and the plastic is peeled away from its interior and the outside of the master model. Now, when the case is re-assembled around the master, there is a narrow gap which is injected with silicone rubber to form the finished mould.

Finally, a secondary case is made to support the mould during casting and, after thorough testing, all these tools are transferred to the production mould-making department to make lots of silicone rubber working moulds.

Visitors to Lilliput Lane can also watch the casting and de-moulding processes which have been refined over many years. Liquid Amorphite is poured into the silicone rubber moulds, which are supported by back-up moulds whilst they are vibrated at low frequency to remove air bubbles.

As the Amorphite is setting, the base of the cast is levelled. It takes just over half an hour for the Amorphite to set to the required degree and the silicone mould is then removed from the back-up and stripped from the cast. It is not as easy as it looks. De-moulding is a very skilled job and great care must be taken to ensure no tall chimneys or spires are broken off.

De-moulding

Fettling, where unwanted pieces of plaster are removed

Many of the craftsmen and women performing these delicate operations seem very young and David Tate is proud of the fact that the average age in the company is only 25. The various Lilliput Lane studios in Cumbria are major employers of youthful talent and, after intensive training and all the relevant work experience, many school leavers are promoted to responsible positions at an early age.

Before the casts of the cottages are completely hard, the fettlers will remove any unwanted remnants of plaster which remain in deep recesses and the piece is allowed to dry for 24 hours before being dipped in a coloured sealant. The colour of the dip is dependent on the original building materials and visitors can see samples of all the base colours and the different effects they produce. A more prolonged drying period in a de-humidifying chamber follows and the piece is then ready for painting.

For many visitors, this is the most exciting department.The carousels of specially formulated paint create a riot of colour and there is something magical about seeing the cottages come to life with the deft touches of the painter's brush. The intense concentration of the artists creates an intimate atmosphere, which is punctuated only by the gasps of delight from collectors as they see their favourite piece or a future introduction being decorated.

Painting

Each painter specialises in just a few different models which enables them to work as efficiently as possible. For reference, they have a master copy which has been created after hours of experimentation by the chief colourist. Sometimes more than thirty different effects are tried out in the Colouring department before a final choice is made.

During the various stages of production, there have been several inspections and sub-standard models are destroyed before they reach the final quality control department. The piece is scrutinised once again and, if satisfactory, is finished with green baize and despatched to Lilliput Lane stockists all over the world.

The Current Range

After an inspirational tour, most collectors want to return to Rose Cottage to buy souvenirs of their visit - a timber-framed and matched life size reproduction of an early Lilliput model,perhaps even a piece they have seen being decorated. The choice is endless as there are representative buildings from every part of the UK - magpie buildings and mills from the Midlands, remote farms and village schools from the North, thatched cottages and pubs from the South-East and seaside cottages from the South-West. Wales is represented by tiny slate-roofed cottages and chapels, Scotland by castles and tenements, and Ireland by crofts and village stores.

The Lilliput Lane studios have also gone further afield for inspiration in response to their growing international audience. In 1986 David Tate and sculptor Tom Raine drove around Northern Europe seeking inspiration for the German collection, which was followed by the French and Dutch collections in 1990 and 1991 respectively. Originally the national collections were only sold in their respective countries.

A log cabin and an adobe village were early, but short lived, introductions to a US series and in 1989 a new direction was taken when Ray Day, one of America's top artists, was commissioned to produce the American Landmarks collection especially for the thousands of Lilliput Lane collectors in the USA.

For collectors conscious of space and budget limitations, a range of miniature cottages, less than 3 inches tall, was added to the range in 1993. The cottages in the Classics collection, now retired, were all inspired by the picturesque village in Blaise Hamlet. Miniature cottages, blanketed in snow (early models have the snow as part of the mould, later ones have "icing sugar" snow applied after painting), have also proved very popular as Christmas gifts and no doubt many new collections will grow from these seasonal 'seeds.'

Building a Collection

Many Lilliput Lane collections grow from chance gifts and, as the delighted recipient gradually succumbs to the infinite charms of the cottages, new purchases follow, sometimes in quick succession! Other collections start from souvenirs purchased at famous British beauty spots and then the fun continues as holidays are spent travelling the country looking for the original buildings which inspired each cottage.

Some collectors become interested in cottages because of their personal associations, for example they have lived in a thatched cottage or been married in a church with the same name or appearance as a Lilliput Lane model. Whatever their starting point, all collectors share the nostalgia for the past which is evoked by all the buildings in the Lilliput range.

It is not unusual for very large collections to be created in comparatively short periods of time as the enthusiasm blossoms. Cabinets and display shelves are built apace and before long it is necessary to convert the spare room or the garage into a showroom! For those aspiring to form a complete collection, it is advisable to keep up with all the introductions to the current range as, once they are discontinued, they can become very elusive. Lilliput Lane regularly retire pieces from the range as David Tate explains, 'We care about collectors and we want to maintain the collectability of our cottages by controlling the numbers rather than just exploiting them.'

Some keen collectors will cross continents in search of retired pieces and stiff competition has led to some meteoric price rises for rare pieces on the secondary market. Auctions of retired pieces have been held at the Lilliput Lane Annual Fair and several specialist dealers are now catering for the demand for discontinued cottages on both sides of the Atlantic. The highest prices are paid for David Tate's first designs with very short production runs. Early versions of cottages with modelling and colour variations also attract a lot of interest. It is hard to believe when the hammer comes down on three- or four-figure prices that the early cottages originally retailed for around £2.50!

Nowadays complex prestige pieces start around £100 in the current price lists, so many collectors need to budget for these special pieces. However, a high price is not a deterrent for spectacular designs as was proved in 1989 with St Peter's Cove, the company's most ambitious and challenging sculpture. The limited edition of 3,000 pieces was sold out within six months and it now changes hands for considerably more than its issue price.

Special commissions with limited distribution, such as the Seven Dwarfs Cottage made for Disney World in 1986 or Mayflower House which was exclusive to the USA in 1989-90 or Out of the Storm (1997), are hard to find today, particularly in the UK. No doubt Counting House Corner, which was produced in a limited edition of 3,093 to mark the company's flotation on the London Stock Exchange, will also be very sought after in the future as the edition was oversubscribed by over 7,000 applications and it was only offered to UK Club members.

The Collectors Club was founded in 1986 and membership grew rapidly from 500 in the first month to over 80,000 members worldwide today. Subscribers receive the

Skirsgill, the home of the Lilliput Lane Collectors Club

informative quarterly magazine *Gulliver's World* as well as annual joining gifts and exclusive cottage offers. Some of the first Club editions, such as Crendon Manor and Yew Tree Farm, now command high premiums, and even past free gifts fetch surprising prices, in particular Packhorse Bridge and Little Lost Dog.

For a brief period the company dabbled in figurative models of clowns and these are now desirable along with the study of Gulliver, the hero of Jonathan Swift's travel tale from which the Lilliput Lane name was taken. Little advertising signs used to promote the company name in retail stores are now sought after and serious collectors are also seeking out all the early sales literature.

One very special collectors piece which all visitors to the Collectors Centre are eligible to purchase is the model of Rose Cottage, Skirsgill, where the Lilliput Lane story began. As only a small proportion of the worldwide Club membership has the chance to make this 'pilgrimage' to the Lake District and few would part with this exclusive souvenir of a memorable day, it is a much coveted collectable.

DATING LILLIPUT LANE MODELS

There are three methods of dating a Lilliput Lane model: the design of the label on the base, the design of the packaging, and the company backstamp.

Labels

The label on the base can be used to identify the approximate age of a model. In the early days from 1982 to 1984, two types of label were used, one had a brown border and the other had a blue border. In 1985 the design of the label was changed with the company name featured prominently in the centre of the label. The labels include the name of the cottage and the words "Handmade in Cumbria UK (or United Kingdom). In the case of the different series, a distinguishing mark or symbol is used. For example, The American Landmarks series has an American flag on the label, and The Irish Collection is indicated by a shamrock in a banner under the words The Irish Collection.

Packaging

The design of the packaging has evolved since 1982 and should the model still have its original packaging then this can aid or even confirm the age of the model. Should a box be required for a model, then it is possible to purchase one of the current boxes through the retailer for a small charge.

Collectors always wonder whether a model is more valuable when it has its original box and its certificate (see page iv for an example) with it. With regard to certificates, certainly a limited edition or Collectors Club model should have its relevant certificate to show its provenance, and in the case of numbered editions a certificate is vital. However, with the other models many of the older ones did not have certificates with them when the model was produced.

Obviously, in an ideal world every collector would like to purchase a retired model complete with its original packaging and certificate. However, as this is not always possible, each collector must decide whether the model they wish to buy warrants the price being asked, or whether they should wait until they can purchase a model which is complete with the box and certificate. A model which does have its original box and certificate certainly will have added attractions to some collectors than a model on its own.

Packaging, from left to right: 1983-1984, Mid-1980s, Mid-1990s, Classic Collection

Backstamps

Backstamps are of great importance when dating a model. To make it easier for the collector to recognize the backstamp on their piece we have assigned a letter to each year that the cottages have been in production. Therefore, backstamp A refers to a cottage modelled in 1982, backstamp B refers to a cottage modelled in 1983, etc. The backstamps for a particular year may come in several sizes depending on the size of the base of the model. If the backstamp alters in appearance during a particular year we have indicated this by using the year's letter followed by a number. For example, in 1992 their was a backstamp with little dots on it and this is referred to as J-1. There was also a backstamp without the dots and this is referred to as J-2. All backstamps have the year of production indicated, as well as the Lilliput Lane logo with the copyright symbol (©), with the excecption of the models produced at the beginning of 1982 which only have the words "Lilliput Lane."

The backstamps from late-1982, 1983 and 1984 are all identical in appearance to the one shown below.

Backstamp D

In 1985 and 1986 the backstamp shape was made more square in appearance. The Lilliput Lane wording was outlined (Lilliput Lane) for the first time.

In 1987 the backstamps took on a less structured shape, and this shape held for two years. 1989 saw the introduction of two backstamps. One was identical to the 1987 version but the second version (H-2) has a raised square border.

Backstamp F

Backstamp H-1

1990 was the first year that Lilliput Lane experimented with 'dots' on the backstamp. This dotted look also was available in 1991 and 1992.

Backstamp J

The words "Lilliput Lane" on the 1993 backstamp were more straight in appearance than in the previous years. This also holds true for the 1994 backstamp.

Backstamp L

A change in appearance of the backstamps took place during 1995 when the letters EEGG were added after the date. This version is referred to as N-2 and is identical in appearance to the 1997 backstamp shown below. EEGG stands for Enesco European Giftware Group who purchased Lilliput Lane in 1995.

Backstamp P

Backstamp	Issued	Backstamp	Issued
A-1	1982	K-1	1992
A-2	1982	K-2	1992
B	1983	L	1993
C	1984	M	1994
D	1985	N-1	1995
E	1986	N-2	1995
F	1987	O-1	1996
G	1988	O-2	1996
H-1	1989	O-3	1996
H-2	1989	P-1	1997
I-1	1990	P-2	1997
I-2	1990	Q-1	1998
J	1991	Q-2	1998

LILLIPUT LANE COLLECTORS CLUB

Details of membership are available from the following offices or from your local Lilliput Lane stockist:

UK (and all other countries not listed below)
Lilliput Lane Collectors Club
Skirsgill, Penrith, Cumbria CA11 0DP
England
Telephone: +44 (0) 1768 212700
Fax: +44 (0) 1768 212601

USA
Lilliput Lane Collectors Club
225 Windsor Drive
Itasca, Illinois
60143
Telephone: (630) 875-5382
Fax: (630) 875-5348

CANADA
Lilliput Lane Collectors Club
N.C. Cameron & Sons Ltd.
7550 Tranmere Drive
Mississauga, Ontario
L5S 1S6
Telephone: (905) 673-9200
Fax: (905) 673-7385

AUSTRALIA
Lilliput Lane Collectors Club
Locked Bag 30
Brunswick, MDC
Victoria 3056
Telephone: (03) 9381 2777
Fax: (03) 9381 9488

NEW ZEALAND
Lilliput Lane Collectors Club
P.O. Box 33-316
Petone, Wellington
Telephone: (04) 568 6619
Fax: (04) 568 6619

JAPAN
Lilliput Lane Collectors Club
Sanario Far East Company Ltd.
1-6-1 Osaki
Shinagawa-Ku
Tokyo 151
Telephone: (03) 3779 8082
Fax: (03) 3779 8050

FURTHER READING

The Cottages of Lilliput Lane, Deborah Scott, Portfolio Press Corporation, 1991

Gulliver's World, published quarterly by the Lilliput Lane Collectors Club

1998/1999 Collectors Club Models: Kiln Cottage and The Pottery

LILLIPUT LANE COTTAGES

Certificates

Deeds

AAN DE AMSTEL
Netherlands Collection

Aan de Amstel (On the Amstel) is typical of the buildings to be found in the city of Amsterdam, which takes its name from the first dam to be built across the River Amstel in the 13th century. Dam Square became the heart of the city and many important municipal buildings were situated there.

Apart from the colouring, Aan de Amstel is similar to De Diamantair. Aan de Amstel's roof and chimneys are white and De Diamantair's are grey.

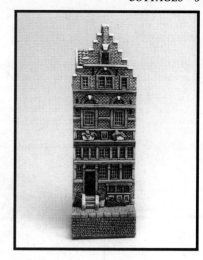

Size:	5 ¾", 14.5 cm
Backstamp:	J
Introduced:	1991
Discontinued:	1998
Variation:	De Diamantair

Description	Can. $	U.S. $	U.K. £
Aan de Amstel	90.00	60.00	30.00

ABERFORD GATE
Special Editions

Aberford Gate Is based upon the gate house to the Gascoigne Almshouses at Aberford in Yorkshire.

The model was launched in September 1993 at the Collectors Meeting at Harewood House, and was only available at that meeting and at the other special events and collectors meetings held from September 1993 to September 1994.

Size:	3 ½", 8.5 cm
Backstamp:	L
Introduced:	1993
Discontinued:	1994

Description	Can. $	U.S. $	U.K. £
Aberford Gate	200.00	125.00	100.00

"A CHERRY COKE - JUST THE PRESCRIPTION"
Coca-Cola™ Country Collection

Based on a shop in Silver Plume, Colorado (an old mining town of the 1870s), this model was designed by Ray Day and was produced under license from the Coca-Cola™ company for the Coca-Cola™ company. Although most of this collection is not advertised as a limited edition, the pieces are all individually numbered by hand. These resin pieces are produced in Ireland and are only available North America.

Size:	3 ¼", 8.0 cm
Backstamp:	N-2
Introduced:	1996
Discontinued:	Current

Description	Can. $	U.S. $	U.K. £
A Cherry Coke	130.00	100.00	N.A.

ACORN COTTAGE

English Collection — South-East

Acorn Cottage was among the original fourteen cottages that launched Lilliput Lane. The cottage, which is located not far from the London-Portsmouth road, would originally have been thatched.

Introduced in September 1982, an early version of this piece (buff and white in colour) either lacked a backstamp or had an A-1 backstamp. The cottage was restyled a few months later, when it became smaller and a boulder at the front was painted grey-blue. On the earlier versions the roof tiling was less refined and the foliage around the base was not as detailed and as well-positioned. By July 1984 it was remodelled again, now larger, the roof had more of a sagging appearance and the bolder to the left front of the cottage was removed, giving it a more refined appearance.

Front View: Version 2 (left),   Version 3 (right)

Side View: Version 2 (left),   Version 3 (right)

Back View: Version 2 (left),   Version 3 (right)

Version	Size	Backstamp	Intro.	Discon.	Can. $	U.S. $	U.K. £
1 - Cream	2″, 5.1 cm	A-1	1982	1982	1000.00	750.00	400.00
2 - Grey-blue	1 7/8″, 4.8 cm	A-1, A-2	1982	1984	225.00	150.00	325.00
3 - Grey-blue	2 1/8″, 5.4 cm	C	1984	1987	225.00	150.00	75.00

ADOBE CHURCH

American Collection

Introduced in October 1984, Adobe Church was one of the thirteen buildings in the American Collection. The series was not very popular, and all of the models now have a high rarity value. Only 475 pieces were produced of Adobe Church.

Size: 2 ¾", 7.0 cm
Backstamp: C
Introduced: 1984
Discontinued: 1985

Description	Can. $	U.S. $	U.K. £
Adobe Church	900.00	600.00	525.00

ADOBE VILLAGE

American Collection

Although it was only in production for a year, two versions of Adobe Village were produced. The original version had three free-standing crosses above the entrance door of the church, and three ladders resting against some of the houses at the various levels; the second version had only one cross above the church door and did not have any ladders resting against the houses. It has been suggested that the ladders and crosses were removed after transportation problems caused the metal additions to break. Only 225 pieces of Adobe Village were produced.

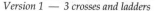

Version 1 — 3 crosses and ladders

Version 2 — 1 cross, no ladders

Version	Size	Backstamp	Intro.	Discon.	Can. $	U.S. $	U.K. £
1 - 3 crosses	4 ¾", 12 cm	C	1984	1985	1800.00	1250.00	725.00
2 - 1 cross	4 ¾", 12 cm	C	1984	1985	1500.00	1000.00	650.00

AFTERNOON TEA

American Landmarks

Afternoon Tea is based on a building in Carthage, Missouri built around 1810.

This Ray Day model was introduced in June 1995 in a limited edition of 1995. Exclusive to the USA, this piece was fully subscribed within the year.

Size:	6", 15.5 cm
Backstamp:	N
Introduced:	1995 in a limited edition of 1995
Discontinued:	1996

Description	Can. $	U.S. $	U.K. £
Afternoon Tea	750.00	500.00	450.00

ALL SAINTS WATERMILLOCK

Lakeland Christmas

This church was constructed in 1881, and is located in the village of Watermillock in the northern fells of Cumbria. There has been a church at Watermillock since the twelve hundreds.

Size:	3 ¼", 7.9 cm
Backstamp:	O-2
Introduced:	1996
Discontinued:	Current

Description	Can. $	U.S. $	U.K. £
All Saints	65.00	50.00	19.95

THE ALMONRY

Founder's Choice Collection

The Almonry, founded by the Bishop of Worcester at the beginning of the 8th century, is located in Evesham, Worcestershire. A large part of the monastery was destroyed in the mid-16th century under the rule of Henry VIII. Fortunately, a small section survived and still stands today. It was first opened to the public in 1957. The Almonry is managed by the Vale of Evesham Historical Society.

The Almonry is the first of a series of Founder's Pieces. It was produced from March to December 1996.

Size:	4 ¾", 11.0 cm
Backstamp:	O-2
Introduced:	1996
Discontinued:	1996

Description	Can. $	U.S. $	U.K. £
The Almonry	450.00	300.00	200.00

ALTE SCHMIEDE

German Collection

Alte Schmiede (Old Smithy) is one of the famous buildings in the Bavarian 16th-century town of Rothenburg on the River Tauber. Perfectly designed to accommodate the harsh winters of its region, the steep roof would play no host to heavy snowfalls.

Size:	4 ½", 11.5 cm
Backstamp:	K-1
Introduced:	1992
Discontinued:	1998

Description	Can. $	U.S. $	U.K. £
Alte Schmeide	180.00	120.00	55.00

AMBERLEY ROSE

Special Editions

Amberley Rose is based on a 16th century thatched cottage from the village of Amberley, north of Arundel, in West Sussex.

Introduced as a special events edition in March 1996, it was available until December of that year. The front door was available in a cream colour, but if a different colour door was required, a choice of colours were available for customers to choose from and were painted on the spot by the "in-house" painters.

Size:	3", 7.8 cm
Backstamp:	O-2
Introduced:	1996
Discontinued:	1997

Description	Can. $	U.S. $	U.K. £
Amberley Rose	225.00	150.00	60.00

AMISFIELD TOWER

Scottish Collection

This stone tower dates back to 1600 and is located in the Nithsdale district of Dumfries and Galloway, Scotland.

Size:	4 ¼", 10.4 cm
Backstamp:	O-2
Introduced:	1995
Discontinued:	Current

Description	Can. $	U.S. $	U.K. £
Amisfield Tower	70.00	50.00	19.95

THE ANCHOR

English Collection — South-East

This pub, once a timber framed house, is located in Wingham, Kent and is still open to the public. The horizontal lines between storeys at the front of the building is evidence that it was once a jettied building.

Size:	3 ¾", 9.5 cm
Backstamp:	O-2
Introduced:	1996
Discontinued:	Current

Description	Can. $	U.S. $	U.K. £
The Anchor	100.00	85.00	29.95

ANNE HATHAWAY'S COTTAGE

English Collection — Midlands

Located at Shottery, a mile to the west of Stratford-upon-Avon, Anne Hathaway's Cottage is in fact a 12-room thatched house. In the parlour is the uncomfortable bench, or settle, where Shakespeare is thought to have courted his future bride.

Based upon the timber-framed cottage, this model was produced in three versions. First introduced in February 1983, the original version, with the name of the cottage embossed in white on the front of the base, is the rarest. In September 1983 it was remodelled without the name on the base, and in September 1984 was remodelled yet again with a larger chimney.

Version 3 — Without Name, Large Chimney

Version	Size	Backstamp	Intro.	Discon.	Can. $	U.S. $	U.K. £
1 - With Name	2 11/16", 6.7 cm	A-1	1983	1983	2250.00	1500.00	825.00
2 - Without Name	2 11/16", 6.7 cm	B	1983	1984	450.00	300.00	200.00
3 - Large Chimney	2 5/8", 6.6 cm	C	1984	1985	200.00	125.00	95.00

ANNE HATHAWAY'S COTTAGE 1989

English Collection — Midlands

Anne Hathaway's Cottage 1989 should not be confused with its predecessor Anne Hathaway's Cottage. Introduced in February 1989, this model has a cottage garden at the front and has more warmth than its predecessor. With its windy steps and fall foliage the new colours help distinguish between early models of Anne Hathaway's Cottage and the 1989 version.

Size: 3 ¼", 8.0 cm
Backstamp: H-1
Introduced: 1989
Discontinued: 1997

Description	Can. $	U.S. $	U.K. £
Anne Hathaway's 1989	225.00	150.00	70.00

ANNE OF CLEVES

English Collection — South-East

This cottage is modelled upon the manor house in Ditchling, Sussex, which Henry VIII gave to his fourth wife Anne of Cleves upon their divorce after only six months of marriage.

Size:	5 ¾", 14.0 cm
Backstamp:	J
Introduced:	1991
Discontinued:	1996

Description	Can. $	U.S. $	U.K. £
Anne of Cleves	375.00	250.00	175.00

APOTHECARY

Victorian Shops Collection

This shop is based on the traditional Victorian Apothecaries. Apothecaries were originally formed as alternatives to customers who could not afford to visit a physician. Their windows were full of remedies, perfumes and toiletries displayed in magnificent containers.

Size:	4", 10.2 cm
Backstamp:	P-1
Introduced:	1997
Discontinued:	Current

Description	Can. $	U.S. $	U.K. £
Apothecary	125.00	90.00	37.95

APPLEBY EAST

British Collection

This railway station was built in 1861 on the Carlisle-Settle line. The line closed in 1983.

Size:	3 ¾", 9.5 cm
Backstamp:	P-1
Introduced:	1997
Discontinued:	Current

Description	Can. $	U.S. $	U.K. £
Appleby East	90.00	70.00	27.95

APPLEJACK COTTAGE

English Collection — South–West

Applejack Cottage can be found close to the famous village of Beaulieu in Hampshire. Built in the 18th century, the cottage is a good example of traditional cottage architecture featuring stone and thatch.

Size:	2 ½", 6.25 cm
Backstamp:	M
Introduced:	1994
Discontinued:	Current

Description	Can. $	U.S. $	U.K. £
Applejack Cottage	55.00	35.00	15.95

APRIL COTTAGE

English Collection — South-East

April Cottage is situated in central Hampshire, not far from the main road between London and Southampton. Built around 1600, the cottage still retains its thatched roof.

Version one is an all over light buff with pale pink foliage. It also has a thick base and a three pot chimney. The model was restyled in late 1982 and made slightly smaller. The base was more refined in appearance. The timbers and base are dark brown and the foliage is lilac. It has a three pot chimney. When it was redesigned in August 1983 the size increased again. This is the one most of us are familiar with. The obvious change is the switch from a three pot to a two pot chimney. The thatched roof and beams on the original version were less refined than the second version; also, the base was thicker and gave more of a 'cut' look than the 'finished' look of the restyled version.

Version 1 — 2 pot chimney

Version 2 — 3 pot chimney

Version	Size	Backstamp	Intro.	Discon.	Can. $	U.S. $	U.K. £
1 - 2 pot chimney	2", 5 cm	A-1	1982	1982	1100.00	750.00	400.00
2 - 3 pot chimney	1 7/8", 4.7 cm	A-1, A-2	1982	1983	975.00	650.00	350.00
3 - 2 pot chimney	2 3/8", 6.0 cm	C	1983	1989	200.00	125.00	70.00

ARBURY LODGE

Special Editions

Arbury Lodge is based on one of the gatehouses to the estate in Arbury Hall, Nuneaton, Warwickshire.

This model is only available to collectors attending the Lilliput Lane Annual Collectors Event (June 7th-8th, 1997). All models had to be pre-reserved with a deposit of £5.00 before May 16th, 1997.

Size:	Unknown
Backstamp:	P-1
Introduced:	1997
Discontinued:	1997

Description	Can. $	U.S. $	U.K. £
Arbury Lodge	N.A.	N.A.	110.00

ARMADA HOUSE

English Collection — Midlands

Built in 1588, the year the English defeated the Spanish armada, Armada House is typical of the buildings found in rural Northamptonshire, on the eastern edge of the Cotswold stone belt.

Size:	4 ¼", 10.5 cm
Backstamp:	J
Introduced:	1991
Discontinued:	1997

Description	Can. $	U.S. $	U.K. £
Armada House	200.00	130.00	70.00

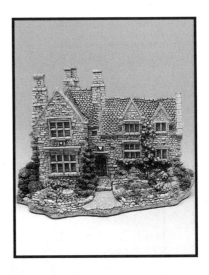

ASHBERRY 92

Special Editions

Ashberry is located in Minchin, Hampton Common, Gloucestershire.

This cottage was produced exclusively for Lilliput Lane collectors who had booked and attended the Lilliput Lane Dinner at the 1992 South Bend Show in the USA. This cottage differs from Cranberry Cottage in its lack of snow and it has the number 10 on the front door (a reference to the 10 year anniversary). 500 pieces were produced in total.

Size:	3 ½", 9.0 cm
Backstamp:	K-1
Introduced:	1992
Discontinued:	1992
Variation:	Cranberry Cottage

Description	Can. $	U.S. $	U.K. £
Ashberry 92	675.00	450.00	325.00

ASHLEIGH DOWN

Paint Your Own

Introduced at the Annual Collectors Fair held at Harewood House, Leeds. It was only available at fairs and events that featured a "paint your own" event. Ashleigh Down was retired a year later at the Chiltern Open Air Museum fair. "Paint Your Owns" are worth more unpainted.

Size:	3 ¼", 8.4 cm
Backstamp:	L
Introduced:	1993
Discontinued:	1994

Description	Can. $	U.S. $	U.K. £
Ashleigh Down (unpainted)	200.00	125.00	100.00

ASH NOOK

English Collection — South-East

Typical of the properties which would have originally been inhabited by the village artisans of Hertfordshire, Ash Nook is built from timber framing and in-filled with plaster and brick; timber cladding gives protection from the sharp winter winds blowing in from the east.

Size:	3", 7.5 cm
Backstamp:	H-1
Introduced:	1989
Discontinued:	1995

Description	Can. $	U.S. $	U.K. £
Ash Nook	90.00	60.00	40.00

L'AUBERGE D'ARMORIQUE

French Collection

L'Auberge d'Armorique (Armorique Guest House) can be found on the rugged north coast of Brittany, and is typical of the buildings in the area.

This model is the second largest in the French Collection.

Size:	5 ½", 14.0 cm
Backstamp:	I-2
Introduced:	1990
Discontinued:	1997

Description	Can. $	U.S. $	U.K. £
L'auberge d'armorique	250.00	170.00	80.00

AUTUMN HUES

A Year in an English Garden

This model is based on a cottage found in a Wiltshire village. The launch of this cottage introduced an interesting new concept to the collecting of cottages. The same cottage is portrayed to show the four seasons — Spring Glory, Summer Impressions, Autumn Hues and Winter's Wonder. Each cottage in the 4-model series has with it a stamp, and all four stamps can be redeemed for a certificate of ownership.

Size:	3 ½", 8.5 cm
Backstamp:	M
Introduced:	1994
Discontinued:	1997

Description	Can. $	U.S. $	U.K. £
Autumn Hues	120.00	85.00	40.00

THE BAKER'S SHOP

Village Shops Collection

Based on two buildings in the village of Broadway, Gloucestershire, built around 1790, The Baker's Shop was introduced in June 1995, along with the China Shop, to complete the Village Shop Collection. As with the other shops it was sold exclusively in the U.K. by the Guild of Specialist China and Glass Retailers during the first six months of production. The model is now in general release.

Size:	3 ½", 8.7 cm
Backstamp:	N-1
Introduced:	1995
Discontinued:	Current

Description.	Can. $	U.S. $	U.K. £
The Baker's Shop	120.00	85.00	34.95

BALLYKERNE CROFT

Irish Collection

Located in the Maumturk Mountains of County Galway, Ballykerne Croft is built firm against the Atlantic weather. With most crofters cottages up until the middle of the 19th century lacking windows and chimneys this would have most certainly been home to a wealthier crofter.

Ballykerne Croft is the first model in the Irish collection.

Size:	2 ½", 6.25 cm
Backstamp:	H-1
Introduced:	1989
Discontinued:	1996

Description	Can. $	U.S. $	U.K. £
Ballykerne Croft	100.00	70.00	45.00

BANQUETING HOUSE

Studley Royal Collection

Banqueting House is located on the Studely Royal Estate near Ripon in Yorkshire. The estate was created between 1716 and 1781 by John Aislabie and his son William.

Banqueting House was one of the five models introduced in 1994 as part of the Studley Royal Collection. The others include Octagon Tower, St. Mary's Church, Temple of Piety and Fountains Abbey. Banqueting House was limited to 5,000 pieces and was sold exclusively in the USA.

Size:	3", 7.9 cm
Backstamp:	M
Introduced:	1994 in a limited edition of 5,000
Discontinued:	Ltd. Ed.

Description	Can. $	U.S. $	U.K. £
Banqueting House	N.A.	65.00	N.A.

BARGATE TEA ROOMS

English Tea Room Collection

Bargate Tea Rooms is located at the entrance of the Longleat Estate, home of the Marquess of Bath near the village of Crocherton, Wiltshire. A lake was constructed just over 200 years ago and Shearwater Lodge (Bargate Tea Rooms) was built approximately 80 years after that.Today it is run as a full-time restaurant and tea room catering to visitors to the lake which is only a stones throw away.

Size:	4", 10.2 cm
Backstamp:	N-1
Introduced:	1995
Discontinued:	Current

Description	Can. $	U.S. $	U.K. £
Bargate Tea Rooms	180.00	120.00	56.95

BAY VIEW

English Collection — South-East

Bay View is typical of the many brick and flint cottages to be found on the North Norfolk coast by Burnham Market, overlooking Brancaster Bay.

Size:	2 ½", 6.25 cm
Backstamp:	E
Introduced:	1986
Discontinued:	1988

Description	Can. $	U.S. $	U.K. £
Bay View	275.00	175.00	100.00

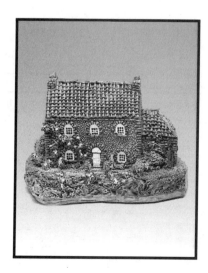

BEACON HEIGHTS

English Collection — Northern

Based upon a mock-Tudor house perched on a hillside in Northumberland, Beacon Heights is typical of properties built during the Victorian era when architects endeavoured to emulate the styles of earlier periods.

Beacon Heights was remodelled in approximately 1990. The noticeable difference is the increase of foliage now covering half of the first set of three windows. On the previous model it only covered a corner of the window.

Version 1 — Less foliage

Version 2 — More foliage

Version	Size	Backstamp	Intro.	Discon.	Can. $	U.S. $	U.K. £
1 - Less foliage	5 ¼", 13.5 cm	F	1987	1990	300.00	200.00	165.00
2 - More foliage	5 ¼", 13.5 cm	F	1990	1992	225.00	150.00	120.00

BEEHIVE COTTAGE

English Collection — Midlands

This cottage, located in the beautiful Cotswolds, is built form local limestone and is typical of the kind of vernacular architecture found within the region.

Size: 3 ¾", 9.5 cm
Backstamp: H-1
Introduced: 1989
Discontinued: 1995

Description	Can. $	U.S. $	U.K. £
Beehive Cottage	150.00	100.00	45.00

BEGIJNHOF
Netherlands Collection

Begijnhof (The Almshouse) was built to provide accommodation for the deserving poor, such as widows. The main house consisted of meeting rooms which were used by the Regents (the city's ruling class who were the almshouses governors), and behind the main house was a courtyard surrounded by small cottages.

Introduced in February 1991, Begijnhof is similar to De Pepermolen apart from the colouring. Begijnhof's roof is brown and De Pepermolen's is grey and white.

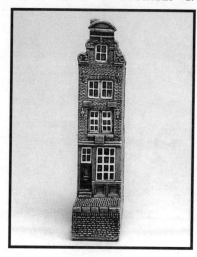

Size:	4 ¾", 12.0 cm
Backstamp:	J
Introduced:	1991
Discontinued:	1998
Variation:	De Pepermolen

Description	Can. $	U.S. $	U.K. £
Begijnhof	55.00	35.00	14.95

LA BERGERIE DU PERIGORD
French Collection

La Bergerie du Perigord (Perigord Farmhouse) is a typical small farm found in the Dordogne region of France. Built of stone on various levels, the ground floor provides storage room and shelter for animals, while the other floors are occupied by the farmer and his family.

Size:	5", 12.5 cm
Backstamp:	I-2
Introduced:	1990
Discontinued:	1997

Description	Can. $	U.S. $	U.K. £
La Bergerie	240.00	170.00	80.00

BERMUDA COTTAGE
Exclusive

Bermuda Cottage was a special commission by a company in Bermuda called The Britannia. Although the model was withdrawn in 1988 it was then re-issued in the same year. Bermuda Cottage carries a plain printed label with details of the cottage. It was produced in blue, pink and yellow with the blue colourway being the most difficult to acquire.

Size:	2", 5.0 cm
Backstamp:	D
Introduced:	1985
Discontinued:	1991

Variation	Can. $	U.S. $	U.K. £
1 - Blue Cottage	525.00	350.00	165.00
2 - Pink Cottage	375.00	250.00	140.00
3 - Yellow Cottage	375.00	250.00	140.00

BEST FRIENDS

British Collection

This quaint cottage, which dates from the late 18th century, is from the small village of Letcombe Basset, Oxfordshire. Letcombe Basset was famous for its watercress industry, and the cry "Basset Cress" was a familiar one at the Old Covent Garden Market.

Best Friends is available in the UK only through H. Samuel (a chain of jewellers), but is generally available elsewhere.

Size:	Unknown
Backstamp:	O-2
Introduced:	1997
Discontinued:	Current

Description	Can. $	U.S. $	U.K. £
Best Friends	35.00	25.00	9.95

BIRCHWOOD COTTAGE

English Collection — South-East

Located in Amberley, West Sussex (also know as the "artist's village because of its beauty") this "chocolate box" cottage was introduced in 1995.

Size:	3", 7.6 cm
Backstamp:	O-2
Introduced:	1995
Discontinued:	Current

Description	Can. $	U.S. $	U.K. £
Birchwood Cottage	80.00	55.00	25.95

BIRDLIP BOTTOM

English Collection — Midlands

Birdlip Bottom is an early 18th century thatched cottage situated at the foot of the Cotswolds in rural Gloucestershire in the location of Witcombe.

Size:	3 ¼", 8.0 cm
Backstamp:	L
Introduced:	1993
Discontinued:	Current

Description	Can. $	U.S. $	U.K. £
Birdlip Bottom	70.00	50.00	19.95

THE BIRDSONG
American Landmarks

The Birdsong is based upon the American Midwest roadside barn, which was traditionally used to advertise products to motorists. The barn was painted by Harley Warrick, who reportedly painted more than 20,000 barns in his 46 year career. Originally owned by the Birdsong family it is now owned by the famous rural American artist Lowell Davis. The advert was added on Ray Day's suggestion after he had visited the building.

This model was available only in North America during 1994, before going into general release in 1995.

Size:	3 ½", 8.5 cm
Backstamp:	M
Introduced:	1994
Discontinued:	1997

Description	Can. $	U.S. $	U.K. £
Birdsong	120.00	90.00	70.00

BLAIR ATHOLL
Scottish Collection

Built in 1269, the building was also known as Blair Castle. Blair Atholl, the ancient home of the Dukes of Atholl, is situated near Pitlochry in Tayside, Scotland. These Dukes were the only British subjects allowed to keep a private army. The official right was granted by Queen Victoria in 1845 (although the army had then been in existence for several years).

Early versions of the Blair Atholl model were patchy on the white areas of the building. This was corrected on later versions. Introduced in July 1989, Blair Atholl was limited to 3,000 pieces which were sold within three years.

Description	Size	Backstamp	Intro.	Discon.	Can. $	U.S. $	U.K. £
Blair Atholl	5", 13.0 cm	H-1	1989	Ltd. Ed.	750.00	500.00	275.00

BLOEMENMARKT

Netherlands Collection

Bloemenmarkt (The Flower Market) is one of the tallest models in the Netherlands Collection. The model is similar to De Zijdewever apart from the colouring. The basement door on Bloemenmarkt is brown while De Zijdewever's is red.

Size:	6 ¼", 15.5 cm
Backstamp:	J
Introduced:	1991
Discontinued:	1998
Variations:	De Zijdewever

Description	Can. $	U.S. $	U.K. £
Bloemenmarkt	90.00	60.00	26.95

BLUEBELL FARM

English Collection — Northern

Built in the 17th century, Bluebell Farm is located in the North Yorkshire village of Hanlith. The farm has a Yorkstone flag roof.

Size:	4", 10.2 cm
Backstamp:	O-3
Introduced:	1996
Discontinued:	Current
Variations:	First Snow at Bluebell

Description	Can. $	U.S. $	U.K. £
Bluebell Farm	320.00	250.00	99.95

THE BLUE BOAR

English Collection — South-East

Located high on the downs on the outskirts of Chievely, The Blue Boar is thought to have been built for two farm workers in the 16th century. The boar which stands outside the Inn is said to have been one of a pair of boars ordered from an Italian sculptor by Lord Ingilby of Yorkshire. Oliver Cromwell and his troops, on the eve of a battle, took one of the boars and left it behind at the inn when they stayed there on Saturday, October 27th, 1644. The other boar now decorates a drinking fountain in Ripley.

Size:	3 ¾", 9.0 cm
Backstamp:	O-1
Introduced:	1996
Discontinued:	Current

Description	Can. $	U.S. $	U.K. £
Blue Boar	120.00	85.00	36.95

BODIAM

Historic Castles of Britain

Although Bodiam, in Sussex, was built in 1386 to discourage French raiders from sailing up the River Rother, the castle was never put to the test as a stronghold. Instead, from the late 1400s, the castle fell into neglect until 1829 when it was saved from demolition. The condition of the castle improved steadily with Lord Curzon finally restoring it when he took possession in 1917.

Size:	3″, 7.5 cm
Backstamp:	M
Introduced:	1994
Discontinued:	1997

Description	Can. $	U.S. $	U.K. £
Bodiam	150.00	95.00	50.00

BOOKSHOP

Victorian Shops Collection

This shop is based on a building in Keswick, Cumbria. It was introduced in January 1997.

Size:	5″, 12.5 cm
Backstamp:	P-1
Introduced:	1997
Discontinued:	Current

Description	Can. $	U.S. $	U.K. £
Bookshop	100.00	75.00	29.95

BO-PEEP TEA ROOM

English Tea Room Collection

Located in Bourton-on-the-Water, Gloucestershire, this tea room was built at the turn of the 18th century and is still open to the public.

Size:	3″, 8.0 cm
Backstamp:	N-1
Introduced:	1995
Discontinued:	1997

Description	Can. $	U.S. $	U.K. £
Bo-Peep Tea Room	120.00	85.00	45.00

BORROWDALE SCHOOL
Lakeland Christmas Collection

Located in Crostwaite, Cumbria this school was built in 1879.

Size:	2 ½", 6.4 cm
Backstamp:	O-2
Introduced:	1996
Discontinued:	Current

Description	Can. $	U.S. $	U.K. £
Borrowdale School	55.00	35.00	15.95

BOWBEAMS
British Collection

Bowbeams is based upon a restaurant in West Tarring, West Sussex.

Size:	3 ¾", 11.25 cm
Backstamp:	P-1
Introduced:	1998
Discontinued:	Current

Description	Can. $	U.S. $	U.K. £
Bowbeams	320.00	180.00	89.95

BOW COTTAGE
English Collection — Midlands

Bow Cottage is situated in the Gloucestershire village of Badminton. The cottage, which was designed by Thomas Wright during the 1750s, has rendered stone walls which gently curve in a bow toward each end.

Size:	3 ½", 8.5 cm
Backstamp:	K-1
Introduced:	1992
Discontinued:	1995

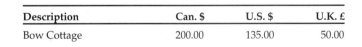

Description	Can. $	U.S. $	U.K. £
Bow Cottage	200.00	135.00	50.00

BOXWOOD COTTAGE

English Collection — South-East

Located in Minstead, Hampshire this small cottage was built around 1590. With its wattle-and-daub infills and timber frame this tiny building was probably used as a farm hands abode as the adjoining building is much larger.

Size:	2 ½", 6.4 cm
Backstamp:	O-2
Introduced:	1996
Discontinued:	Current

Description	Can. $	U.S. $	U.K. £
Boxwood Cottage	45.00	30.00	14.95

BRAMBLE COTTAGE

English Collection — Midlands

Bramble Cottage can be found in a tiny village in Berkshire, where a number of similar cottages can be found set around the village green and pond. All of the cottages were built during the 16th and 17th centuries.

Size:	3 ¼", 8.0 cm
Backstamp:	I-1
Introduced:	1990
Discontinued:	1995

Description	Can. $	U.S. $	U.K. £
Bramble Cottage	125.00	75.00	40.00

DE BRANDERIJ

Netherlands Collection

As gin had become a very popular drink towards the end of the 17th century, De Branderij (The Distillery) is the type of house that a distiller would have been able to afford.

Apart from the colouring, De Branderij is similar in appearance to De Wolhandelaar. De Branderij's roof is white while De Wolhandelaar's is grey.

Size:	5 ¼", 13.5 cm
Backstamp:	J
Introduced:	1991
Discontinued:	1998
Variations:	De Wolhandelaar

Description	Can. $	U.S. $	U.K. £
De Branderij	80.00	55.00	24.95

BRECON BACH

Welsh Collection

Brecon Bach can be found close to Pen-y-Fan, which at 2,906 feet is the highest peak in the Brecon Beacons. Typical of the small farmhouses in this region of Wales, Brecon Bach is constructed of stone and slate.

Size:	3", 7.5 cm
Backstamp:	E
Introduced:	1986
Discontinued:	1993

Description	Can. $	U.S. $	U.K. £
Brecon Bach	150.00	95.00	75.00

BREDON HOUSE

English Collection — Midlands

Located close to Stratford-upon-Avon, Bredon House was named after a well-known local hill which, in early days, was believed to be a magic or mystical place. Using a variety of materials, the house has a distinctive 'magpie' style.

Size:	4 ¼", 11.0 cm
Backstamp:	G
Introduced:	1988
Discontinued:	1990

Description	Can. $	U.S. $	U.K. £
Bredon House	300.00	195.00	110.00

THE BRIARY

English Collection — South-West

The Briary is one of the Gothic buildings which can be found at Stourhead in Wiltshire.

Size:	2 ¾", 7.0 cm
Backstamp:	H-1
Introduced:	1989
Discontinued:	1995

Description	Can. $	U.S. $	U.K. £
The Briary	125.00	75.00	50.00

BRIDGE HOUSE

Dealer Sign
Style One

Introduced in late September 1982 as a promotional 'dealer sign' for use by Lilliput Lane retailers, the inscription at the foot of the bridge reads: BRIDGE HOUSE LILLIPUT LANE. However, only six weeks after introduction, the model was replaced by a new flat-back version for use by retailers, and was also modified and introduced into the general range.

Size:	2 ½", 7.0 cm
Backstamp:	None
Introduced:	1982
Discontinued:	1982

Description	Can. $	U.S. $	U.K. £
Bridge House Sign	1800.00	1250.00	675.00

BRIDGE HOUSE

Dealer Sign
Style Two

The second promotional 'dealer sign' was introduced in November 1982 and was intended to stand flat against a wall, on the front was the wording: THE LILLIPUT LANE COLLECTION MADE IN THE BORDERS. In August 1983, the model was restyled when it was made thinner and the wording changed to: THE LILLIPUT LANE COLLECTION MADE IN ENGLAND.

Version	Size	Backstamp	Intro.	Discon.	Can. $	U.S. $	U.K. £
1 - Thicker model	4", 10.25 cm	None	1982	1983	1,100.00	750.00	525.00
2 - Thinner model	4", 10.25 cm	None	1983	1984	900.00	600.00	350.00

BRIDGE HOUSE

English Collection — Northern
Style Three

Bridge House spans Stock Ghyll in Ambleside, Cumbria. It was bought in 1926 by The National Trust. Bridge House was thought to have been built originally as a summer-house or apple store. Some reports suggest a builder wanted to avoid large land tax bills of the 16th century, and by building the house across the river only the footing of the bridge was liable for land tax. The inscription at the foot of the bridge reads: BRIDGE HOUSE. For the Dream Cottage Miniature version of this model see page 74.

Size:	2 ½", 7.0 cm
Backstamp:	None
Introduced:	1982
Discontinued:	1990

Description	Can. $	U.S. $	U.K. £
Bridge House	150.00	95.00	40.00

BRIDGE HOUSE 1991

English Collection — Northern
Style Four

Slightly larger and more refined than the original model, Bridge House 1991 was introduced in February 1991. On the side of the wall is the inscription: BRIDGE HOUSE 1991.

Size:	3", 7.5 cm
Backstamp:	None
Introduced:	1991
Discontinued:	Current

Description	Can. $	U.S. $	U.K. £
Bridge House 1991	30.00	20.00	8.50

BRIDGE HOUSE IN WINTER

English Collection — Northern
Style Five

This remodelled version has a special plaque at the foot of the bridge and a holly wreath on the door. It was available in Holland, Belgium and the U.S. as a gift with purchase. 2,225 of the 3,000 pieces made were allocated to the U.S.. New Zealand customers were able to obtain one of these cottages through the Collector's Club if they purchased another cottage in the last two months of 1995. New Collector Club members were put into a draw for the cottage, 50 were made available.

Size:	3", 8.0 cm
Backstamp:	None
Introduced:	1995 in a limited edition of 3,000
Discontinued:	1995

Description	Can. $	U.S. $	U.K. £
Bridge House	75.00	50.00	120.00

BRIDLE WAY

Collectors Club

Bridle Way publicized the craft of thatching and featured a thatcher at work on the roof. This cottage is located in Oxfordshire, and was built around the 16th century.

Bridle Way was only available to members of the Lilliput Lane Collectors Club for a 12-month period, and was never generally available.

Size:	3 ¾", 9.5 cm
Backstamp:	H-1
Introduced:	1990
Discontinued:	1991

Description	Can. $	U.S. $	U.K. £
Bridle Way	375.00	250.00	185.00

BRO DAWEL

Welsh Collection

Bro Dawel is typical of the cob and thatch cottages once found in Dyfed in the west of Wales; unfortunately, only a few of these cottages still exist in the less mountainous parts of the region.

Size:	2", 5.0 cm
Backstamp:	J
Introduced:	1991
Discontinued:	1998

Description	Can. $	U.S. $	U.K. £
Bro Dawel	45.00	30.00	15.00

BROCKBANK

English Collection — South-East

Set in the county of Surrey and originally a timber-framed, jettied building from the 17th century, in later times Brockbank has had walls built outside the timber frame on the ground floor, and then tiles hung to provide extra weather protection on the upper floors.

Size:	3 ½", 8.5 cm
Backstamp:	G
Introduced:	1988
Discontinued:	1993

Description	Can. $	U.S. $	U.K. £
Brockbank	150.00	100.00	40.00

BRONTË PARSONAGE

English Collection — Northern

Standing high on the moors at Haworth, Yorkshire, this Georgian house was once the home of the Brontë family. The model was originally known as The Parsonage. Early production pieces had window surrounds which were very thin and almost non-existent, whereas on pieces produced after a few months the window surrounds were noticeably thicker.

Version 2 — Thick surrounds

Version	Size	Backstamp	Intro.	Discon.	Can. $	U.S. $	U.K. £
1 - Thin surrounds	3 ¾", 9.5 cm	D	1985	1985	450.00	300.00	400.00
2 - Thick surrounds	3 ¾", 9.5 cm	D	1985	1987	375.00	250.00	100.00

DER BÜCHERWURM

German Collection

Der Bücherwurm (The Bookworm) is typical of the medieval buildings found in the ancient university town of Tübingen. Situated on the River Neckar in the Baden-Württemberg region of Germany, Tübingen, which was founded in 1477, is full of bustling, narrow streets running between attractive medieval buildings.

Size: 4 ¼", 11.0 cm
Backstamp: K-1
Introduced: 1992
Discontinued: 1998

Description	Can. $	U.S. $	U.K. £
Der Bücherwurm	140.00	100.00	45.00

BUMBLE BEE COTTAGE

British Collection

This thatched building of grey stone and white-washed walls can be found in Treworthal, Cornwall.

Size:	2 ¼", 5.5 cm
Backstamp:	P-1
Introduced:	1997
Discontinued:	Current

Description	Can. $	U.S. $	U.K. £
Bumble Bee Cottage	50.00	35.00	14.95

BURNS COTTAGE, ALLOWAY

Scottish Collection

This gardener's cottage at Alloway, 2 miles south of Ayr in Scotland, was the birthplace of Robert Burns. Born on January 25th, 1759, Burns is regarded as Scotland's greatest poet, and each year - on Burns Night - his birth date is celebrated by Scots throughout the world. Burns Cottage is now a museum.

Size:	2", 5.0 cm
Backstamp:	D
Introduced:	1985
Discontinued:	1988

Description	Can. $	U.S. $	U.K. £
Burns Cottage	200.00	125.00	90.00

BURNSIDE

English Collection — Northern

Based in the village of Glenridding at the top of Ullswater in the Lake District, Burnside was first introduced in November, 1982 and was also known as Burnside Cottage.

After slight restyling in 1982, when the model was made smaller and the backstamp was changed from A-1 to A-2, the colours of the roof and rocks are noticeably darker and the chimney pots changed from grey to sienna. The cottage was remodelled again in 1985 and backstamp was repositioned further to the right of the rear of the base.

Version	Size	Backstamp	Intro.	Discon.	Can. $	U.S. $	U.K. £
1 - Grey chimney	2 ½ ", 6.0 cm	A-1	1982	1982	1,300.00	900.00	425.00
2 - Sienna chimney	2 ¼", 5.7 cm	A-2	1982	1985	1,200.00	750.00	275.00
3 - Right rear backstamp	2 ¼", 5.7 cm	B	1985	1985	1,200.00	750.00	250.00

BUTTERCUP COTTAGE

English Collection — Midlands

Buttercup Cottage, which can be found in Gloucestershire, is a simple cruck-framed cottage built in the mid-1700s.

Introduced in February 1990, the cottage had a short production run and was retired in December 1992.

Size:	2 ¾", 7.0 cm
Backstamp:	I-1
Introduced:	1990
Discontinued:	1992

Description	Can. $	U.S. $	U.K. £
Buttercup Cottage	125.00	75.00	40.00

BUTTERMILK FARM

British Collection

A traditional farmstead, this 16th century building is located in Tivington, Somerset. Tivington is one of nine villages, along with thousands of acres of countryside, which forms the Holnicoate Estate. The National Trust was given the Estate in 1944 by Sir Richard Acland and has continued to preserve the traditional villages.

Size:	4", 10.0 cm
Backstamp:	P-1
Introduced:	1997
Discontinued:	Current

Description	Can. $	U.S. $	U.K. £
Buttermilk Farm	180.00	120.00	49.95

BUTTERWICK

English Collection — South-West

Butterwick is reminiscent of the type of thatched cottage that would have been built around 1830 in the North Devon and Somerset areas, when picturesque styles based on the vernacular were very popular.

Size:	2 ¾", 7.0 cm
Backstamp:	H-1
Introduced:	1989
Discontinued:	1997

Description	Can. $	U.S. $	U.K. £
Butterwick	85.00	65.00	45.00

BUTTON DOWN

English Collection — Midlands

Built around 1650, this little cottage from Gloucestershire has a roof in reed thatch with a sedge ridge.

Size:	2 ½", 6.0 cm
Backstamp:	N-1
Introduced:	1995
Discontinued:	1998

Description	Can. $	U.S. $	U.K. £
Button Down	45.00	30.00	13.95

BWTHYN BACH GWYN

British Collection

Bwythn Bach Gwyn, which translates as Little White Cottage, is based upon a tiny cottage in Merthyr Mawr, Wales.

Size:	2 ½", 6.0 cm
Backstamp:	P-2
Introduced:	1998
Discontinued:	Current

Description	Can. $	U.S. $	U.K. £
Bwythn Bach Gwyn	60.00	35.00	16.95

Photograph not
available
at press time

BY DAWN'S EARLY LIGHT

Allegiance Collection

By Dawn's Early Light is based on the Mukilteo Lighthouse at Point Elliot in Puget Sound, Washington.

Size:	3 ¾", 9.5 cm
Backstamp:	Unknown
Introduced:	1998
Discontinued:	Current

Description	Can. $	U.S. $	U.K. £
By Dawn's Early Light	N.A.	70.00	N.A.

LA CABANE DU GARDIAN

French Collection

La Cabane du Gardian (The Horsekeeper's Hut) is found in the wide, flat land of the Camargue in the south of France. The Camargue is famous for its colonies of flamingoes and its wild horses.

This is the smallest model in the French Collection.

Size:	2", 5.0 cm
Backstamp:	I-2
Introduced:	1990
Discontinued:	1997

Description	Can. $	U.S. $	U.K. £
La Cabane du Guardian	60.00	45.00	25.00

CALENDAR COTTAGE

English Collection — South-East

Calendar Cottage, located in Amberely, West Sussex, was built around the 17th century.

Size:	3 ¼", 8.3 cm
Backstamp:	O-2
Introduced:	1996
Discontinued:	Current

Description	Can. $	U.S. $	U.K. £
Calendar Cottage	80.00	55.00	25.95

CAMOMILE LAWN

English Collection — South-East

Therfield, winner on many occasions of the title Best Kept Village in Hertfordshire, was once owned by Henry VIII, who in 1541 presented the village to Catherine Howard. Camomile Lawn, a 17th century house close to Therfield, is a half-timbered building with white plaster in-fill, oak-framed leaded windows and thatched roof.

Size:	3 ¼", 8.0 cm
Backstamp:	M
Introduced:	1994
Discontinued:	1997

Description	Can. $	U.S. $	U.K. £
Camomile Lawn	130.00	90.00	45.00

CANTERBURY BELLS

British Collection

This 17th century cottage can be found in a little village on the edge of the northern Weald in Kent. Although not strictly Wealden in style, it does have the familiar jettied ends.

Size:	3 ½", 9.0 cm
Backstamp:	P-1
Introduced:	1997
Discontinued:	Current

Description	Can. $	U.S. $	U.K. £
Canterbury Bells	240.00	170.00	64.95

CAPE COD COTTAGE

American Collection

Cape Cod Cottage is a clapboard building with a tiled roof, typical of the buildings in the New England coastal areas of the USA.
Only 225 pieces of this model were produced.

Size:	2 ½", 6.5 cm
Backstamp:	C
Introduced:	1984
Discontinued:	1985

Description	Can. $	U.S. $	U.K. £
Cape Cod Cottage	1,100.00	750.00	350.00

CARRICK HOUSE

Scottish Collection

Carrick House is typical of the many houses to be found in the Lowlands of Scotland, south of Edinburgh. Originally the properties would have been built to house the workers on the laird's estate.

Size: 2 ½", 6.5 cm
Backstamp: H-1
Introduced: 1989
Discontinued: Current

Description	Can. $	U.S. $	U.K. £
Carrick House	55.00	35.00	15.95

CASTELL COCH

Historic Castles of Britain

Castell Coch (the 'Red Castle') is 5 miles north-west of Cardiff, overlooking the River Taff. Just over 100 years old, Castell Coch was built on the site of a ruined medieval castle. In 1865, Lord Bute (the Third Marquess of Bute) asked the architect William Burges to rebuild the castle.

The Castell Coch piece was remodelled in August 1994 and the tips of the turrets were modified, leaving it a simple cone without the knob.

Version 1 — With Knobs

Version	Size	Backstamp	Intro.	Discon.	Can. $	U.S. $	U.K. £
1 - With knobs	5 ½", 14 cm	M	1994	1994	500.00	350.00	175.00
2 - Without knobs	5 ½", 14 cm	O	1994	Current	200.00	120.00	56.95

CASTLE STREET

English Collection — Northern

Castle Street is typical of an area where development has centred around a Pele tower or castle. In the Middle Ages, the wooden buildings would have been ransacked and burnt by invaders, but other dwellings would then have been built in the safety and security of the tower.

Introduced in November 1982, within a few months Castle Street was restyled: the rock base at the rear was filled in and the company backstamp added to the rock; the street name was embossed instead of engraved; and the rock base to the left of the entrance, which was originally filled in, was cut away so that the moat was more easily seen. However, although the restyling took place in December 1983, the original mould was still used until Autumn 1984. Production of Castle Street was halted for 6 months in 1984, and in December 1986 the model was retired.

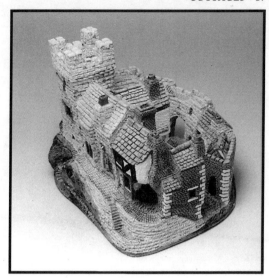

Version 2 — Embossed Name

Version	Size	Backstamp	Intro.	Discon.	Can. $	U.S. $	U.K. £
1 - Engraved name	5 ½", 14 cm	A-1, A-2	1982	1984	1,300.00	850.00	400.00
2 - Embossed name	5 ½", 14 cm	B, C	1984	1986	975.00	650.00	325.00

CATKIN COTTAGE

British Collection

An early Victorian gatehouse with an amalgam of architectural features from the Picturesque, Victorian and Classical styles, Catkin Cottage is located in Woolston, Devon.

Size: 3", 7.25 cm
Backstamp: P-1
Introduced: 1997
Discontinued: Current

Description	Can. $	U.S. $	U.K. £
Catkin Cottage	100.00	70.00	27.95

CAT'S COOMBE COTTAGE

English Collection — South-West

Cat's Coombe Cottage can be found in 'Thomas Hardy country' near Wool in Dorset. Hardy used his native county as the location for most of his novels. Cats Coombe Cottage is an example of the early 'natural' cottage design, where natural materials were used in the construction.

Size:	2 ¾", 7.0 cm
Backstamp:	L
Introduced:	1993
Discontinued:	1995

Description	Can. $	U.S. $	U.K. £
Cat's Coombe Cottage	125.00	95.00	45.00

CAWDOR CASTLE

Scottish Collection

Cawdor Castle, near Inverness, is well known as the castle in Shakespeare's play Macbeth. In its 600-year history, Cawdor has been extended and modified a number of times. Originally built and owned by the Cawdor family, in 1510 it passed into the ownership of the Campbells.

Cawdor Castle's production was limited to 3,000 pieces.

Size:	6", 15.0 cm
Backstamp:	I-2
Introduced:	1990 in a limited edtion of 3,000
Discontinued:	1994

Description	Can. $	U.S. $	U.K. £
Cawdor Castle	1,100.00	750.00	350.00

CHALK DOWN

English Collection — South-East

Located in Amberely, West Sussex, this cottage was inspired by a small 17th century thatched cottage known as the "studio."

Size:	2 ½", 5.7 cm
Backstamp:	O-2
Introduced:	1996
Discontinued:	Current

Description	Can. $	U.S. $	U.K. £
Chalk Down	45.00	35.00	14.95

CHANTRY CHAPEL

Exclusive

Located in Wakefield, parts of the building (mainly underground) date back as early as 1356. Many visible parts of the building date back to the 19th century. This is one of only four surviving chapels in England.

Chantry Chapel was commissioned in 1988 by an English company, Peter Jones China, and was only available through their stores. Chantry was remodelled in December 1988 due to breakage problems. The appearance of the spires are noticeably different, with those on version two being taller.

Version 2 — 3 cm spires

Version	Size	Backstamp	Intro.	Discon.	Can. $	U.S. $	U.K. £
1 - 2 cm spires	4 ¼", 10.8 cm	G	1988	1988	500.00	400.00	350.00
2 - 3 cm spires	4", 10.2 cm	G	1988	1991	450.00	350.00	250.00

CHATSWORTH VIEW

English Collection — Northern

Close to Chatsworth House (the home of the Duke of Devonshire), at Edensor in Derbyshire, is Chatsworth View. Built in the 19th century, Chatsworth View is an attractive lodge house. Timber framed on stone, one of its major features is its scalloped slate roof and stone chimneys.

Size: 5", 12.5 cm
Backstamp: J
Introduced: 1991
Discontinued: 1996

Description	Can. $	U.S. $	U.K. £
Chatsworth View	275.00	175.00	90.00

LA CHAUMIERE DU VERGER

French Collection

La Chaumière du Verger (Orchard Cottage) is a typical close-studded timber-framed farmhouse which can be found on the Normandy coast. Roofed with local thatch, wild irises are planted in a clay ridge to bind the individual reeds together.

Size: 3 ¼", 8.5 cm
Backstamp: I-2
Introduced: 1990
Discontinued: 1997

Description	Can. $	U.S. $	U.K. £
La Chaumière du Verger	120.00	95.00	50.00

CHERRY BLOSSOM COTTAGE

English Collection — South-East

Built around the 18th century and located in Barton Mills, Suffolk this cottage has lime-washed walls and a thatched roof.

Teething problems with the first models resulted in trees which had to be moulded and painted separately and then secured to the model.

Size:	3 ½", 9.2 cm
Backstamp:	N-1
Introduced:	1995
Discontinued:	1997

Description	Can. $	U.S. $	U.K. £
Cherry Blossom Cottage	150.00	95.00	50.00

CHERRY COTTAGE

English Collection — South-East

Cherry Cottage, located in the valley of the river Stour, is typical of the colour washed plaster, traditionally white, pink or buff, found on many of the buildings in Suffolk

Size:	2 ¾", 7.0 cm
Backstamp:	I-2
Introduced:	1990
Discontinued:	1995

Description	Can. $	U.S. $	U.K. £
Cherry Cottage	55.00	40.00	25.00

CHESTNUT COTTAGE

Christmas Collection

Chestnut Cottage is situated close to the village of Bibury in Gloucestershire.

Introduced in March 1992, a new, effective technique of 'icing sugar' snow was used.

Size:	2 ½", 6.0 cm
Backstamp:	K-1
Introduced:	1992
Discontinued:	1996

Description	Can. $	U.S. $	U.K. £
Chestnut Cottage	60.00	45.00	25.00

CHILTERN MILL

English Collection — Midlands

Chiltern Mill is a 17th-century post mill, which was pivoted on sunken poles and used for milling wheat and barley.

Introduced in July 1989, initially Chiltern Mill was exclusive to H. Samuel, the UK chain of jewellery stores. The model was later incorporated into the general range and available worldwide.

Size:	6 ¾", 16.5 cm
Backstamp:	H-1
Introduced:	1989
Discontinued:	1995

Description	Can. $	U.S. $	U.K. £
Chiltern Mill	125.00	80.00	55.00

THE CHINA SHOP

Village Shops Collection

This village shop was built around 1845 and is located in the village of Burford, Oxfordshire.

This model was generally available worldwide, but in the United Kingdom it was only available through the Guild of Specialist China and Glass Retailers for the first 6 months of production. After this time it went into general release.

Size:	3 ½", 9.0 cm
Backstamp:	N-1
Introduced:	1995
Discontinued:	Current

Description	Can. $	U.S. $	U.K. £
China Shop	120.00	85.00	34.95

CHINE COT

English Collection — South-East

"Chine" is a steep wooded valley leading to the sea, and "Cot" is a small dwelling. Chine Cot is typical of the sandstone cottages which can be found on the Isle of Wight.

Introduced in July 1987, the cottage was restyled in December 1989, when four windows were removed and bricked up (although it is still noticeable that the windows were originally there), and the doors became solid (originally the front and back doors had 'glass effect' panes). The colouring used on the steps at the front of the cottage and on the footpath was also changed, from grey to buff.

Front View: Version 1 — Grey Steps, Version 2 — Buff Steps

Side View: Version 1, Version 2

Version	Size	Backstamp	Intro.	Discon.	Can. $	U.S. $	U.K. £
1 - Grey steps	2 ½", 6.5 cm	H-1	1987	1989	150.00	100.00	75.00
2 - Buff steps	2 ½", 6.5 cm	H-1	1989	1996	60.00	40.00	25.00

CHIPPING COOMBE

English Collection — South-West

This model is inspired by the village of Castle Combe, Wiltshire. This village was the centre of the woolen industry in the Middle Ages. Chipping Coombe shows buildings such as Archway cottage, The Old Post Office, and a medieval gatehouse.

Demand exceeded supply of this limited edition (3,000 pieces) and orders were not fulfilled until the later half of the year.

Size:	5 ½", 14.0 cm
Backstamp:	Special Limited Edition
Introduced:	1995 in a limited edition of 3,000
Discontinued:	1995

Description	Can. $	U.S. $	U.K. £
Chipping Coombe	725.00	500.00	375.00

THE CHOCOLATE HOUSE

English Collection — Northern

The Chocolate House is based upon a stone cottage which can be found just off the Market Place in Kendal, Cumbria. Built in 1630, the building has been used for a variety of purposes, but today it is the only contemporary chocolate house in England, evoking memories of the mid-1600s when the first English chocolate shop opened, and solid chocolate for making the drink cost between 10 and 15 shillings per pound. For the Dream Cottage Miniature version of this model see pg. 74.

Size:	4 ½", 11.5 cm
Backstamp:	K-1
Introduced:	1992
Discontinued:	Current

Description	Can. $	U.S. $	U.K. £
Chocolate House	130.00	90.00	42.95

CHRISTMAS PARTY

Christmas Specials

Based on a Victorian lodge-house in a Derbyshire village, this model is only available from June to December 1997.

Size:	4", 10.5 cm
Backstamp:	P-1
Introduced:	1997
Discontinued:	1997

Description	Can. $	U.S. $	U.K. £
Christmas Party	N.A.	150.00	59.95

CIDER APPLE COTTAGE
Collectors Club

Cider Apple is based on a cottage found close to the Somerset village of Selworthy.

This cottage superseeds Nursery Cottage as the free cottage in the "Much Valued Customer Scheme." Collectors Club members who purchased £250 ($400 US) of current cottages were given this cottage for free. Receipts totalling the specified value were taken to a retailer in the special wallet provided in the members packs. There was no limit to the number of cottages a collector could obtain.

Size: 3 ¾", 9.5 cm
Backstamp: P-1
Introduced: 1997
Discontinued: 1998

Description	Can. $	U.S. $	U.K. £
Cider Apple Cottage	N.A.	N.A.	N.A.

CIRCULAR COTTAGE
Style One
Blaise Hamlet Collection

All of the cottages in Blaise Hamlet (near Bristol) were designed by the architects John Nash and George Repton, and were built around 1810. Circular Cottage is probably the most unusual design in Blaise Hamlet, with its sweeping semi-circular feature, a Dorset-type thatch and lean-to's running down from the main eaves.

Size: 4 ½", 11.5 cm
Backstamp: H-1
Introduced: 1989
Discontinued: 1993

Description	Can. $	U.S. $	U.K. £
Circular Cottage	175.00	125.00	80.00

CIRCULAR COTTAGE

Style Two
Classics Collection

All of the nine miniature cottages in the Classics Collection are based upon the buildings in the village of Blaise Hamlet which has already provided the subjects for the Blaise Hamlet Collection. Circular Cottage is an unusual design with a sweeping semi-circular feature.

Size:	2 ½", 6.0 cm
Backstamp:	L
Introduced:	1993
Discontinued:	1995

Description	Can. $	U.S. $	U.K. £
Circular Cottage	100.00	60.00	40.00

CLARE COTTAGE

English Collection — South-East

Based upon the thatched cottages to be found in the village of Clare in Suffolk, Clare Cottage is modelled upon a building which dates from 1658. The cottage has examples on its front and gable ends of the decorated relief plaster work known as pargeting. First used in Elizabethan times, pargeting is unique to this area of England.

Size:	3", 7.5 cm
Backstamp:	D
Introduced:	1985
Discontinued:	1993

Description	Can. $	U.S. $	U.K. £
Clare Cottage	85.00	65.00	35.00

CLAYPOTTS CASTLE

Scottish Collection

Claypotts Castle, which is now a well-preserved ruin, stands overlooking the Tay, near Dundee. Built in 1588, the castle was once the home of James Graham of Claverhouse. It was bought in the 1920s, in a derelict state, by Mrs. Wilson whose family used it as a holiday home. It is still run by the family as a guest house.

Size:	5 ", 13.0 cm
Backstamp:	H-1
Introduced:	1989
Discontinued:	1997

Description	Can. $	U.S. $	U.K. £
Claypotts Castle	100.00	75.00	45.00

CLEY-NEXT-THE-SEA

English Collection — South-East

This 18th-century windmill, which overlooks Blakeney harbour in Norfolk, is a well-known coastal landmark.

In the UK, this model (which was limited to a total of 3,000 pieces) was only available to members of the Lilliput Lane Collectors Club. 150 pieces were produced for a United States mail order company (numbers 50-200). The difference in these models can be seen in the boat to the left of the mill. The US mail order company version has a red brimmed boat, and in all other models, it is a yellow brimmed boat. Cley-next-the-Sea was fully subscribed by December 1995.

Variation	Size	Backstamp	Intro.	Discon.	Can. $	U.S. $	U.K. £
1 - Red boat	8 ½", 22 cm	K-1	1992	1995	1,500.00	1,000.00	650.00
2 - Yellow boat	8 ½", 22 cm	K-1	1992	1995	750.00	500.00	365.00

CLIBURN SCHOOL

Special Editions

Located in Cliburn village, near Penrith, this school was built in 1860 and closed in 1983. Cliburn School is one of the three rarest Lilliput Lane cottages (the others being Drapers and Old Mill). 64 pieces were produced for the closing of the school and given to the remaining 17 pupils, and the teachers. The rest were sold to former staff and pupils. The model carried its own special label which read: LILLIPUT LANE CLIBURN SCHOOL SPECIAL EDITION 1860-83 A GENUINE LILLIPUT LANE PRODUCT.

Size: 2 ½", 6.5 cm
Backstamp: A-1
Introduced: 1983 in a limited edition of 64
Discontinued: 1983

Description	Can. $	U.S. $	U.K. £
Cliburn School	4,500.00	3,000.00	2,125.00

CLOCKMAKER'S COTTAGE

Exclusive

This former cottage would normally have been found at the entrance of a large country estate. As estates became too expensive to maintain, the worker's homes would have been sold off.

Clockmaker's Cottage was only available through H. Samuel (a chain of jewellery stores) in the UK, and through Peoples Jewellers in Canada.

Size: 4", 10.0 cm
Backstamp: F
Introduced: 1987
Discontinued: 1990

Description	Can. $	U.S. $	U.K. £
Clockmaker's Cottage	375.00	250.00	190.00

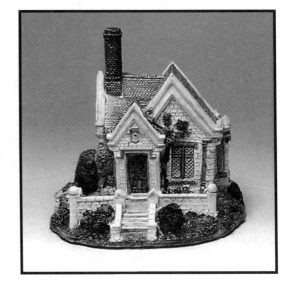

CLOVER COTTAGE

English Collection — South-West

Clover Cottage, a half-hip shaped thatch, is typical of many cottages to be found in Devon. The walls are of cob - a mixture of mud, straw and cow dung - which is then lime-washed.

Two variations of this cottage exist. The first was introduced in July 1987 and remodelled in 1988. The foliage and grass on Variation 1 were beige and orange, while on Variation 2 they were green.

Variation	Size	Backstamp	Intro.	Discon.	Can. $	U.S. $	U.K. £
1 - Orange foliage	2", 5.0 cm	F	1987	1988	75.00	50.00	65.00
2 - Green foliage	2 ½", 6.1 cm	G	1988	1994	75.00	50.00	35.00

COACH AND HORSES, THE

British Collection

Brunton Street in London is the locale of this traditional inn.

Size: 5", 13.0 cm
Backstamp: P-1
Introduced: 1997
Discontinued: Current

Description	Can. $	U.S. $	U.K. £
Coach and Horses	150.00	90.00	44.95

COACH HOUSE

English Collection — South-East

Introduced in September 1982, Coach House was remodelled in December 1982. The chimneys were remodelled; and the lattice work across the front of the building was changed from a criss-cross style to a distinctive tudor panelling Other noticeable differences on the second version are the lack of white window sills and the pathway which lay on top of the cobbles was removed. Version 1 lacked a backstamp and version 2 had either an A-1 or A-2 backstamp. 67 models of version 1 were produced prior to renovation. Major renovations occurred in December 1982. 870 models were produced in total.

Version	Size	Backstamp	Intro.	Discon.	Can. $	U.S. $	U.K. £
1 - Pathway	4", 10.5 cm	None	1982	1982	2,600.00	1,750.00	1,500.00
2 - No pathway	4", 10.2 cm	A-1, A-2	1982	1985	1,800.00	1,250.00	600.00

COBBLERS COTTAGE

English Collection — Midlands

Cobblers Cottage is typical of the cottages to be found in Northamptonshire. Built of mellow Cotswold limestone and thatched with reeds, the cottage may well have been occupied by a shoemaker in an area long famed for its leatherwork.

Size: 2 ½", 6.5 cm
Backstamp: E
Introduced: 1986
Discontinued: 1994

Description	Can. $	U.S. $	U.K. £
Cobblers Cottage	125.00	75.00	40.00

COCKLESHELLS
British Collection

This thatched cottage from Hope Cove, Devon was undoubtedly home to a fisherman.

Size: 2″, 5.0 cm
Backstamp: P-1
Introduced: 1997
Discontinued: Current

Description	Can. $	U.S. $	U.K. £
Cockleshells	35.00	25.00	9.95

COMFORT COTTAGE
Special Editions

Comfort Cottage was produced as a sales promotion piece, and was available only in those retail outlets who held in-house promotions during 1998.

Size: 2 ½″, 6.5 cm
Backstamp: Q-2
Introduced: 1998
Discontinued: Current

Description	Can. $	U.S. $	U.K. £
Comfort Cottage	N.A.	N.A.	N.A.

CONVENT IN THE WOODS
English Collection — South-West

Based upon a cottage in the grounds of Stourhead, near Mere, in Wiltshire, Convent in the Woods is typical of the many unusual buildings which were designed to enhance the large parks and gardens of the 18th century. With its gardens, lakes and temples, Stourhead is regarded as one of the finest landscape designs of that time.

Size: 4 ½″, 11.5 cm
Backstamp: I-2
Introduced: 1990
Discontinued: 1996

Description	Can. $	U.S. $	U.K. £
Convent in the Woods	300.00	200.00	85.00

COOPERS

English Collection — South-East

Typical of the cottages to be found in the forested areas of West Sussex, Coopers is built of local flint with a curved clay tile roof.

Introduced in February 1983, Coopers was restyled in October 1983, when it was reduced in size by about a quarter, and the appearance of the base became more pitted.

Front View: Version 1 — Large, Version 2 — Small

Back View: Version 1 — Large, Version 2 — Small

Version	Size	Backstamp	Intro.	Discon.	Can. $	U.S. $	U.K. £
1 - Large	3 ½", 8.75 cm	A-1	1983	1983	750.00	500.00	300.00
2 - Small	2 ¾", 7 cm	A-2	1983	1986	500.00	350.00	200.00

CORNFLOWER COTTAGE
Special Editions

Built in the 18th century and located in Cuddington, Buckinghamshire this cottage was only available at the annual fair in Chichester in August 1996.

The cottage was available to those who had reserved it with a £5 deposit when ordering their tickets to the fair. Two cottages were allowed per person.

Size:	3 ¼", 8.1 cm
Backstamp:	O-2
Introduced:	1996
Discontinued:	1996

Description	Can. $	U.S. $	U.K. £
Cornflower Cottage	250.00	175.00	120.00

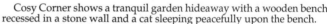

COSY CORNER
Collectors Club

Cosy Corner shows a tranquil garden hideaway with a wooden bench recessed in a stone wall and a cat sleeping peacefully upon the bench.

Introduced in March 1990, Cosy Corner was a free gift for members who joined the Collectors Club during the 12 months from March 1990 to February 1991, at which time it was retired.

Size:	2 ¾", 7.0 cm
Backstamp:	I-1
Introduced:	1990
Discontinued:	1991

Description	Can. $	U.S. $	U.K. £
Cosy Corner	150.00	95.00	80.00

COTMAN COTTAGE
Anniversary Editions

Situated in the north-west corner of Suffolk, Cotman Cottage dates from the early 18th century. Heavily timber framed, the walls have been plastered and then lime-washed.

As with all anniversary models, Cotman Cottage was only available for one year. For the Dream Cottage Miniature, please see page 74.

Size:	4", 10.0 cm
Backstamp:	L
Introduced:	1993
Discontinued:	1993

Description	Can. $	U.S. $	U.K. £
Cotman Cottage	375.00	250.00	150.00

COUNTING HOUSE CORNER

Collectors Club

Counting House Corner was based upon the early Victorian-style buildings reminiscent of Dickensian London.

Produced to commemorate Lilliput Group plc becoming a publicly quoted company, the production run was limited to 3,093, which was the level of the Financial Times Stock Exchange 100 Index at the close of business on the first day that Lilliput Group plc shares were traded (November 25th,1993).

Only UK members of the Lilliput Lane Collectors Club were allowed to apply for the model, and from the 10,270 member applications, 3,093 lucky names were randomly drawn. A further 365 pieces were also mounted on plinths and distributed to the new Lilliput Group shareholders who purchased on that day.

Variation 1 is mostly grey in colour with grey windows and frames. This cottage is mounted on a plinth, which was not taken into account when the height was measured. Variation 2 has a sienna roof with black window frames and doors.

Variation	Size	Backstamp	Intro.	Discon.	Can. $	U.S. $	U.K. £
1 - Grey windows	4 ½", 11.5 cm	M	1993	Ltd. Ed. 3,093	1,500.00	1,000.00	700.00
2 - Black windows	4 ½", 11.5 cm	M	1993	Ltd. Ed. 365	1,000.00	750.00	550.00

COUNTRY CHURCH

Style One
American Collection

Introduced in October 1984, Country Church was soon undergoing colour changes. Initial production pieces had a brown building, white windows, white bell tower, brown door and brown steps. The colours were then changed to white building, brown windows, brown bell tower and white door. Of the 500 pieces produced, the majority were in the second colourway; pieces in the original colourway are quite rare.

Variation 1

Variation 2

Variation	Size	Backstamp	Intro.	Discon.	Can. $	U.S. $	U.K. £
1 - Brown building	2 ¾", 7 cm	C	1984	1984	1,500.00	1,000.00	650.00
2 - White building	2 ¾", 7 cm	C	1984	1985	750.00	500.00	525.00

COUNTRY CHURCH

Style Two
American Landmarks

This typical American church, built in Shelbyville, Indiana around 1872, recalls memories of summer with the roses climbing up the red building towards the steeple. Sadly, the church was demolished in 1991.

Size:	4", 10.0 cm
Backstamp:	H-1
Introduced:	1989
Discontinued:	1992

Description	Can. $	U.S. $	U.K. £
Country Church	200.00	125.00	95.00

"COUNTRY FRESH PICKINS"

Coca-Cola™ Country Collection

Inspired by structures located along Old State Highway 335 in southern Indiana, this model was designed by Ray Day under license from the Coca-Cola™ Company for the Coca-Cola™ Company. The pieces in this collection, although not known as limited editions, are all hand-numbered. Made of resin and manufactured in Ireland, these pieces are exclusively available in North America.

Size:	3 ½", 9.0 cm
Backstamp:	N-2
Introduced:	1996
Discontinued:	Current

Description	Can. $	U.S. $	U.K. £
"Country Fresh Pickins"	200.00	160.00	N.A.

COUNTRYSIDE BARN

American Landmarks

This traditional American wooden barn was introduced in June, 1989, and was retired in December 1992. It was sold exclusively in the USA for the first year of production before being released worldwide.

Size:	3 ½", 9.0 cm
Backstamp:	H-1
Introduced:	1989
Discontinued:	1992

Description	Can. $	U.S. $	U.K. £
Countryside Barn	175.00	110.00	85.00

COVERED BRIDGE
American Collection

Introduced in October 1984, Covered Bridge was only available for 12 months. As with the other models in the American Collection, Covered Bridge was not very popular, and although the actual number of pieces produced is not known, it is believed that the model is quite rare.

Size:	2 ½", 6.5 cm
Backstamp:	C
Introduced:	1984
Discontinued:	1985

Description	Can. $	U.S. $	U.K. £
Covered Bridge	1,500.00	1,000.00	1,250.00

COVERED MEMORIES
American Landmarks

Based upon the well-known, historic wooden covered bridge (which is now a protected building in the USA), this model was introduced in March 1990. It was sold exclusively in the USA for the first year before being released worldwide.

Size:	3 ½", 9.0 cm
Backstamp:	I-1
Introduced:	1990
Discontinued:	1993

Description	Can. $	U.S. $	U.K. £
Covered Memories	300.00	200.00	90.00

COWSLIP COTTAGE
British Collection

Cowslip Cottage is based upon a cottage in Munslow, Shropshire.

Size:	3", 7.5 cm
Backstamp:	Q-2
Introduced:	1998
Discontinued:	Current

Description	Can. $	U.S. $	U.K. £
Cowslip Cottage	140.00	120.00	39.95

CRADLE COTTAGE

English Collection — South East

Located in the Pang Valley, Sulham, Berkshire, this cottage was built in the picturesque style in the 19th century by the vicar of Sulham. The remains of a Romano-British villa and farmhouse were found in the vicinity in the 1970s.

Size:	4", 10.5 cm
Backstamp:	O-2
Introduced:	1996
Discontinued:	Current

Description	Can. $	U.S. $	U.K. £
Cradle Cottage	140.00	100.00	49.95

CRAIGIEVAR CASTLE

Scottish Collection

Craigievar Castle, situated about 30 miles west of Aberdeen, is a small, high-turreted, fairy-tale castle practically unchanged since it was completed in 1626. Built by the Forbes family, the walls are harled in the distinct and unusual colour of pale apricot which adds to the castle's fairy-tale appearance.

Size:	6 ¾", 17.0 cm
Backstamp:	H-1
Introduced:	1989
Discontinued:	1991

Description	Can. $	U.S. $	U.K. £
Craigievar Castle	450.00	300.00	190.00

CRANBERRY COTTAGE

Christmas Collection

From Minchinhampton common, this Cottage can be seen clinging to the slopes of the Cotswolds. Built from golden-coloured stone and with a thatched roof, the cottage enjoys spectacular views across the surrounding countryside.

This model is the same as Ashberry Cottage except with snow, and it lacks the South Bend backstamp and the number 10 on the door.

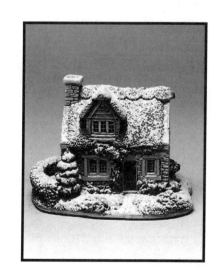

Size:	2 ½", 6.0 cm
Backstamp:	K-1
Introduced:	1992
Discontinued:	1996
Variations:	Ashberry Cottage

Description	Can. $	U.S. $	U.K. £
Cranberry Cottage	75.00	50.00	35.00

CRATHIE CHURCH

British Collection

The foundation stone of this church in Balmoral, Scotland was laid by Queen Victoria in 1893. The Royal Family has worshipped at this church ever since.

Size :	4", 10.0 cm
Backstamp:	P-1
Introduced:	1997
Discontinued:	Current

Description	Can. $	U.S. $	U.K. £
Crathie Church	90.00	60.00	24.95

CREEL COTTAGE

English Collection — South-West

Based upon a similar building in Polperro, Cornwall, this granite-built, white-washed fisherman's cottage has been tile-hung on the corner facing the prevailing wind to give added protection against the severe Atlantic weather.

Size:	2 ½", 6.0 cm
Backstamp:	M
Introduced:	1994
Discontinued:	1997

Description	Can. $	U.S. $	U.K. £
Creel Cottage	55.00	35.00	20.00

CRENDON MANOR
Collectors Club

Crendon Manor was based upon a late 16th/early 17th-century building in Long Crendon, Buckinghamshire.

Crendon Manor has the distinction of being the first model to be offered exclusively to Lilliput Lane Collectors Club members (who numbered around 3,500 at that time). Production was limited to 1,500 pieces. Each piece was individually numbered and carried a distinctive label in gold lettering.

Size:	4 ½", 11.5 cm
Backstamp:	E
Introduced:	1986 in a limited edition of 1,500
Discontinued:	1989

Description	Can. $	U.S. $	U.K. £
Crendon Manor	1,875.00	1,250.00	550.00

CRISPIN COTTAGE
English Collection — South-East

This cottage is located in Westmarsh, Kent and dates back to the 15th century.

Size:	3", 7.5 cm
Backstamp:	0-2
Introduced:	1996
Discontinued:	Current

Description	Can. $	U.S. $	U.K. £
Crispin Cottage	65.00	50.00	19.95

CROFTER'S COTTAGE / THE CROFT
Scottish Collection

Typical of the stone cottages found in the Highlands and Islands region of Scotland, Crofter's Cottage was introduced in September 1982 in a light grey version without sheep. In late 1982 it was renamed The Croft, and the backstamp was repositioned to the side of the cottage base. It was a slate grey colour and it also lacked sheep. The Croft was remodelled in July 1984 and the chimney pots were removed, sheep were added and the colouring was a very light grey. The backstamp was positioned at the rear.

Front View: Version 2 — Dark Grey   Version 3 — Very Light Grey

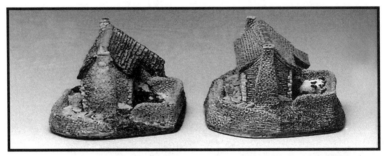

Side View: Version 2 — Without Sheep   Version 3 — With Sheep

Rear View: Version 2 — Without Sheep   Version 3 — With Sheep

Version	Size	Backstamp	Intro.	Discon.	Can. $	U.S. $	U.K. £
1 - Light grey	2 ¼", 5.75 cm	A-1, None	1982	1982	1,875.00	1,250.00	500.00
2 - Dark grey	2 ¼", 5.75 cm	B	1982	1984	1,100.00	750.00	400.00
3 - Very light grey	2 ½", 6.75 cm	C	1984	1991	200.00	125.00	75.00

CROWN INN

English Collection — South-East

Situated in Chiddingfold, Surrey, the Crown Inn is constructed of timber framing in-filled with plaster and brick. The main roof, pent roofs and gable end are covered with clay tiles.

Size:	4 ½", 11.5 cm
Backstamp:	G
Introduced:	1988
Discontinued:	1992

Description	Can. $	U.S. $	U.K. £
Crown Inn	275.00	175.00	100.00

CRUCK END

Anniversary Editions

Based on a cottage in Didbrook, Gloucestershire, Cruck End was built over 5 centuries ago. When the house was first built it would not have had a first storey or any windows, all these were added at a later date.

Size:	3 ¾", 9.0 cm
Backstamp:	O-1
Introduced:	1996
Discontinued:	1996

Description	Can. $	U.S. $	U.K. £
Cruck End	200.00	135.00	75.00

THE CUDDY

English Collection — South-West

Based on a cottage in Chiswell, Dorset this dwelling dates back to 1690 and would have been home to a fisherman. The lobster pots and boat outside the house confirm this.

Size:	2 ½", 6.0 cm
Backstamp:	O-2
Introduced:	1996
Discontinued:	Current

Description	Can. $	U.S. $	U.K. £
The Cuddy	45.00	30.00	13.95

CULLODEN COTTAGE
Scottish Collection

In the windswept north-east corner of Scotland many cottages similar to Culloden Cottage can be found. Built of thick stone, the single-storey cottage provides protection from the North Sea weather.

Size:	2 ½", 6.0 cm
Backstamp:	H-1
Introduced:	1989
Discontinued:	Current

Description	Can. $	U.S. $	U.K. £
Culloden Cottage	55.00	35.00	15.95

CULROSS HOUSE
Scottish Collection

With its crow-stepped gables, pantile roofs, outside stairways and decorative stone lintels, Culross House is typical of Scottish vernacular architecture.

Size:	3", 9.5 cm
Backstamp:	K-1
Introduced:	1992
Discontinued:	1997

Description	Can. $	U.S. $	U.K. £
Culross House	100.00	75.00	45.00

CURLEW COTTAGE
Collectors Club

Curlew Cottage was based upon a South Yorkshire dwelling which was built in 1885 by a local shepherd.
Introduced in March 1993, Curlew Cottage was offered at a preferential price to Club members who enrolled a friend; the cottage was not obtainable through retailers.

Size:	3", 9.5 cm
Backstamp:	L
Introduced:	1993
Discontinued:	1994

Description	Can. $	U.S. $	U.K. £
Curlew Cottage	225.00	150.00	190.00

DAISY COTTAGE

English Collection — South-East

Daisy Cottage is based upon the 17th-century single-storey timber-framed thatched cottages which were abundant in Hertfordshire.

Size: 2″, 5.0 cm
Backstamp: J
Introduced: 1991
Discontinued: 1997

Description	Can. $	U.S. $	U.K. £
Daisy Cottage	80.00	60.00	40.00

DALE FARM

English Collection — Northern

Dale Farm was first introduced in September 1982 and was light in colour and weight and had an A-1 or no backstamp. In the latter half of 1982 it was remodelled and the colours were darkened and the backstamp was changed to an A-2 version. The two early versions have 17 windows. The farm was remodelled again in September 1983. This version reduced the number of windows to 15, added a bush on the left side of the building and the backstamp changed to a B version.

Version 1

Version 2

Version	Size	Backstamp	Intro.	Discon.	Can. $	U.S. $	U.K. £
1 - 17 windows	2 ¼″, 5.7 cm	A-1, None	1982	1982	2,250.00	1,500.00	575.00
2 - 17 windows	2 ¼″, 5.7 cm	A-2	1982	1983	1,500.00	1,000.00	400.00
3 - 15 windows	2 ¼″, 5.4 cm	B	1983	1986	1,200.00	750.00	325.00

DALE HEAD

English Collection — Northern

Built from local York stone (which is a warm, yellow sandstone), Dale Head is typical of the farms and buildings to be found in Yorkshire.

Size:	2 ¾″, 7.0 cm
Backstamp:	E
Introduced:	1986
Discontinued:	1988

Description	Can. $	U.S. $	U.K. £
Dale Head	300.00	200.00	95.00

DALE HOUSE

English Collection — Northern

The original version of Dale House, which was introduced in September 1982, was sculpted by David Tate, the founder of Lilliput Lane. In September 1983 it was remodelled in a more detailed style: the windows and doorways were larger and better proportioned; the stairway was wider and had fewer steps; at the top of the steps a window was added parallel to the door; the ivy/foliage at the front of the building was extended up to the top of the first floor window; and more foliage was added at the rear of the building. As well as these changes, the restyled version was also a third larger in size than the original.

Version	Size	Backstamp	Intro.	Discon.	Can. $	U.S. $	U.K. £
1 - Small windows	2 ½″, 6 cm	A-1, A-2, None	1982	1983	2,250.00	1,500.00	415.00
2 - Large windows	2 ¾″, 7 cm	C	1983	1996	1,500.00	1,000.00	315.00

THE DALESMAN

The English Collection — Northern

The Dalesman is based on a popular pub, "The Foresters Arm," found in Carlton-in-Coverdale, North Yorkshire. Originally used as a coaching inn in the mid 16th century, the inn has been used as a pub since the beginning of the 18th century.

Size:	3 ¾, 9.5 cm
Backstamp:	O-2
Introduced:	1996
Discontinued:	Current

Description	Can. $	U.S. $	U.K. £
The Dalesman	120.00	95.00	36.95

DAYDREAMS

An American Journey

This model was inspired by the Smith Bridge, built in 1887, which spans the Flatrock River in Rush County, Indiana.

Size:	3 1/8", 8.0 cm
Backstamp:	P-1
Introduced:	1997
Discontinued:	Current

Description	Can. $	U.S. $	U.K. £
Daydreams	N.A.	75.00	34.95

DEER PARK HALL

Christmas Specials

Standing high on the East Sussex Downs, Deer Park Hall has a sturdy oak frame in-filled with herring-bone brickwork.
This was the first Christmas model to be produced.

Size:	5 ¼", 13.0 cm
Backstamp:	G
Introduced:	1988
Discontinued:	1989

Description	Can. $	U.S. $	U.K. £
Deer Park Hall	425.00	75.00	190.00

DERWENT-LE-DALE

English Collection — Northern

An example of an 18th century cottage building, Derwent-le-Dale, is a thatched limestone cottage situated on a tributary of the River Derwent.

Size:	2 ¾", 7.0 cm
Backstamp:	K-1
Introduced:	1992
Discontinued:	Current

Description	Can. $	U.S. $	U.K. £
Derwent-Le-Dale	80.00	55.00	25.95

DEVON LEIGH

British Collection

This cob cottage hails from a little village near Kingsbridge, Devon.

Size:	3 ½", 8.5 cm
Backstamp:	P-1
Introduced:	1997
Discontinued:	Current

Description	Can. $	U.S. $	U.K. £
Devon Leigh	140.00	80.00	39.95

DIAL COTTAGE

Style One
Blaise Hamlet Collection/
English Collection — South-West

Dial Cottage is unique amongst the buildings in Blaise Hamlet, near Bristol, in that it is the only one where brick has been conspicuously used in the main wall.

Initially one of the nine cottages which made up the Blaise Hamlet Collection, in 1994 Dial Cottage and the other five Blaise Hamlet cottages were transferred to the English Collection — South-West.

Size:	4 ½", 11.0 cm
Backstamp:	I-1
Introduced:	1990
Discontinued:	1995

Description	Can. $	U.S. $	U.K. £
Dial Cottage	225.00	150.00	70.00

DIAL COTTAGE

Style Two
Classics Collection

Taking its name from the focal point of the village green —
a water pump and sun dial — Dial Cottage, in Blaise Hamlet,
near Bristol, was designed by John Nash and George Repton.

Size: 2 ½", 6.0 cm
Backstamp: L
Introduced: 1993
Discontinued: 1995

Description	Can. $	U.S. $	U.K. £
Dial Cottage	150.00	95.00	40.00

DE DIAMANTAIR

Netherlands Collection

This large house shows the wealth gained from one of
Amsterdam's most famous industries — diamonds. The
Amsterdam diamond industry has always been dominated by
the city's Jewish residents. In 1748 about 600 Jewish families
were engaged in the trade, but after 1870 when diamonds were
being shipped in from South Africa the number increased to
over 3,000.

De Diamantair (The Diamond Merchant), is similar to Aan
de Amstel apart from the colouring. The roof on De Diamantiar
is grey and the roof on Aan de Amstel is white.

Size: 5 ¾", 14.5 cm
Backstamp: J
Introduced: 1991
Discontinued: 1998
Variation: Aan de Amstel

Description	Can. $	U.S. $	U.K. £
De Diamantair	90.00	60.00	25.00

DIAMOND COTTAGE

Style One
Blaise Hamlet Collection

Situated in Blaise Hamlet, Diamond Cottage has a very geometric design, topped by tiles of stone and the type of chimney normally seen on old manor houses. The architects of Blaise Hamlet — John Nash and George Repton — had special bricks moulded for this and the other cottages in the village.

Size:	4 ¾", 12.0 cm
Backstamp:	H-1
Introduced:	1989
Discontinued:	1993

Description	Can. $	U.S. $	U.K. £
Diamond Cottage	275.00	175.00	80.00

DIAMOND COTTAGE

Style Two
Classics Collection

Based upon the model previously issued as part of the Blaise Hamlet Collection, this Classics Collection cottage is a miniature version of its predecessor.

Size:	2 ½", 6.0 cm
Backstamp:	L
Introduced:	1993
Discontinued:	1995

Description	Can. $	U.S. $	U.K. £
Diamond Cottage	150.00	95.00	40.00

DOG DAYS OF SUMMER

An American Journey

This model was inspired by a Kirbyville, Missouri farm.

Size:	2 ½", 6.5 cm
Backstamp:	P-2
Introduced:	1997
Discontinued:	Current

Description	Can. $	U.S. $	U.K. £
Dog Days of Summer	N.A.	55.00	25.95

DONEGAL COTTAGE

Irish Collection

Donegal Cottage can be found on the north-west coast of Ireland. With walls built of stone, mud and limewash, and thatched with marram grass, the building stands up well to the fierce Atlantic weather.

Slight changes occurred to the model in the late 1980s when it was made more refined. The most obvious difference is in the colouring. The earlier variation had dark blue-grey windows and a slate grey path to the front. The second variation had light grey-blue windows and a buff pathway and lighter sienna doors.

Variation	Size	Backstamp	Intro.	Discon.	Can. $	U.S. $	U.K. £
1 - Grey pathway	2", 5 cm	F	1987	1989	125.00	75.00	65.00
2 - Buff pathway	2", 5 cm	F	c.1989	1992	100.00	50.00	40.00

DORMOUSE COTTAGE

Special Editions

Located in Inberrow, Worcestershire, this cottage was available at Special Events during 1997. The front door of Dormouse Cottage was available in a standard cream/off white, but the customer could choose another colour and this would then be painted by one of the in-house painters at the event.

Size:	3 ½", 8.5 cm
Backstamp:	P-1
Introduced:	1997
Discontinued:	1997

Description	Can. $	U.S. $	U.K. £
Dormouse Cottage	N.A.	N.A.	N.A.

DOUBLE COTTAGE

Style One
English Collection — South-West

Originally designed by John Nash and George Repton, and built in 1810 by John Scandrett Harford, Double Cottage stands at one end of Blaise Hamlet village green. The largest of the buildings in the hamlet, the cottage was originally designed as two dwellings, and the different window styles show the two parts of the building.

Size:	5", 12.5 cm
Backstamp:	J
Introduced:	1991
Discontinued:	1996

Description	Can. $	U.S. $	U.K. £
Double Cottage	375.00	250.00	75.00

DOUBLE COTTAGE

Style Two
Classics Collection

A miniature version based upon the larger model of Double Cottage, this cottage as well as the others in the Classics Collection can be seen at Blaise Hamlet, Hewbury, near Bristol.

Size:	2 ½", 6.0 cm
Backstamp:	L
Introduced:	1993
Discontinued:	1995

Description	Can. $	U.S. $	U.K. £
Double Cottage	150.00	100.00	50.00

DOVE COTTAGE

English Collection — Northern

Prior to 1793 this cottage was an inn called The Dove and Olive. Renowned as the home of William Wordsworth, Dove Cottage at Grasmere in the Lake District was built in the early 17th century using local materials, including green Westmorland slate for the roof. The Cottage is now a museum dedicated to the life of Wordsworth, who wrote most of his major works whilst living there from 1799-1810.

Introduced in February 1983, Dove Cottage was restyled in September 1983, when the embossed name across the front of the base was removed.

Version 1

Version 2

Version	Size	Backstamp	Intro.	Discon.	Can. $	U.S. $	U.K. £
1 - With name	2 ½", 6 cm	A-1	1983	1983	1,900.00	1,250.00	450.00
2 - Without name	2 ½", 6 cm	B, C	1983	1988	200.00	125.00	80.00

DOVECOT

Collectors Club

Based upon a building in the south-west of England, Dovecot was modelled complete with white doves.

Dovecot was the joining gift for members of the Collectors Club from March 1989 to February 1990 (the fourth year of the Club).

Size:	3", 7.5 cm
Backstamp:	H-1
Introduced:	1989
Discontinued:	1990

Description	Can. $	U.S. $	U.K. £
Dovecot	200.00	125.00	80.00

DOVETAILS

English Collection — Northern

Based upon a building in the centre of Ilkley, in Yorkshire, Dovetails was originally a school. Built in 1635, the building was used as a school until 1869, when it was sold to a cabinetmaker. Having been used for a variety of purposes since the cabinetmaker left the building, it is today an antique shop.

Size:	3 ¼", 8.0 cm
Backstamp:	J
Introduced:	1991
Discontinued:	1996

Description	Can. $	U.S. $	U.K. £
Dovetails	100.00	65.00	35.00

DRAPERS

English Collection — Midlands

Located in Lincoln, and known as "The Jews House," this building was originally built in the 12th century and a flourishing Jewish community would have lived in and around the area.

One of the rarest models produced by Lilliput Lane, Drapers was introduced in September 1982. On the original version, there is a window to the left side wall. When it was remodelled in late 1982 the window was removed. Colour variations of Drapers have come on the market. Some are beige (probably first version), some have beige-yellow windows and some have red windows. Only 360 pieces had been produced when Drapers was retired.

Version	Size	Backstamp	Intro.	Discon.	Can. $	U.S. $	U.K. £
1 - Without windows	2 ¾", 7 cm	A-1	1982	1982	5,250.00	3,500.00	1,625.00
2 - With windows	2 ¾", 7 cm	A-1	1982	1983	4,500.00	3,000.00	1,350.00

DREAM COTTAGES
Exclusive Editions

These tiny cottages were produced for Lilliput Lane's sister company, Hamilton Gallery. They are miniature versions of existing Lilliput Lane models. Cotman Dream Cottage and Honeysuckle Dream Cottage were given to customers who spent over £29.95 on current models. The rest of the series were released during 1997 and were available from The Hamilton Gallery at £7.95 each. A wooden display stand was given free of charge if all the Dream Cottages were purchased. In 1997 The Hamilton Gallery was purchased by The Bradford Group all remaining stock of the miniatures were offered to retailers.

Bridge House

The Chocolate House

Cotman Cottage

Honeysuckle Cottage

Old Mother Hubbard's

Paradise Lodge

Rose Cottage

St. Lawrence Church

Summer Haze

Titmouse Cottage

The Toy Shop

Vine Cottage

Name	Size	Intro.	Discon.	Can. $	U.S. $	U.K. £
Bridge House	1 ½", 3.5 cm	1997	Current	N.A.	N.A.	7.95
The Chocolate House	1 ½", 3.8 cm	1997	Current	N.A.	N.A.	7.95
Cotman Cottage	1 ½", 3.5 cm	1996	1996	375.00	250.00	150.00
Honeysuckle Cottage	1 ½", 3.5 cm	1996	1996	40.00	25.00	20.00
Old Mother Hubbards	1 ½", 3.5 cm	1997	Current	N.A.	N.A.	7.95
Paradise Lodge	1 ½", 3.5 cm	1997	Current	N.A.	N.A.	7.95
Rose Cottage	1 ½", 3.2 cm	1997	Current	N.A.	N.A.	7.95
St. Lawerence Church	1 ½", 3.8 cm	1997	Current	N.A.	N.A.	7.95
Summer Haze	1 ¼", 3.0 cm	1997	Current	N.A.	N.A.	7.95
Titmouse Cottage	1 ½", 4.0 cm	1997	Current	N.A.	N.A.	7.95
The Toy Shop	1 ½", 3.5 cm	1997	Current	N.A.	N.A.	7.95
Vine Cottage	1 ½", 3.5 cm	1997	Current	N.A.	N.A.	7.95

Note: None of these models have backstamps.

DUART CASTLE

Scottish Collection

Standing proudly on the Isle of Mull, Duart Castle is the 13th century home of the Maclean's of Duart.

Duart Castle was limited to 3,000 pieces.

Size:	5", 13.0 cm
Backstamp:	K-1
Introduced:	1992 in a limited edition of 3,000
Discontinued:	1995

Description	Can. $	U.S. $	U.K. £
Duart Castle	500.00	350.00	260.00

DUCKDOWN COTTAGE

English Collection — South-West

Built around 1890 the long "catslide" roof is very distinctive on this piece. This cottage is situated in Ramsbury, Whiltshire.

Size:	3 ½", 8.7 cm
Backstamp:	N-1
Introduced:	1995
Discontinued:	1997

Description	Can. $	U.S. $	U.K. £
Duckdown Cottage	100.00	75.00	40.00

EAMONT LODGE

Christmas Lodge Collection

Eamont Lodge can be found at the entrance to Lowther Castle in Penrith, Cumbria. Built in 1877 of pink sandstone quarried on the estate, and roofed with Cumbrian slate, Eamont Lodge is a fine example of Victorian Gothic.

Eamont Lodge was the second in a series of four lodge houses.

Size:	4 ¼", 11.0 cm
Backstamp:	L
Introduced:	1993
Discontinued:	1993

Description	Can. $	U.S. $	U.K. £
Eamont Lodge	375.00	250.00	80.00

EAST NEUK

Scottish Collection

Situated in an area known as the East Neuk of Fife, which is immediately opposite Edinburgh, across the Firth of Forth, this little cottage is built of stone with a pantile roof. 'Neuk' is taken from the Old Scots and means 'a comfortable or cosy place.'

Size:	2", 5.0 cm
Backstamp:	F
Introduced:	1987
Discontinued:	1991

Description	Can. $	U.S. $	U.K. £
East Neuk	75.00	50.00	45.00

EDZELL SUMMER-HOUSE

Scottish Collection

Set in the grounds of Edzell Castle, about 5 miles north of Brechin, Edzell Summer-House is a tiny pavilion which was built in 1604. Constructed of red sandstone with slate tiles (95% of which are original), the building is a marvel of Scottish architecture.

Size:	4", 10.0 cm
Backstamp:	L
Introduced:	1993
Discontinued:	1997

Description	Can. $	U.S. $	U.K. £
Edzell Summer-House	100.00	50.00	40.00

EILEAN DONAN CASTLE

Scottish Collection

Built by Alexander II of Scotland in 1220 on an island at the meeting points of Lochs Duich, Alsh and Long, Eilean Donan Castle was bombarded by the English warship *Worcester* in 1719 and was destroyed. The ruin was rebuilt in 1932 by the MacRae family at a cost of almost £250,000, and is now a clan war memorial and museum run by the Conchra Charitable Trust.

Description	Size	Backstamp	Intro.	Discon.	Can. $	U.S. $	U.K. £
Eilean Donan	5", 13 cm	H-1	1990	Current	240.00	170.00	77.95

ELM COTTAGE

English Collection — Midlands

Located in a village near Chippenham, Wiltshire, this small lodge house was built more than 200 years ago. Constructed of Cotswold stone, the roof is also of stone and probably weighs in excess of 2 tons; the ornately carved wooden gables are a prominent feature.

Size:	2 ¾", 7.0 cm
Backstamp:	M
Introduced:	1994
Discontinued:	1997

Description	Can. $	U.S. $	U.K. £
Elm Cottage	50.00	35.00	25.00

ERISKAY CROFT

Scottish Collection

Eriskay, a small island in the Hebrides, between Barra and South Uist, takes the full force of the Atlantic weather, so the crofts (which are affectionately known as 'black houses') are sturdily built of stone with a turf roof.

Size:	2 ¼", 5.5 cm
Backstamp:	K-1
Introduced:	1992
Discontinued:	Current

Description	Can. $	U.S. $	U.K. £
Eriskay Croft	60.00	40.00	18.95

ESSEX COTTAGE

Paint Your Own

Introduced in September 1993 at the Collector's Event held at Harewood House, Leeds, this piece was only available at this event and other events throughout the 12 months. Please note that "Paint Your Owns" are worth more unpainted.

Size:	3", 7.6 cm
Backstamp:	L
Introduced:	1993
Discontinued:	1994

Description	Can. $	U.S. $	U.K. £
Essex Cottage (unpainted)	150.00	100.00	85.00

EVERGREENS

Christmas Collection (1997 Annual Ornament)

The north end of the famous street, The Shambles, York is home to this old building.

Size:	2 ¾", 7.0 cm
Backstamp:	P-1
Introduced:	1997
Discontinued:	1997

Description	Can. $	U.S. $	U.K. £
Evergreens	N.A.	30.00	12.95

FALLS MILL

American Landmarks

Falls Mill was built around 1873 and is located in south-east Tennessee near Belvedere. It is now privately owned and open to the public.

Falls Mill, which is finely detailed, was sold exclusively in the USA in its first year of issue before going into general release worldwide.

Size:	4 ¾", 12.0 cm
Backstamp:	H-1
Introduced:	1989
Discontinued:	1992

Description	Can. $	U.S. $	U.K. £
Falls Mill	375.00	275.00	140.00

DER FAMILIENSCHREIN

German Collection

Der Familienschrein (The Family Chapel) was introduced in September 1988, and was retired in December 1991.

Size:	4", 10.0 cm
Backstamp:	G
Introduced:	1988
Discontinued:	1991

Description	Can. $	U.S. $	U.K. £
Der Familienschrein	200.00	125.00	115.00

FARRIERS

English Collection — Midlands

Based upon a cottage found in Worcestershire, in this model the farrier (who shod horses and whose trade had evolved from the blacksmith) has only a small part of his house remaining as a stable and workshop.

Size: 2 ½", 6.5 cm
Backstamp: D
Introduced: 1985
Discontinued: 1990

Description	Can. $	U.S. $	U.K. £
Farriers	150.00	100.00	65.00

FARTHING LODGE

English Collection — Midlands

Originally a toll-keeper's house, the windows of Farthing Lodge were positioned to give a clear view of the turnpike and approaching travellers.

Size: 2 ½", 6.5 cm
Backstamp: J
Introduced: 1991
Discontinued: 1996

Description	Can. $	U.S. $	U.K. £
Farthing Lodge	75.00	45.00	25.00

FIDDLER'S FOLLY

English Collection — Midlands

Located in Pershore, Worcestershire, this home was built for farm hands in the 16th century.

Size: 2 ½", 6.4 cm
Backstamp: O-2
Introduced: 1996
Discontinued: Current

Description	Can. $	U.S. $	U.K. £
Fiddler's Folly	45.00	35.00	14.95

'FILL'ER UP & CHECK THE OIL

Coca-Cola™ Country Collection

This is typical of gasoline (petrol) service stations that were built before World War II along USA highways.

Introduced in 1996 under license from the Coca-Cola™ company for the Coca-Cola™ company. Although not issued as a limited edition, all pieces in the series are hand-numbered. These pieces, manufactured in Ireland, are exclusively available in North America.

Size:	3", 8.0 cm
Backstamp:	N-2
Introduced:	1996
Discontinued:	Current

Description	Can. $	U.S. $	U.K. £
'Fill'er Up...	180.00	140.00	N.A.

FINCHINGFIELD

English Collection — South -East

The village of Finchingfield, near Saffron Walden in Essex, is well-known for its attractive blend of architecture. Finchingfield is timber framed and thatched with Norfolk reed, but its most striking feature is the front elevation which is plastered and decorated with elaborate ornamental designs. The technique used for this form of decoration is know as pargetin.

Size:	3 ½", 8.5 cm
Backstamp:	K-1
Introduced:	1992
Discontinued:	1995

Description	Can. $	U.S. $	U.K. £
Finchingfield	150.00	100.00	40.00

FIR TREE COTTAGE

Christmas Collection (1996 Annual Ornament)

Located in Grasmere, Cumbria, this piece was introduced as the fifth annual Christmas ornament.

Size:	2 ¾", 7.0 cm
Backstamp:	O-2
Introduced:	1996
Discontinued:	1996

Description	Can. $	U.S. $	U.K. £
Fir Tree Cottage	45.00	30.00	25.00

FIRE HOUSE 1
American Landmarks

Constructed around 1890 and situated in the New England state of Maine, the Victorian architectural influence upon Fire House 1 is evident in the design of the hose-drying tower and the bell tower.

It was sold exclusively in the USA first year of issue before going into worldwide release.

Size:	4 ¼", 11.0 cm
Backstamp:	J
Introduced:	1991
Discontinued:	1997

Description	Can. $	U.S. $	U.K. £
Fire House	125.00	85.00	65.00

FIRE STATION 105
Exclusive

Based on a building on Main St., Disneyland, Anaheim, California, this piece was designed by Ray Day for the Annual Disneyanna Collectable Convention in Disneyworld, Orlando, Florida. Produced in a limited edition of 501, this piece sold out within the course of the day. An interesting feature of this piece is the base label in the shape of a silhouette of Mickey Mouse, both the ears of 'Mickey' are signed by David Tate (founder) and Ray Day.

Size:	4 ½", 11.5 cm
Backstamp:	Special Ltd. Ed. Disney Stamp
Introduced:	1995 in a limited edition of 501
Discontinued:	1995

Description	Can. $	U.S. $	U.K. £
Fire Station 105	1,200.00	800.00	720.00

FIRST SNOW AT BLUEBELL
British Collection

Size:	4", 10.0 cm
Backstamp:	Unknown
Introduced:	1997 in a limited edition of 3,500
Discontinued:	1997
Variations:	Bluebell Farm

Description	Can. $	U.S. $	U.K. £
First Snow at Bluebell	325.00	250.00	125.00

FISHERMAN'S BOTHY

Scottish Collection

In a country where fishing provides a livelihood for many of the people, Fisherman's Bothy provides a summer home for the salmon fisher.

Size:	2", 5.0 cm
Backstamp:	H-1
Introduced:	1990
Discontinued:	Current

Description	Can. $	U.S. $	U.K. £
Fisherman's Bothy	55.00	35.00	15.95

FISHERMAN'S COTTAGE

English Collection — South-West

Located in Boscastle, Fisherman's Cottage is reminiscent of the cottages to be found in the coves and harbours of Cornwall. These sturdy, heavily slated dwellings have withstood centuries of Atlantic storms.

Size:	2", 5.0 cm
Backstamp:	D
Introduced:	1985
Discontinued:	1989

Description	Can. $	U.S. $	U.K. £
Fisherman's Cottage	125.00	85.00	70.00

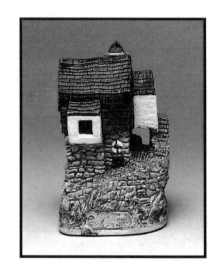

FIVEWAYS

English Collection — Midlands

Built 300 years ago, when the major routes were simple dirt tracks, cottages such as this were situated at the junctions of the tracks and typical of the cottages to be found in Shropshire and Cheshire, Fiveways was probably the home of a craftsman who was dependent upon the passing trade.

Size:	2 ¾", 6.5 cm
Backstamp:	H-1
Introduced:	1989
Discontinued:	1995

Description	Can. $	U.S. $	U.K. £
Fiveways	75.00	50.00	35.00

FLAXTON BECK

Paint Your Own

Introduced in September 1993 at the Annual Collectors Fair held at Harewood House, Leeds, this piece was only available at the Fair, special events featuring "Paint Your Own" and at the Collectors Club Centre.

This piece was retired at the Annual Fair held in the Chiltern Open - Air Museum September 1994. Please note unpainted version of "Paint Your Owns" are worth more unpainted.

Size:	2 ¾", 7.0 cm
Backstamp:	L
Introduced:	1993
Discontinued:	1994

Description	Can. $	U.S. $	U.K. £
Flaxton Beck (unpainted)	125.00	100.00	70.00

FLOWERPOTS

English Collection — South East

Flowerpots is based on "Fordcombe Cottage" situated between Penshurst and Groombridge in Kent.

Size:	3 ½", 8.5 cm
Backstamp:	O-2
Introduced:	1996
Discontinued:	Current

Description	Can. $	U.S. $	U.K. £
Flowerpots	75.00	55.00	25.95

FLOWER SELLERS

English Collection — South-East

Built in the early 1800s this timber-framed house provides a most unusual sight in London's Soho Square.

Size:	4", 10.5 cm
Backstamp:	J
Introduced:	1991
Discontinued:	1996

Description	Can. $	U.S. $	U.K. £
Flower Sellers	140.00	90.00	45.00

FORGE BARN
American Collection

Introduced in October 1984, only 275 pieces were produced before Forge Barn was retired.

Size:	2 ½", 5.75 cm
Backstamp:	B
Introduced:	1984
Discontinued:	1985

Description	Can. $	U.S. $	U.K. £
Forge Barn	1,100.00	750.00	600.00

FORGET-ME-NOT
Collectors Club

The cottage portrayed the story of a couple who are soon to be married, and who have just bought their first home. Although the thatched cottage is in a somewhat dilapidated condition, their intention is to renovate it and try to restore it to its former glory. There is a broken down car buried amongst the foliage; and there is a solitary badger in the undergrowth at the front of the cottage on the left. (See also Heaven Lea Cottage, page 106).

Forget-Me-Not was only available to members of the Collectors Club during the 1992-1993 club year.

Size:	3 ¼", 9.5 cm
Backstamp:	K-1
Introduced:	1992
Discontinued:	1993

Description	Can. $	U.S. $	U.K. £
Forget-Me-Not	350.00	250.00	200.00

Photograph
not available
at press time

FOURTH OF JULY, THE
Allegiance Collection

This model was inspired by a Victorian bandstand in Bellville, Ohio.

Size:	3", 7.6 cm
Backstamp:	Unknown
Introduced:	1998 in a limited edition of 1,776
Discontinued:	Current

Description	Can. $	U.S. $	U.K. £
Fourth of July	N.A.	70.00	N.A.

FOUNTAINS ABBEY

Studley Royal Collection

Fountains Abbey is located on the Studley Royal Estate in Yorkshire and provides the inspiration for the collection as a whole. It was produced in a limited edition of 3,500 pieces. The other pieces (Octagon Tower, Temple of Piety, Banqueting House, St. Mary's Church) are all limited to 5,000. It is constructed in an unusual way, comprising of 17 sections which were put together after painting. Approximately 20 pieces were produced per month initially.

Size	Backstamp	Intro.	Discon.	Can. $	U.S. $	U.K. £
6", 15.2 cm	Special Limited Edition	1995	Ltd. Ed.	N.A.	395.00	N.A.

FOUR SEASONS

English Collection — Midlands

Built in the 16th century, this timber-framed house from Warwickshire has Cotswold stone at ground level to protect the timber framing from rising damp.

Size:	4", 10.0 cm
Backstamp:	F
Introduced:	1987
Discontinued:	1991

Description	Can. $	U.S. $	U.K. £
Four Seasons	225.00	150.00	80.00

FOXGLOVE FIELDS

English Collection — Midlands

This cottage of 17th century origin can be found near Credenhill, Herefordshire. Foxglove Fields combines stone, timber and thatch, and epitomises the local vernacular style.

Size:	3 ¼", 8.0 cm
Backstamp:	L
Introduced:	1993
Discontinued:	1997

Description	Can. $	U.S. $	U.K. £
Foxglove Fields	125.00	85.00	45.00

FRESH BREAD

American Landmarks

Fresh Bread is located in the old silver mining town of Silver Plume, Colorado. With the growing population of the 1850s, the need for specialist grocery stores became apparent as immigrants flocked to the west in search of their fortune. Most of the wooden structures in this area were destroyed by fire in 1884. Fresh Bread most certainly dates back to that time. This bakery is still in operation today and serves the local community whose population has dropped to less than 300 residents.

Size:	3 ½", 9.0 cm
Backstamp:	M
Introduced:	1994
Discontinued:	Current

Description	Can. $	U.S. $	U.K. £
Fresh Bread	150.00	100.00	74.95

FROSTY MORNING

Christmas Specials

This model is based on an impressive 17th century dwelling in Queniborough, Leicestershire. It is the third piece in the Christmas Specials Collection and is available during 1998 only.

Size:	4 ¼", 11.0 cm
Backstamp:	Q-2
Introduced:	1998
Discontinued:	1998

Description	Can. $	U.S. $	U.K. £
Frosty Morning	200.00	150.00	59.95

FRY DAYS

English Collection— Northern

This model is based on a building in Kendal, Cumbria, birth place of Catherine Parr (6th wife of Henry VIII).

The traditional English supper, "fish n' chips," is the topic of this Cumbrian cottage.

It was only available through the Guild Of Specialist China and Glass Retailers in the UK during the first 6 months of production it was put into general release worldwide

Size:	3 ¾", 9.5 cm
Backstamp:	O-2
Introduced:	1996
Discontinued:	Current

Description	Can. $	U.S. $	U.K. £
Fry Days	100.00	70.00	34.95

FUCHSIA COTTAGE

English Collection — South West

Built during the 17th century, Fuschia Cottage is located in Corfe, Dorset.

Size:	2 ¼", 5.7 cm
Backstamp:	O-1
Introduced:	1996
Discontinued:	Current

Description	Can. $	U.S. $	U.K. £
Fuchsia Cottage	45.00	30.00	14.95

THE GABLES

English Collection — South-East

Typical of the Gothic style of architecture which flourished in the 19th century through the efforts of Prince Albert, consort of Queen Victoria, this Victorian family house is aptly named with its carved gables and front porch.

Size:	5 ¼", 13.5 cm
Backstamp:	F
Introduced:	1987
Discontinued:	1992

Description	Can. $	U.S. $	U.K. £
The Gables	425.00	275.00	160.00

GAMEKEEPER'S COTTAGE

Special Editions

Gamekeeper's Cottage can be found on the estate of Ragley Hall in Warwickshire, and was built in 1872 by the 5th Marquess of Hertford.

When 350 pieces were first released in July 1991 at the South Bend Show in the USA, Gamekeeper's Cottage had a red roof and white doors and a special stamp: SOUTH BEND 1991. This South Bend edition was given to people attending the South Bend International and Collectables Exhibition.

The cottage was then issued in September 1991 without the South Bend backstamp as a Collectors Club events cottage; it had a light sienna roof, and the front door and flowers were painted in the colours of the members choice.

Variation	Size	Backstamp	Intro.	Discon.	Can. $	U.S. $	U.K. £
1 - Red roof	3 ½", 9 cm	J	1991	1991	600.00	400.00	250.00
2 - Sienna roof	3 ½", 9 cm	J	1991	1992	200.00	125.00	115.00

GARDENER'S COTTAGE
Collectors Club

Introduced in March 1991 as an exclusive cottage only available for one year to members of the Collectors Club.

Size: 3 ¾", 9.5 cm
Backstamp: J
Introduced: 1991
Discontinued: 1992

Description	Can. $	U.S. $	U.K. £
Gardener's Cottage	375.00	250.00	150.00

DAS GEBIRGSKIRCHLEIN
German Collection

With its onion-shaped towers, wooden tiles and plain white walls, Das Gebirgskirchlein is typical of the buildings seen on the borders of southern Germany and Austria.

Size: 5", 13.0 cm
Backstamp: F
Introduced: 1987
Discontinued: 1998

Description	Can. $	U.S. $	U.K. £
Das Gebirgskirchlein	180.00	120.00	54.95

GENERAL STORE

American Collection

Introduced in October 1984, the initial production pieces of General Store had a diagonal, ribbed store sign with lettering in red. At some time during production (which was only for a year), the store sign changed to a horizontal, timber-mounted sign with white embossed lettering, larger and easier to read than the initial red lettering.

Approximately 50 pieces of the 150 pieces produced in total are version 1 models.

Version	Size	Backstamp	Intro.	Discon.	Can. $	U.S. $	U.K. £
1 - Red lettering	2 ¾", 7 cm	C	1984	Unknown	1,500.00	1,000.00	800.00
2 - White lettering	2 ¾", 7 cm	C	Unknown	1985	1,350.00	900.00	550.00

GEORGE INN, THE

British Collection

Dating from 1250 this formidable building from Somerset once belonged to the Carhusian priory of Hinton. It was originally built as a hostelry for wool and cloth merchants.

Size: 4", 10.0 cm
Backstamp: Unknown
Introduced: 1997
Discontinued: Current

Description	Can. $	U.S. $	U.K. £
George Inn	320.00	225.00	94.95

GERTRUDE'S GARDEN

Anniversary Editions

Lilliput Lanes version of Gertrude's Garden is based on a cottage found in the village of Badminton which was once home to the famous Edwardian designer/gardener 'Gertrude Jekyll' who published 13 gardening books, over 1000 articles and designed over 2,000 gardens. Her home was designed by Thomas Wright, the 18th century architect, the windows on this piece typify his work.

Gertrude's Garden was the fourth Anniversary Cottage.

Size:	3 ¾", 9.5 cm
Backstamp:	N-1
Introduced:	1995
Discontinued:	1995

Description	Can. $	U.S. $	U.K. £
Gertrude's Garden	300.00	200.00	80.00

GINGERBREAD SHOP

Christmas Collection

The Christmas Collection adopts the theme of a traditional village at Christmastime, and the Gingerbread Shop portrays the baker's shop, a popular place at Christmastime, where the villagers stock up in readiness for the festivities.

Gingerbread Shop features 'icing sugar' snow which is painted on after production.

Size:	2 ½", 6.5 cm
Backstamp:	L
Introduced:	1993
Discontinued:	1997

Description	Can. $	U.S. $	U.K. £
Gingerbread Shop	50.00	35.00	25.00

GLENLOCHIE LODGE
Scottish Collection

The highland lodge, reflecting a grand baronial style, stands at the entrance to the laird's estate, where each year the local highland games are held.

Size: 4 ¾", 12.0 cm
Backstamp: H-1
Introduced: 1990
Discontinued: 1993

Description	Can. $	U.S. $	U.K. £
Glenlochie Lodge	275.00	175.00	60.00

GOLDEN MEMORIES
British Collection

The basis for this model is a 17th century home in Barthomley, Chesire.

Size: 3 ¾", 11.0 cm
Backstamp: Q-2
Introduced: 1998
Discontinued: Current

Description	Can. $	U.S. $	U.K. £
Golden Memories	140.00	90.00	39.95

GOLDEN YEARS
British Collection

This traditional East Anglian dwelling sports ornate thatch and lime-washed walls.

Size: 2 ½", 6.0 cm
Backstamp: P-1
Introduced: 1997
Discontinued: Current

Description	Can. $	U.S. $	U.K. £
Golden Years	50.00	25.00	9.95

GOLD MINER'S CLAIM
American Landmarks

Bringing back memories of the days when thousands of prospectors hoped to 'strike it lucky' panning for gold, Gold Miner's Claim shows the disused mine, derelict cabin and rusting equipment which were left behind once the mine ran out.

Approximately 15 pieces were released from the factory without the 'snow'. Although retailers were asked to return the pieces for the 'snow' to be added, it is not known if they were all returned, or whether some were actually sold; if so, these pieces could be valuable. Exclusive to the USA in the first year of issue it went into general release in 1993.

Version One — With Snow

Version Two — Without Snow

Version	Size	Backstamp	Intro.	Discon.	Can. $	U.S. $	U.K. £
1 - With snow	3 ¼", 8 cm	K-1	1992	1992	2,000.00	1,250.00	875.00
2 - Without snow	3 ¼", 8 cm	K-1	1992	1997	125.00	85.00	65.00

GOSSIP GATE

English Collection — South East

Located in Lansing Village, Sussex (found between Worthing and Brighton), early parts of this building date back as far as 1445, some parts of the beam (when additions were added) came from the Spanish Armada (1588). It is rumoured that en route to London, James II and Elizabeth I stayed at this cottage. This cottage also has a priest's hole in the rafters where persecuted Tudor catholics could hide.

Size:	4", 10.4 cm
Backstamp:	O-1
Introduced:	1996
Discontinued:	Current

Description	Can. $	U.S. $	U.K. £
Gossip Gate	240.00	170.00	82.95

GRANDMA BATTY'S TEA ROOM

English Tea Room Collection

This model is based on a building in York which dates back to the late 13th century.

Size:	3 ¾", 9.5 cm
Backstamp:	N-1
Introduced:	1995
Discontinued:	Current

Description	Can. $	U.S. $	U.K. £
Grandma Batty's	130.00	90.00	39.95

GRANNY SMITHS

English Collection — Midlands

Surrounded by Worcestershire orchards, this 16th-century cottage typifies the architecture of the area.

Size:	2 ¾", 7.0 cm
Backstamp:	K-1
Introduced:	1992
Discontinued:	1996

Description	Can. $	U.S. $	U.K. £
Granny Smiths	70.00	45.00	25.00

GRANNY'S BONNET

British Collection

Built in the early 18th century in Buckinghamshire, the name of the cottage originated from the cottage garden flower 'aquilegia' which is commonly known as Granny's Bonnet.

Size:	2 ¼", 5.5 cm
Backstamp:	P-1
Introduced:	1997
Discontinued:	Current

Description	Can. $	U.S. $	U.K. £
Granny's Bonnet	35.00	25.00	9.95

GRANTCHESTER MEADOWS

English Collection — South-East

Grantchester Meadows is an 18th-century timber-framed cottage, situated in a little hamlet close to Cambridge. The hamlet has long been a favourite haunt of both students and dons. Reached by a bridge over a tributary of the River Cam, the cottage is roofed with East Anglian thatch and is surrounded by meadows.

The model is finely detailed, including willows, a swan and a punt.

Size:	4", 10.0 cm
Backstamp:	K-1
Introduced:	1992
Discontinued:	1996

Description	Can. $	U.S. $	U.K. £
Grantchester Meadows	300.00	195.00	100.00

GREAT EXPECTATIONS

Christmas Collection (1998 Annual Ornament)

This Christmas Ornament is a model of a Toy Shop in Grassington, Yorkshire.

Size:	2 ½", 6.5 cm
Backstamp:	Q-2
Introduced:	1998
Discontinued:	1998

Description	Can. $	U.S. $	U.K. £
Great Expectations	50.00	35.00	13.95

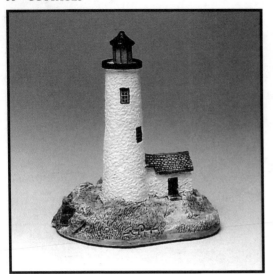

GREAT POINT LIGHT

American Landmarks

Built in 1818, this lighthouse stood firm until in 1984 it was brought down by a very severe storm.

Introduced in March 1990, Great Point Light is only the second lighthouse to have been produced by Lilliput Lane.

There are colour differences between the first issued and the later models. Variation 1 has brown windows and brown light housing. Variation 2 has blue windows and blue light housing. Approximately 500 to 800 were produced with the first colour variation.

Variation	Size	Backstamp	Intro.	Discon.	Can. $	U.S. $	U.K. £
1 - Brown housing	4", 10 cm	I-2	1990	1990	250.00	175.00	115.00
2 - Blue housing	4", 10 cm	I-2	1990	Current	60.00	50.00	24.95

GREEN GABLES

British Collection

This Victorian house can be found in Wiveliscombe, Somerset.

Size: 4 ¾", 12.0 cm
Backstamp: P-1
Introduced: 1997
Discontinued: Current

Description	Can. $	U.S. $	U.K. £
Green Gables	320.00	225.00	94.95

THE GREENGROCER'S

Village Shops Collection

Based upon traditional Cotswold stores, The Greengrocer's was one of the first three models launched in a series of six. In the UK, the model was initially exclusive to the UK Guild of Specialist China & Glass Retailers before being put into general release.

Size:	3 ¾", 9.5 cm
Backstamp:	J
Introduced:	1991
Discontinued:	1998

Description	Can. $	U.S. $	U.K. £
The Greengrocer's	125.00	85.00	35.00

GREENSTED CHURCH

English Collection — South-East

St Andrew's, at Greensted-juxta-Ongar in Essex, certainly dates from 845 AD, and could even date from 645 AD. An outstanding example of a Saxon church, it is unique in having its original split oak log walls intact, and is believed to be the oldest wooden church in the world as well as the oldest surviving example of timber framing in England. Dorma windows would have added at a later date to let in more light.

Size:	4", 10.4 cm
Backstamp:	H-1
Introduced:	1989
Discontinued:	1995

Description	Can. $	U.S. $	U.K. £
Greensted Church	150.00	95.00	60.00

GRIST MILL
American Collection

Although introduced in October 1984, due to the lack of popularity of the American Collection, all thirteen of the models in the collection were retired in October 1985. As a result very few pieces were produced and hence each model is quite rare. Only 150 pieces were made of Grist Mill.

Front View

Side View

Description	Size	Backstamp	Intro.	Discon.	Can. $	U.S. $	U.K. £
Grist Mill	2 ½", 6.5 cm	C	1984	1985	1,350.00	900.00	750.00

GUILDHALL
Special Editions

Built in the 14th century Guildhall is based on the Guildhall found in Thaxted, Essex.

Commissioned in the UK by the UK Guild of Specialist China & Glass Retailers for sale exclusively in their stores.

Size: 5", 12.5 cm
Backstamp: F
Introduced: 1987
Discontinued: 1989

Description	Can. $	U.S. $	U.K. £
Guildhall	450.00	300.00	250.00

HABERDASHERY
Victorian Shops Collection

In the Victorian era the Haberdashery catered to all the dressmaking needs of its patrons.

Size: 4", 9.9 cm
Backstamp: P-1
Introduced: 1997
Discontinued: Current

Description	Can. $	U.S. $	U.K. £
Haberdashery	125.00	90.00	37.95

HALCYON DAYS
British Collection

Situated in Stagsden, Bedforshire, this Victorian Lodge House has been open to the public since 1965.

Size: 4 ¼", 10.5 cm
Backstamp: P-1
Introduced: 1997
Discontinued: Current

Description	Can. $	U.S. $	U.K. £
Halcyon Days	200.00	150.00	59.95

THE HALL OF PRESIDENTS
Exclusive

Hall of Presidents is based on the building located in Disneyworld Resort, Orlando, Florida. Inside the building in Disneyworld, robotic former presidents educate visitors about American history.

This "Hall" was introduced at the Disneyanna Collectables Convention held between September 4th and September 7th, 1996 and was limited to 500 pieces. Note the label which is a silhouette of Mickey Mouse with one ear signed by Ray Day and the other by David Tate.

Size: 4 ¾", 12.1 cm
Backstamp: O-2
Introduced: 1996 in a limited edition of 500
Discontinued: 1996

Description	Can. $	U.S. $	U.K. £
The Hall of Presidents	1,100.00	750.00	600.00

HAMPTON MANOR

Collectors Club

Hampton Moat forms part of the gatehouse leading to Hampton Manor.

This is the first time we have seen the members free joining gift (Hampton Moat) and the main Collectors Club cottage (Hampton Manor) released in this way, and marketed as a set. Once a member of the club you are entitled to the main Collectors Club piece and this can be ordered via a retailer using the redemption card. The two cottages are displayed together as they would be in their true location which is in Lower Brockhampton, Herefordshire.

Size:	4", 10.0 cm
Backstamp:	P-1
Introduced:	1997
Discontinued:	1998

Description	Can. $	U.S. $	U.K. £
Hampton Manor	N.A.	N.A.	N.A.

HAMPTON MOAT

Collectors Club

Available as a free Collectors Club joining gift from March 1997 to February 1998. Based on a timber gatehouse that leads to the main building, Hampton Manor. (See description of Hampton Manor for details).

Size:	2 ½", 6.25 cm
Backstamp:	P-1
Introduced:	1997
Discontinued:	1998

Description	Can. $	U.S. $	U.K. £
Hampton Moat	N.A.	N.A.	N.A.

HARRIET'S COTTAGE

English Collection — South-West

This cottage is located in Lyndhurst, Hampshire.

It was offerred as an exclusive to H. Samuel (chain of jewellers) in the UK but available in general release elsewhere.

Size:	3 ½", 8.5 cm
Backstamp:	O-2
Introduced:	1996
Discontinued:	Current

Description	Can. $	U.S. $	U.K. £
Harriet's Cottage	100.00	85.00	33.95

HARVEST HOME

British Collection

Harvest Home is inspired by a traditional oast house near Bearsted, Kent. Oast houses first appeared in Kent around 1805.

This model will be produced in a limited edition of 4,950.

Size:	5", 13.0 cm
Backstamp:	Unknown
Introduced:	1997 in a limited of 4,950
Discontinued:	Ltd. Ed.

Description	Can. $	U.S. $	U.K. £
Harvest Home	420.00	250.00	125.00

HARVEST MILL

American Landmarks

Based upon the Old Mill at Pigeon Forge in Tennessee, which has been a working mill for over 160 years, Harvest Mill was introduced in January 1994.

Limited to 3,500 pieces, the model was only available in North America during 1994; however, it was generally available from 1995 onwards.

Size:	4 ¼", 11.0 cm
Backstamp:	M
Introduced:	1994
Discontinued:	Current

Description	Can. $	U.S. $	U.K. £
Harvest Mill	450.00	400.00	195.00

THE HAUNTED HOUSE

Exclusive

This is the third in the series of pieces released at Disneyana events. This model was released in a limited edition of 500 during the event held on September 2nd-6th, 1997.

Size:	5", 12.7 cm
Backstamp:	P-1
Introduced:	1997 in a limited edition of 500
Discontinued:	1997

Description	Can. $	U.S. $	U.K. £
The Haunted House	700.00	500.00	350.00

HAUS IM RHEINLAND

German Collection

Haus im Rheinland is typical of the buildings to be found in the land of the Lorelei (a large rock in the River Rhine near Sankt Goarshausen) where according to legend a beautiful maiden drowned herself in despair, only to rise as a siren to lure fishermen to their doom on the rock.

Available only in central Europe first year of issue before general release.

Size:	7", 18.0 cm
Backstamp:	F
Introduced:	1987
Discontinued:	1998

Description	Can. $	U.S. $	U.K. £
Haus Im Rheinland	275.00	215.00	95.00

HAZARDS OF THE ROAD
Coca-Cola™ Country Collection

Designed by Ray Day and produced under licence from the Coca Cola™ . Although not issued as a limited edition all pieces in this collection are hand-numbered, made of resin and manufactured in Ireland. Available exclusively in North America.

Front View

Rear View

Description	Size	Backstamp	Intro.	Discon.	Can. $	U.S. $	U.K. £
Hazards of the Road	3 ¾", 8.5 cm	N-2	1996	Current	70.00	55.00	N.A.

HEAVEN LEA COTTAGE

Collectors Club

Heaven Lea Cottage continues the story which began with Forget-Me-Not (see page 86). The newlyweds have now renovated the cottage to its former glory and renamed it Heaven Lea Cottage; the car has been restored and now sits proudly outside the cottage; and the family of badgers are more than pleased with their new surroundings.

Heaven Lea Cottage was exclusive to Collectors Club members.

Size:	3 ¼", 9.5 cm
Backstamp:	L
Introduced:	1993
Discontinued:	1994

Description	Can. $	U.S. $	U.K. £
Heaven Lea Cottage	350.00	225.00	135.00

HEBRIDEAN HAME

Scottish Collection

Originally a 'black house' which had no windows or chimney (smoke from the peat fire just filtered through the thatch, which was replaced each year), this sturdy cottage from the Outer Hebrides, has had windows and chimneys added later.

Size:	2 ½", 6.0 cm
Backstamp:	H-1
Introduced:	1990
Discontinued:	1992

Description	Can. $	U.S. $	U.K. £
Hebridean Hame	150.00	95.00	85.00

HEGARTY'S HOME

Irish Collection

Typical of the buildings in County Donegal, this working family home might also have served as a hideaway for the drinking of poteen (the illicit alcohol made from potatoes).

In 1990, painting changes were made. The original version has beige windows, grey window sills and white out building and side walls. The second version has black windows, black window sills and buff/grey out building and side walls, as well as the same colour for wall and pathway.

Version	Size	Backstamp	Intro.	Discon.	Can. $	U.S. $	U.K. £
1 - Beige windows	2", 5.5 cm	H-1	1989	1990	250.00	175.00	140.00
2 - Black windows	2", 5.5 cm	J	1990	1992	200.00	125.00	95.00

HELMERE COTTAGE

English Collection — Northern

With its distinctive green slate roof, Helmere Cottage can be found in the Lakeland fells.

Size:	3 ¼", 8.0 cm
Backstamp:	H-1
Introduced:	1989
Discontinued:	1995

Description	Can. $	U.S. $	U.K. £
Helmere Cottage	130.00	85.00	40.00

HERMITAGE
Welsh Collection

From around 150 BC Anglesey has been the centre of Celtic culture and religion, and the island is still remembered as the place where the Druids made the fiercest stand against their Roman conquerors. Hermitage can be found in a remote corner of the island, and although in poor repair has provided shelter for its various occupants over the past 200 years.

Introduced in July 1985, Hermitage was remodelled in December 1986. Major changes were made including a lean-to being added to the main building, more foliage around the base, repositioning of the steps leading up to the cottage. The second version was also larger in size than the original version.

Front View: Version 1 — Without Lean-to, Version 2 — With Lean-to

Back View: Version 1 — Less Foliage, Version 2 — More Foliage

Version	Size	Backstamp	Intro.	Discon.	Can. $	U.S. $	U.K. £
1 - Without lean-to	2 ¼", 5.7 cm	D	1985	1986	475.00	325.00	200.00
2 - With lean-to	2 ½", 6.5 cm	E	1986	1990	125.00	75.00	85.00

HESTERCOMBE GARDENS

Garden Series

The landscape design is based on the gardens at Hestercombe House, Somerset. These gardens were created between 1903 and 1908 under the guidance of architect Sir Edwin Lutyens and landscape gardener Gertrude Jekyll.

Hestercombe Gardens is due to be produced in a limited of 3,950. This is the fourth model in the Garden Series.

Size: 4 ½", 11.5 cm
Backstamp: Unknown
Introduced: 1997 in a limited of 3,950
Discontinued: Ltd. Ed.

Description	Can. $	U.S. $	U.K. £
Hestercombe Gardens	500.00	350.00	150.00

HIGH GHYLL FARM

English Collection — Northern

Using an amalgam of various farm buildings which can still be found in the Lake District today, High Ghyll Farm shows how a typical Cumbrian farm would have appeared in the 17th century.

Size: 5", 12.5 cm
Backstamp: K-1
Introduced: 1992
Discontinued: Current

Description	Can. $	U.S. $	U.K. £
High Ghyll Farm	350.00	250.00	110.00

HIGHLAND LODGE

Christmas Lodge Collection

Built around the 1850s, Highland Lodge can be found close to the Highland village of Kinloch Laggan. Constructed of local stone and roofed with slate, the most striking feature of the lodge is the round tower which is topped with a conical roof.

Highland Lodge was the first model in the Christmas Lodge Collection.

Size: 5 ¼", 13.5 cm
Backstamp: K-1
Introduced: 1992
Discontinued: 1992

Description	Can. $	U.S. $	U.K. £
Highland Lodge	450.00	300.00	250.00

HOLLY COTTAGE

English Collection — Northern

Holly Cottage is based upon a small Victorian cottage to be found in that part of Cumbria which was formerly Westmorland (which was combined with Cumberland to form Cumbria).

Introduced in February 1983, Holly Cottage was remodelled in July 1984, when the height of the chimneys was reduced and the base around the conservatory was made thinner. Other noticeable differences between the two versions were that the original version was duller in colour and was also less refined in appearance than the remodelled version.

Version 1 — Tall Chimney

Version 2 — Short Chimney

Version	Size	Backstamp	Intro.	Discon.	Can. $	U.S. $	U.K. £
1 - Tall chimney	3 ½", 8.9 cm	A-1, A-2	1983	1984	1,100.00	750.00	340.00
2 - Short chimney	3 ¼", 8.2 cm	C	1984	1988	225.00	150.00	80.00

HOLLYTREE HOUSE

Christmas Collection

Introduced in February 1992 as part of the miniature Christmas Collection, Hollytree House continued the theme of a traditional village at Christmastime.

Size: 2 ½", 6.0 cm
Backstamp: K-1
Introduced: 1992
Discontinued: 1996

Description	Can. $	U.S. $	U.K. £
Hollytree House	70.00	45.00	30.00

HOLME DYKE

English Collection — Northern

This house is typical of those built in the 17th century in the vicinity of York. The walls are of local stone and it is tiled with Flemish pantiles.

Size: 2 ½", 6.5 cm
Backstamp: F
Introduced: 1987
Discontinued: 1990

Description	Can. $	U.S. $	U.K. £
Holme Dyke	150.00	95.00	65.00

HOLY NIGHT

American Landmarks

Constructed in 1887 and based in Louisville, Kentucky, this church, which replaced another church on the same site, was built for $20,000 and has been serving the community since then.

This model was available only in the USA for the first six months and then released worldwide.

Size: 4 ½", 11.5 cm
Backstamp: M
Introduced: 1994
Discontinued: Current

Description	Can. $	U.S. $	U.K. £
Holy Night	240.00	180.00	95.00

Photograph
not available
at press time

HOME FOR THE HOLIDAYS

Christmas in America

This style of building, dating from 1820, can be found in western Indiana and Gastin, Illinois.

This limited edition of 2,596 was only available in North America during the first six months of production. The model became available in the UK in January of 1997. It is designed by Ray Day.

Size:	4", 10.5 cm
Backstamp:	Ltd. Ed.
Introduced:	1996 in a limited edition of 2,596
Discontinued:	Current

Description	Can. $	U.S. $	U.K. £
Home For The Holidays	600.00	375.00	195.00

HOME OF THE BRAVE

American Landmarks

Designed by Ray Day, Home of the Brave forms part of the Allegiance Collection whose overall theme is patriotism, demonstrated here by the flying of the American Flag.

Size:	3 ¼", 8.0 cm
Backstamp:	O-2
Introduced:	1997
Discontinued:	Current

Description	Can. $	U.S. $	U.K. £
Home of the Brave	N.A.	75.00	34.95

HOMETOWN DEPOT

American Landmarks

Situated in New Albany, Indiana, this station revives memories of the days when the train was the only means that people had of travelling long distances. Built in 1839 and used up until 1962, it was destroyed by fire in 1981.

Introduced in March 1990, it was available only in the USA the first year of issue before going into general worldwide release.

Size:	3", 7.5 cm
Backstamp:	I-1
Introduced:	1990
Discontinued:	1993

Description	Can. $	U.S. $	U.K. £
Hometown Depot	190.00	125.00	70.00

HONEY POT COTTAGE

English Collection — South East

Fondly known as the "Round House" in Finchingfield, Essex, this cottage was built circa 1800.

Size:	3 ¾", 9.5 cm
Backstamp:	O-1
Introduced:	1996
Discontinued:	Current

Description	Can. $	U.S. $	U.K. £
Honey Pot Cottage	100.00	60.00	29.95

HONEYSUCKLE COTTAGE

English Collection — South-East

Based upon a 17ᵗʰ-century thatched cottage in the village of Oakhanger in Hampshire, this building was quite a substantial house for its time. The oak frame would have been in-filled with clay on oak staves and then painted with lime wash. When the roof comes down to ground level and almost touches the floor, it is known as a 'catslide' roof.

Honeysuckle Cottage was among the very first Lilliput Lane models to be introduced.The window frames were thin, the base thick, and there was no retaining wall around the dovecot. It was remodelled in November 1982 with one row of bricks around the base of the dovecot and the window frames also seem thicker. Many variations of colour are apparent with version 2, some very dark. Honeysuckle was again remodelled in December 1983 and two rows of bricks were added to the base of the dovecot. It now had a more refined appearance.

Version 1 — No bricks

Version 2 — One row of brick

Version	Size	Backstamp	Intro.	Discon.	Can. $	U.S. $	U.K. £
1 - No bricks	3 ", 7.9 cm	A-1	1982	1982	1,875.00	1,250.00	415.00
2 - One row of brick	3 ", 7.8 cm	A-2	1982	1983	1,500.00	1,000.00	325.00
3 - Two rows of brick	3", 7.6 cm	C	1983	1987	275.00	175.00	90.00

HONEYSUCKLE COTTAGE 1992

Anniversary Editions

Based upon the original Honeysuckle Cottage, this model was produced to commemorate the 10ᵗʰ anniversary of the launch of Lilliput Lane.

For the Dream Cottage Miniature please see page 74.

Size:	2 ¾", 7.0 cm
Backstamp:	K-1
Introduced:	1992
Discontinued:	1992

Description	Can. $	U.S. $	U.K. £
Honeysuckle 1992	375.00	250.00	250.00

HONEYSUCKLE COTTAGE III

Special Editions

This cottage is based on the newly built visitors centre and is only available to personal callers.

Remodelling of this cottage took place very soon after its introduction. The dovecot found at the front of the cottage (although a metal addition) was prone to dislodge and even break. The solution was to build a retaining wall around the base of the dovecot to give it more support.

Approximately 60-70 models of the first version exist. It is already becoming a much sought after cottage.

Version	Size	Backstamp	Intro.	Discon.	Can. $	U.S. $	U.K. £
1 - Without wall	2 ½", 6.5 cm	P-1	1997	1997	1,000.00	750.00	500.00
2 - One row of brick	2 ½", 6.5 cm	P-1	1997	1997	750.00	500.00	300.00
3- Two rows of brick	2 ½", 6.5 cm	P-1	1997	Current	N.A	N.A	24.95

HOOK, LINE AND SINKER

Coca-Cola™ Country Collection

Hook, Line and Sinker is based on a typical 1930s / 1940s bait and tackle shop in a rural part of the midwest.

Designed by Ray Day under license from the Coca-Cola™ Company for the Coca-Cola™ Company and manufactured in Ireland, Hook, Line and Sinker was introduced in January 1996 and is exclusively available in North America.

Size:	3 ½ ", 8.5 cm
Backstamp:	N-2
Introduced:	1996
Discontinued:	Current

Description	Can. $	U.S. $	U.K. £
Hook, Line And Sinker	130.00	100.00	N.A.

HOPCROFT COTTAGE

English Collection — South-East

The neat mid-Victorian village of Old Warden in Bedfordshire was rebuilt by the last Lord Ongley (who died in 1877) as a model village for his tenants. Hopcroft Cottage is based upon a building in Old Warden.

Size:	4″, 10.0 cm
Backstamp:	J
Introduced:	1991
Discontinued:	1995

Description	Can. $	U.S. $	U.K. £
Hopcroft Cottage	200.00	125.00	55.00

HOROLOGIST

Victorian Shops Collection

The Horologist made sure that the nations clocks kept chiming in hourly unison during the emerging industrial workforce of the Victorian era.

Size:	5 ″, 13.0 cm
Backstamp:	P-1
Introduced:	1997
Discontinued:	Current

Description	Can. $	U.S. $	U.K. £
Horologist	100.00	75.00	29.95

HUBBLE-BUBBLE

British Collection

There are plenty of witchcraft signs around this house in Pendleton, Lancashire.

Size:	2 ¾", 7.0 cm
Backstamp:	P-1
Introduced:	1998
Discontinued:	Current

Description	Can. $	U.S. $	U.K. £
Hubble-Bubble	60.00	35.00	16.95

Photograph
not available
at press time

I'LL BE HOME FOR CHRISTMAS

Allegiance Collection

The setting for this World War II era train station is Ottawa Junction, southeast of Topeka, Kansas. This model was designed by Ray Day.

Size:	3 ½", 8.9 cm
Backstamp:	Unknown
Introduced:	1998
Discontinued:	Current

Description	Can. $	U.S. $	U.K. £
I'll Be Home . . .	N.A.	70.00	N.A.

INGLEWOOD

English Collection — Northern

Buildings similar to Inglewood can be found in the fertile farming land to the west and north of York. The cottage has hardly changed since it was originally built of York stone with a pantiled roof.

Introduced in July 1987, Inglewood was remodelled in December 1989 when a window at the rear was removed, and the model was made slightly larger; the windows on the remodelled version were also more pronounced and more finely detailed.

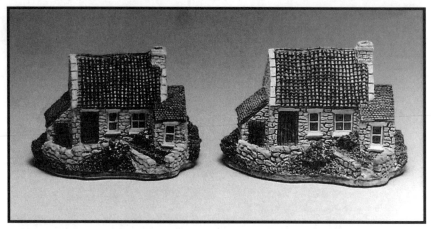

Front View: Version 1 — Less Detail, Version 2 — More Detail

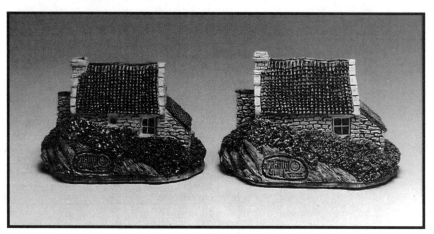

Back View: Version 1 — Two Rear Windows, Version 2 — One Rear Window

Version	Size	Backstamp	Intro.	Discon.	Can. $	U.S. $	U.K. £
1 - 2 rear windows	2", 5 cm	F	1987	1994	150.00	100.00	85.00
2 - 1 rear window	2", 5.2 cm	F	1989	1994	75.00	50.00	35.00

IN REMEMBERANCE
Allegiance Collection

This model is based on a small Missouri post office.

Size: 2 ¾", 7.0 cm
Backstamp: O-2
Introduced: 1997
Discontinued: Current

Description	Can. $	U.S. $	U.K. £
In Rememberance	N.A.	75.00	34.95

Photograph
not available
at press time

INVERLOCHIE HAME
Scottish Collection

To be found on the west coast of the Scottish Highlands and Islands region, this fisherman's cottage is a rugged building solidly constructed of granite to provide protection from the Atlantic weather.

Size: 2 ½", 6.0 cm
Backstamp: H-1
Introduced: 1989
Discontinued: Current

Description	Can. $	U.S. $	U.K. £
Inverlochie Hame	60.00	40.00	18.95

> Photograph
> not available
> at press time

I PLEDGE ALLEGIANCE
Allegiance Collection

This Indiana schoolhouse model was designed by Ray Day.

Size:	3 ½", 8.5 cm
Backstamp:	O-2
Introduced:	1997
Discontinued:	Current

Description	Can. $	U.S. $	U.K. £
I Pledge Allegiance	N.A.	75.00	34.95

IVY HOUSE
Christmas Collection (1994 Annual Ornament)

Based on a 19th century building, Ivy House was the third in the Annual Ornament collection. Introduced in February 1994, the model was only available until December of that year.

Size:	3", 7.5 cm
Backstamp:	M
Introduced:	1994
Discontinued:	1994

Description	Can. $	U.S. $	U.K. £
Ivy House	70.00	45.00	35.00

IZAAK WALTON'S COTTAGE
English Collection — Midlands

Izaak Walton (1593-1683) is well-known as the 'father' of fly fishing and the author of *The Compleat Angler*. Born in Stafford (at 92 Eastgate Street), Walton later lived in a half-timbered cottage at Shallowford, with the River Meece flowing through the grounds.

For the first twelve months the model was exclusive to Church's China in the UK, before becoming generally available.

Size:	3 ½", 9.0 cm
Backstamp:	F
Introduced:	1987
Discontinued:	1989

Description	Can. $	U.S. $	U.K. £
Izaak Walton's Cottage	300.00	200.00	100.00

JAGDHÜTTE
German Collection

Jagdhütte is a building where hunters gather to eat, drink and practice blowing their horns in readiness for the festival parades.

This cottage was introduced in February 1987 and was available only in Europe during the first year of issue before going into worldwide release.

Size:	4 ½", 11.5 cm
Backstamp:	F
Introduced:	1987
Discontinued:	Current

Description	Can. $	U.S. $	U.K. £
Jagdhütte	110.00	85.00	37.50

JASMINE COTTAGE
Style One
English Collection — South-West

Designed in 1810 and based upon the buildings at Blaise Hamlet, Henbury near Bristol, Jasmine Cottage is one of the three thatched cottages in the hamlet. It is situated between Diamond Cottage and Double Cottage, and its unusual double thatched roof provides an interesting contrast to the slate roofs of its neighbours.

Size:	5", 12.5 cm
Backstamp:	J
Introduced:	1991
Discontinued:	1996

Description	Can. $	U.S. $	U.K. £
Jasmine Cottage	225.00	150.00	75.00

JASMINE COTTAGE
Style Two
Classics Collection

The entire range of miniature cottages in the Classics Collection is based upon the buildings to be found in Blaise Hamlet, at Henbury, near Bristol. Jasmine Cottage is one of three thatched cottages in the hamlet, and John Nash's early designs refer to it as 'Dutch Cottage,' but no-one knows why its name was changed.

Size:	2 ¾", 6.0 cm
Backstamp:	L
Introduced:	1993
Discontinued:	1995

Description	Can. $	U.S. $	U.K. £
Jasmine Cottage	150.00	95.00	40.00

JEWELLER
Victorian Shops Collection

This Victorian shop is based on a building in Knightsbridge, London. There are two versions of this model. The first version sports an "H. Samuel" sign on the front of the building, while the second version says "Jeweller." In the UK this model is exclusive to the jeweller H. Samuel.

Jeweller

H.Samuel

Version	Size	Backstamp	Intro.	Discon.	Can. $	U.S. $	U.K. £
1 - H. Samuel	4 ¾", 10 cm	P-1	1997	Current	N.A.	N.A.	29.95
2 - Jeweller	4 ¾", 10 cm	P-1	1997	Current	100.00	75.00	29.95

JOHN BARLEYCORN COTTAGE

English Collection — South-East

John Barleycorn Cottage is another of the cottages based upon buildings in the mid-Victorian village of Old Warden, near Biggleswade, in Bedfordshire. Old Warden was rebuilt in its present form by the last Lord Ongley as a model village for his tenants.

Size:	4 ¼", 11.0 cm
Backstamp:	J
Introduced:	1991
Discontinued:	1995

Description	Can. $	U.S. $	U.K. £
John Barleycorn Cottage	225.00	150.00	50.00

JOHN KNOX HOUSE

Scottish Collection

Situated within Edinburgh's Royal Mile (the name given to the ancient streets which run eastwards from Castle Street to the gates of Holyroodhouse), John Knox House is a 15th-century building where Knox, the leader of the Protestant Reformation in Scotland, is believed to have lived. The house has a timber gallery and is now preserved as a museum.

Size:	5 ¾", 14.5 cm
Backstamp:	H-1
Introduced:	1989
Discontinued:	1992

Description	Can. $	U.S. $	U.K. £
John Knox House	225.00	150.00	85.00

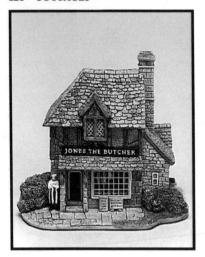

JONES THE BUTCHER

Village Shops Collection

The Village Shops Collection is based upon traditional Cotswold stores, and is a sub-collection of the English-Midlands series. The Butcher's shop was built in 1861. It was not unusual to convert your house into a business, utilising the ground floor as a shop and the second floor as living quarters.

In the UK, it was initially exclusive to the UK Guild of Specialist China & Glass Retailers for 6 months before general release.

Size:	3 ¾", 9.5 cm
Backstamp:	L
Introduced:	1993
Discontinued:	1998

Description	Can. $	U.S. $	U.K. £
Jones The Butcher	120.00	80.00	34.95

JUNK AND DISORDERLY

English Collection — Midlands

Pembridge is a village in Herefordshire which still has a wide and varied selection of ancient buildings. One of these buildings is a medieval cross-passage Hall which was built in 1382. Known as 'Junk and Disorderly,' part of the building is used to sell local crafts and items of bric-a-brac.

Size:	4", 10.0 cm
Backstamp:	L
Introduced:	1993
Discontinued:	1998

Description	Can. $	U.S. $	U.K. £
Junk And Disorderly	160.00	110.00	49.95

KEEPER'S LODGE

English Collection — Northern

Similar to the many gatekeepers' houses which can be found at the entrances to large country estates, this small Victorian cottage displays many of the features of the Gothic style which was so popular in the 19th century. Built of stone, an interesting feature is the small tower.

Size:	3 ½", 9.0 cm
Backstamp:	F
Introduced:	1987
Discontinued:	1988

Description	Can. $	U.S. $	U.K. £
Keeper's Lodge	275.00	175.00	70.00

KENDAL TEA HOUSE

English Tea Room Collection

Located in Stricklandgate, Kendal in the Lake District and originally used as an inn in 1639, this building became a Tea Room in 1819. Visitors can still visit the Tea Room and some of the original tea storage tubs and fittings are proudly displayed and used today.

Size:	3 ¾", 9.5 cm
Backstamp:	N-1
Introduced:	1995
Discontinued:	Current

Description	Can. $	U.S. $	U.K. £
Kendal Tea House	120.00	85.00	37.95

KENMORE COTTAGE

Scottish Collection

Kenmore, a picturesque village at the eastern end of Loch Tay, was built by the philanthropist the Marquis of Breadalbane. Kenmore Cottage was built in the Victorian Rustic style.

Size:	3 ½ ", 8.5 cm
Backstamp:	H-1
Introduced:	1989
Discontinued:	1993

Description	Can. $	U.S. $	U.K. £
Kenmore Cottage	190.00	125.00	60.00

KENNEDY HOMESTEAD

Irish Collection

In 1820, Patrick Kennedy was born in a small stone cottage in Dunganstown, County Wexford. He emigrated to America in 1849 and became the founding father of the Kennedy dynasty. His great-grandson, John F. Kennedy,was one of America's best-remembered presidents. Kennedy Homestead is based upon the small stone cottage that Patrick Kennedy left and which is now a major tourist attraction.

Size:	2 ¼", 5.5 cm
Backstamp:	H-1
Introduced:	1989
Discontinued:	1996

Description	Can. $	U.S. $	U.K. £
Kennedy Homestead	50.00	35.00	25.00

KENTISH COTTAGE

Paint Your Own

Kentish Cottage was introduced at the Collectors Fair at Grimsthorpe Castle in September 1995. It was also available through the Collectors Club Mail Order Department, events which featured "Paint Your Own Events" and at the Visitors Centre in Penrith for the following year. Sometimes, stock of the "Paint Your Owns" take longer than a year to sell. This one was still available mid year 1997. As with any of the "Paint Your Owns," they are worth more unpainted.

Size:	2 ¾", 7.0 cm
Backstamp:	N-1
Introduced:	1995
Discontinued:	Current

Description	Can. $	U.S. $	U.K. £
Kentish Cottage	40.00	30.00	20.00

KENTISH OAST HOUSE

English Collection — South-East

Based upon a derelict building near Tunbridge Wells in Kent, oast houses with circular kilns were introduced in the early 1800s, but around 1900 square kilns became more normal.

Introduced in July 1985, and using 7,500 tiles to cover the roof and the drying kilns, the original version had plastic vaines on the cowl; however, from December 1986 the vaines were made of metal.

Version	Size	Backstamp	Intro.	Discon.	Can. $	U.S. $	U.K. £
1 - Plastic vaines	3 ¾", 9.5 cm	D	1985	1990	600.00	450.00	300.00
2 - Metal vaines	3 ¾", 9.5 cm	D	1986	1990	200.00	125.00	110.00

KERRY LODGE

Christmas Lodge Collection

Kerry Lodge is based on Deenagh Lodge, Killarney, Ireland which was built around 1834 as the gate lodge for the Kenmare Estate, which is now the entrance to the Killarney National Park.

Only available until December 1995, this was the last "lodge" to be produced in the Collection.

Size:	4", 10.2 cm
Backstamp:	N-1
Introduced:	1995
Discontinued:	1995

Description	Can. $	U.S. $	U.K. £
Kerry Lodge	200.00	125.00	65.00

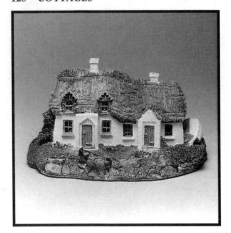

KILMORE QUAY

Irish Collection

As with most coastal areas in the 18th century, smuggling was very prominent around this coastal region. The first Irish Coast Guard Station was set up around the 1840s and was used to assist ships in difficulty. Kilmore Quay is typical of the cottages that the fishermen of County Wexford live in.

Size:	2 ¾″, 7.0 cm
Backstamp:	H-1
Introduced:	1989
Discontinued:	1992

Description	Can. $	U.S. $	U.K. £
Kilmore Quay	150.00	100.00	75.00

KILN COTTAGE

Collectors Club

This potter's cottage, based on a property in Devon, is the 1998-99 Collector's Club Symbol of Membership. It is a companion piece to the Club Special Edition for 1998-99, The Pottery (see page 171).

Size:	2 ¾″, 7.0 cm
Backstamp:	Q-2
Introduced:	1998
Discontinued:	1999

Description	Can. $	U.S. $	U.K. £
Kiln Cottage	N.A.	N.A.	N.A.

THE KING'S ARMS

English Collection — South-East

A fine example of 17th century architecture, The King's Arms is based upon the coaching inns which once stood beside the Great North Road (from London to York).

When this model was introduced in June 1990 demand was so great that it was not readily available until January 1991.

Size:	5 ½″, 14.0 cm
Backstamp:	I-1
Introduced:	1990
Discontinued:	1995

Description	Can. $	U.S. $	U.K. £
The King's Arms	675.00	450.00	200.00

KINLOCHNESS
Scottish Collection

A typical gamekeeper's lodge built of granite with a slate roof and crow-stepped gables.

Size:	4″, 10.0 cm
Backstamp:	H-1
Introduced:	1990
Discontinued:	1993

Description	Can. $	U.S. $	U.K. £
Kinlochness	150.00	95.00	70.00

KIRKBRAE COTTAGE
Scottish Collection

Situated in Banffshire, Kirkbrae Cottage is a hillside cottage with attractive views of the rocky coastline.
Apart from a slight colour change on later pieces no other variation exist.

Size:	2 ½″, 6.0 cm
Backstamp:	H-1
Introduced:	1990
Discontinued:	1993

Description	Can. $	U.S. $	U.K. £
Kirkbrae Cottage	150.00	95.00	65.00

DIE KLEINE BACKEREI
German Collection

A common sight in the 1600s across Germany and Europe, this typical 17th-century German bakehouse would serve a dozen farms and was located away from the main house to avoid the danger of fire. Many now are sights of historical interest only. The Industrial Revolution put an end to small bakeries like this.

Size:	3 ½″, 8.5 cm
Backstamp:	G
Introduced:	1988
Discontinued:	1994

Description	Can. $	U.S. $	U.K. £
Die Kleine Backerei	125.00	85.00	45.00

LACE HOUSE

An American Journey

This model was inspired by an American Gothic style home in Black Hawk, Colorado.

Size:	3 ¾″, 9.5 cm
Backstamp:	P-1
Introduced:	1997
Discontinued:	Current

Description	Can. $	U.S. $	U.K. £
Lace House	??.00	85.00	54.95

LACE LANE

English Collection — Midlands

After a threat of destruction in 1969, this home was moved near to Nottingham's Royal Castle. Nottingham is renowned as the 'City of Lace,' and this classic 15th century timber-framed building was purchased in 1980 by a lifetime lacemaker. It is now a museum to the city's lace industry, housing an abundance of historical lace.

Size:	4″, 10.0 cm
Backstamp:	J
Introduced:	1991
Discontinued:	1997

Description	Can. $	U.S. $	U.K. £
Lace Lane	80.00	60.00	40.00

LADYBANK LODGE

Scottish Collection

Based upon a building which can be found in the village of Ladybank, north of Glenrothes, Fife, Ladybank Lodge was built during the mid-19th century. Built of ironstone with a slate roof, it has the usual Scottish feature of crow-stepped gables, one of which leads into the round tower.

Size:	3 ½″, 9.0 cm
Backstamp:	M
Introduced:	1994
Discontinued:	1998

Description	Can. $	U.S. $	U.K. £
Ladybank Lodge	90.00	60.00	27.95

LADYBIRD COTTAGE

English Collection — Midlands

Located in Warkton, Northamptonshire. this cottage is typical of a 17th century Cotswold Stone Cottage. Less than fifty homes exist in this tiny village.

Size:	2 ½", 6.0 cm
Backstamp:	N-1
Introduced:	1995
Discontinued:	Current

Description	Can. $	U.S. $	U.K. £
Ladybird Cottage	55.00	35.00	15.95

LADY JANE'S COTTAGE

British Collection

This model is based upon a mock-timbered frame cottage at Eglinton Castle, near Irvine, in Scotland.

Size:	2 ¼", 5.5 cm
Backstamp:	Q-2
Introduced:	1998
Discontinued:	Current

Description	Can. $	U.S. $	U.K. £
Lady Jane's Cottage	60.00	35.00	17.95

LAKESIDE HOUSE

English Collection — Northern

As the Lake District became increasingly popular amongst the Victorians as an area to visit, many new dwellings were built (using local stone and slate) to provide accommodation for them. The houses were substantially constructed and many are still in use today as guest houses.

There are three versions of Lakeside House. Version 1 was introduced in September 1982 and has 27 windows, 10 roof tiles and carries no backstamp or an A-1 backstamp. Remodeling took place in November, 1982 resulting in Version 2, with 17 windows, 10 roof tiles and an A-1 backstamp. Version 3 was introduced in February 1983, it has 17 windows, 6 roof tiles and carries an A-2 backstamp.

Version	Size	Backstamp	Intro.	Discon.	Can. $	U.S. $	U.K. £
1 - 27 windows	4", 10.2 cm	A-1, None	1982	1982	3,000.00	2,000.00	1,100.00
2 - 17 windows	4", 10.2 cm	A-1	1982	1983	2,600.00	1,750.00	450.00
3 - 6 roof tiles	3 ½", 9.2 cm	A-2	1983	1986	1,500.00	1,000.00	325.00

LANGDALE COTTAGE

Lakeland Christmas Collection

This 19th century cottage is not based on a particular cottage but is typical of homes found in the Lake District.

This was one of three cottages first introduced in the Lakeland series in February 1995.

Size:	2 ½", 6.4 cm
Backstamp:	N-1
Introduced:	1995
Discontinued:	1998

Description	Can. $	U.S. $	U.K. £
Langdale Cottage	60.00	35.00	15.95

LAPWORTH LOCK

English Collection — Midlands

Built around 1815 on the Lapworth section of the Stratford-upon-Avon Canal, there are six of these delightful barrel-roofed cottages to be seen. The roofs were constructed in the same way as the bridges and tunnels on the canal.

Size:	2 ¾", 6.5 cm
Backstamp:	J
Introduced:	1991
Discontinued:	1993

Description	Can. $	U.S. $	U.K. £
Lapworth Lock	150.00	100.00	40.00

LARKRISE

English Collection — Midlands

Located in Weekley, Northamptonshire, Larkrise was originally part of a larger building built around 1652. Around the mid-18th century, the area of Weekley was owned by the Dukes of Buccleuch. These cottages were built and maintained by the Dukes for the workers.

Size:	2 ¾", 7.0 cm
Backstamp:	N-1
Introduced:	1995
Discontinued:	Current

Description	Can. $	U.S. $	U.K. £
Larkrise	60.00	45.00	17.95

LAVENDER COTTAGE

Collectors Club

Based upon cottages to be found in Bishops Cannings, Wiltshire, Lavender Cottage is a small thatched cottage built of Cotswold stone in the 16th/17th century.

Introduced in October 1989, Lavender Cottage was offered exclusively to members of the Lilliput Lane Collectors Club.

Size:	2 ¾", 7.0 cm
Backstamp:	H-1
Introduced:	1989
Discontinued:	1991

Description	Can. $	U.S. $	U.K. £
Lavender Cottage	275.00	175.00	120.00

LAZY DAYS

English Collection — South West

Located in Letcombe Regis, Oxfordshire, the village dates back to the 9th century. One of it's famous owners was William the Conqueror, it was then given to the French Abbey of Cluny by King Stephen in 1136. The cottage was built around 1540.

Size:	3", 7.6 cm
Backstamp:	N-1
Introduced:	1995
Discontinued:	1998

Description	Can. $	U.S. $	U.K. £
Lazy Days	100.00	60.00	30.00

LEAGRAVE COTTAGE

Special Editions

Leagrave Cottage was based upon a building at the Chiltern Open Air Museum in Buckinghamshire, where a number of traditional buildings from the area have been re-erected. Condemned, repaired and rebuilt, the costs amounted to £40,000.

Launched at the 1994 Lilliput Lane Annual Fair, Leagrave Cottage was only available at that meeting and at the other special events held during the following twelve months.

Size:	3 ½", 8.5 cm
Backstamp:	M
Introduced:	1994
Discontinued:	1995

Description	Can. $	U.S. $	U.K. £
Leagrave Cottage	275.00	175.00	65.00

LEONORA'S SECRET GARDEN

Garden Series

Leonora's Secret depicts a magnificent walled garden where a young woman contemplates her future. Leonora's Secret was a very finely detailed model which was time-consuming and complex to produce. Priority was given to collectors club members. This piece was fully subscribed very quickly and final orders were dispatched in December, 1995. As with any piece that is first in a series this has become much sought after. 1000 pieces were available in the UK, the rest of the edition going to the USA and Europe.

Size:	4 ½", 11.5 cm
Backstamp:	Limited Edition
Introduced:	1994 in a limited edition of 2,500
Discontinued:	1995

Description	Can. $	U.S. $	U.K. £
Leonora's Secret Garden	900.00	600.00	375.00

LET HEAVEN AND NATURE SING

Christmas in America

This imposing Catholic church is located in Port Gamble, Washington. The model was designed by Ray Day.

Size:	5", 12.7 cm
Backstamp:	P-1
Introduced:	1997
Discontinued:	1997

Description	Can. $	U.S. $	U.K. £
Let Heaven. . .	N.A.	160.00	50.00

LIGHTHOUSE

American Collection

Located around the New England shore line, these lighthouses were built around the late 1800s.

Lighthouse was in production for a fairly short period of time. As a result, approximately only 200 pieces were produced. It was only sold in the USA.

Size:	4", 10.0 cm
Backstamp:	C
Introduced:	1984
Discontinued:	1985

Description	Can. $	U.S. $	U.K. £
Lighthouse	1,500.00	1,000.00	550.00

LILAC LODGE

British Collection

Located in Lyme Regis, Dorset, Lilac Lodge is popularly known as the "umbrella house" because of its domed thatched roof.

Size:	3", 7.5 cm
Backstamp:	P-1
Introduced:	1997
Discontinued:	Current

Description	Can. $	U.S. $	U.K. £
Lilac Lodge	100.00	60.00	27.95

LIMERICK HOUSE
Irish Collection

In Adare, County Limerick, the villagers represent a good cross-section of society, it is likely that Limerick House would have been owned by a well-to-do family.

Size:	3 ¾", 9.5 cm
Backstamp:	H-1
Introduced:	1989
Discontinued:	1992

Description	Can. $	U.S. $	U.K. £
Limerick House	225.00	150.00	80.00

LITTLE BIRCH
Paint Your Own

Introduced at the annual fair held at Arbury Hall, Warwickshire on June 7th and 8th, 1997, Little Birch is only available at the Visitor's Centre in Penrith, through the Collector's Club and at Paint Your Own events. As with all "Paint Your Owns," this model is worth more unpainted.

Size:	3 ½", 8.0 cm
Backstamp:	Unknown
Introduced:	1997
Discontinued:	Current

Description	Can. $	U.S. $	U.K. £
Little Birch (unpainted)	N.A.	N.A.	11.95

LITTLE HAY
English Collection — Midlands

Little Hay is based on a builiding constructed during the 18th century in Newnham, Northamptonshire.

Size:	2 ½", 6.3 cm
Backstamp:	N-1
Introduced:	1995
Discontinued:	Current

Description	Can. $	U.S. $	U.K. £
Little Hay	25.00	50.00	19.95

LITTLE LUPINS

English Collection — South-East

The original Little Lupins is built of local materials found around the Hamlet of Bridge Street, Suffolk.

Size:	2 ¾", 7.0 cm
Backstamp:	O-1
Introduced:	1996
Discontinued:	Current

Description	Can. $	U.S. $	U.K. £
Little Lupins	70.00	40.00	19.95

LITTLE SMITHY

English Collection - Midlands

This building was built around 1570 in the village of Claverdon, Warwickshire. Note the "horse shoe" entrance made of pearwood and the detailed work area of the farrier. In the 1940s, Robin Loman took over the business. He was so proficient at his craft, that he memorised the specifications of over 400 horses.

Size:	2 ½", 6.4 cm
Backstamp:	N-1
Introduced:	1995
Discontinued:	Current

Description	Can. $	U.S. $	U.K. £
Little Smithy	100.00	60.00	28.95

LOBSTER AT THE PIER

American Landmarks

This model is typical of the restaurants found in the fishing ports along the New England coast.

Size:	4 ¼", 11.0 cm
Backstamp:	P-1
Introduced:	1997
Discontinued:	Current

Description	Can. $	U.S. $	U.K. £
Lobster At The Pier	N.A.	90.00	44.95

LOCMARIA

French Collection

Lo cmaria (Mary Cottage), with its strong granite walls and 'eyebrow' roof window, can be found in south-west Brittany, which is still an area of distinctive Celtic culture.

Size: 4", 10.0 cm
Backstamp: I-2
Introduced: 1990
Discontinued: 1997

Description	Can. $	U.S. $	U.K. £
Locmaria	75.00	50.00	25.00

LOG CABIN

American Collection

Introduced in October 1984, Log Cabin was produced in two versions. Originally, the model had snow on it; however, the second version did not have snow (this was painted not applied). When it was retired in October 1985, only 150 pieces of Log Cabin had been produced, of which the original version was the rarest. It is only sold in the USA.

Version 1 — With Snow

Version 2 — Without Snow

Version	Size	Backstamp	Intro.	Discon.	Can. $	U.S. $	U.K. £
1 - With snow	1 ¾", 4.5 cm	C	1984	1985	1,500.00	1,000.00	500.00
2 - Without snow	1 ¾", 4.5 cm	C	1985	1985	1,125.00	750.00	375.00

LOXDALE COTTAGE

English Collection — Northern

Loxdale Cottage is located in Thornton-le-Dale, North Yorkshire. With most of the history of the village dating back before the Doomsday Book of 1086, this 17th century building seems almost modern.

Size:	3 ¾", 9.0 cm
Backstamp:	O-1
Introduced:	1996
Discontinued:	Current

Description	Can. $	U.S. $	U.K. £
Loxdale Cottage	60.00	35.00	17.95

"THE LUNCH LINE"

Coca-Cola™ Country Collection

This is a renovated old train carriage that has been converted into a small café/snack bar. It was designed by Ray Day and produced under license from the Coca-Cola™ company. This cottage is produced in resin and manufactured in Ireland. Although not produced in a limited edition, all the cottages is the range are hand-numbered on the base label. This piece is available only in North America.

Size:	2 ½", 6.35 cm
Backstamp:	O-2
Introduced:	1997
Discontinued:	Current

Description	Can. $	U.S. $	U.K. £
"The Lunch Line"	60.00	42.00	N.A.

MAGILLIGAN'S

Irish Collection

This simple two-bedroomed house in County Derry would have been a typical home for a family of labourers.

Size: 2", 5.0 cm
Backstamp: H-1
Introduced: 1989
Discontinued: 1996

Description	Can. $	U.S. $	U.K. £
Magilligan's	55.00	40.00	25.00

MAGPIE COTTAGE

English Collection — Midlands

Typical of the Herefordshire area, this cruck-framed cottage has wattle and daub infills of the timber frame, which have then been lime-washed to provide additional weather protection. The small extension would have been added at a later date.

Two variations exist of Magpie Cottage. The first version has a cream shed and the second has a pink shed.

Variation	Size	Backstamp	Intro.	Discon.	Can. $	U.S. $	U.K. £
1 - Cream shed	3 ¼", 8 cm	F	1987	1989	200.00	125.00	110.00
2 - Pink shed	3 ¼", 8 cm	F	1989	1990	150.00	100.00	80.00

MAIL POUCH BARN
American Landmarks

Mail Pouch Barn, located on Highway 36 in Hendricks County west of Indianapolis, Indiana, is a typical tobacco factory that mail carriers would often stop at for a 'chew,' as well as taking a little bit extra for their 'mail pouch.'

Mail Pouch Barn is one of the first group of four models introduced in the American Landmarks collection in June 1989.

Size: 3 ¼", 8.0 cm
Backstamp: H-1
Introduced: 1989
Discontinued: 1993

Description	Can. $	U.S. $	U.K. £
Mail Pouch Barn	225.00	150.00	70.00

MAIR HAVEN
Scottish Collection

These sturdy fishermen's cottages are typical of the properties to be found in the villages on the eastern side of Scotland, along the North Sea coastline.

Size: 2 ½", 6.5 cm
Backstamp: K-1
Introduced: 1992
Discontinued: Current

Description	Can. $	U.S. $	U.K. £
Mair Haven	55.00	35.00	15.95

MANGERTON MILL
British Collection

This 17th century mill can be found in Bridport, Dorset.

Size: 4", 10.0 cm
Backstamp: Unknown
Introduced: 1997
Discontinued: Current

Description	Can. $	U.S. $	U.K. £
Mangerton Mill	300.00	185.00	84.95

LE MANOIR DE CHAMPFLEURI

French Collection

Situated in the beautiful Loire Valley, Le Manoir de Champfleuri (Pasture Lodge) marks the entrance to a Duke's estate. Built in the 18th century, the lodge has the same charm and elegance as the many chateaux which are to be found in the surrounding area.

Size:	6 ¾", 17.0 cm
Backstamp:	I-2
Introduced:	1990
Discontinued:	1997

Description	Can. $	U.S. $	U.K. £
Le Manoir De Champfleuri	275.00	215.00	100.00

MARCHE HOUSE

Paint Your Own

Introduced at the annual fair held at Arbury Hall, Warwickshire on June 7th and 8th, 1997, Marche House is only available at the Visitor's Centre in Penrith, through the Collector's Club and at Paint Your Own events. As with all "Paint Your Owns," this model is worth more unpainted.

Size:	2 ¾", 7.0 cm
Backstamp:	Unknown
Introduced:	1997
Discontinued:	Current

Description	Can. $	U.S. $	U.K. £
Marche House (unpainted)	N.A.	N.A.	7.95

MARIGOLD MEADOW

English Collection — South-East

Based upon a cottage in Hampshire, Marigold Meadow is a 14th century oak-framed building with wattle and daub infill (although some has been replaced with brick), and a half-hip thatched roof. The large brick chimney houses a bread oven which the original occupier would have used to good effect.

Size:	3 ½", 8.5 cm
Backstamp:	L
Introduced:	1993
Discontinued:	1998

Description	Can. $	U.S. $	U.K. £
Marigold Meadow	125.00	80.00	40.00

LE MAS DU VIGNERON

French Collection

Le Mas du Vigneron (The Vine Grower's House) can be found on the high slopes of Provence where fine wines have been produced for centuries. Built from local stone and covered with yellow plaster, the house is reminiscent of the villas that were built here by the Romans, when the Roman civilisation spread throughout Provence in 10 BC.

Size:	3 ½", 9.0 cm
Backstamp:	I-2
Introduced:	1990
Discontinued:	1997

Description	Can. $	U.S. $	U.K. £
Le Mas Du Vigneron	120.00	85.00	45.00

LA MASELLE DE NADAILLAC

French Collection

La Maselle de Nadaillac (Nadaillac Shelter) can be found among the forests of the Dordogne. Built of local limestone, the thick walls support the weight of large stone slabs which make up the roof; the conical building now houses the family pig. Pigs in this region are not used for food but as workers for hunting truffles.

Size:	4", 10.0 cm
Backstamp:	I-2
Introduced:	1990
Discontinued:	1997

Description	Can. $	U.S. $	U.K. £
La Maselle De Nadaillac	135.00	95.00	50.00

MAYFLOWER HOUSE

Special Editions

This building with it's distinctive chimneys and windows date back to the Tudor period. Located in Lavenham, Suffolk and named after the famous ship "The Mayflower" that took the pilgrim fathers to the New World and landed at Plymouth Rock.

It was produced exclusively for sale in the USA. The model had a fairly short production run before being retired in December 1990. The early versions of this model have grey lattice windows while later versions were blue. Mayflower House is a difficult model to obtain in the UK because of the distribution and production limitations mentioned above.

Variation	Size	Backstamp	Intro.	Discon:	Can. $	U.S. $	U.K. £
1 - Grey windows	4 ½", 11.4 cm	H-1	1989	1990	750.00	500.00	350.00
2 - Blue windows	4 ½", 11.4 cm	H-1	1989	1990	700.00	475.00	290.00

MEADOWSWEET COTTAGE

Collectors Club

Meadowsweet Cottage was built in the 17th century at Elmley Castle in the Vale of Evesham.

It was introduced in March 1996 and was only available to collectors club members through retailers special order.

Size:	3 ¾", 9.0 cm
Backstamp:	O-2
Introduced:	1996
Discontinued:	1997

Description	Can. $	U.S. $	U.K. £
Meadowsweet Cottage	135.00	110.00	60.00

MEDWAY MANOR

British Collection

This half-timbered Wealden house can be found in the village of Smarden, Kent.

Size:	4 1/8", 10.5 cm
Backstamp:	P-1
Introduced:	1998
Discontinued:	Current

Description	Can. $	U.S. $	U.K. £
Medway Manor	200.00	120.00	59.95

MEERSBURGER WEINSTUBE

German Collection

Meersburger (roughly translated to Sea Castle) which overlooks Lake Constance (also known as the Bodensee, with a population of 5,200) between Germany and Switzerland, is bedecked with flowers.
It was sold only in Central Europe the first year of issue.

Size:	4 ¾", 12.0 cm
Backstamp:	F
Introduced:	1987
Discontinued:	1998

Description	Can. $	U.S. $	U.K. £
Meersburger Weinstube	100.00	75.00	35.00

MICKLEGATE ANTIQUES

English Collection — Northern

Micklegate Antiques is typical of the 17th century buildings to be found in the Shambles (from the Old English shamel, meaning a slaughterhouse), in York. A favourite place for visitors to the city, across the short, narrow Shambles old timber-framed buildings lean towards one another.

Size:	4 ¼", 11.0 cm
Backstamp:	J
Introduced:	1991
Discontinued:	1997

Description	Can. $	U.S. $	U.K. £
Micklegate Antiques	120.00	95.00	45.00

MIDWEST BARN
American Collection

This distinctive country barn, with its red and white striped boarding, was introduced in October, 1984. Seemingly one of the more popular models in the American Collection, 400 pieces had been produced by the time it was retired in October, 1985.

Size:	2 ½", 6.5 cm
Backstamp:	C
Introduced:	1984
Discontinued:	1985

Description	Can. $	U.S. $	U.K. £
Midwest Barn	1,125.00	750.00	315.00

MILESTONE COTTAGE
English Collection — Midlands

Located in Harlestone, Northampshire, Milestone Cottage was originally a peasants home, and is a typical example of northern Cotswold architecture.

Size:	2 ½", 6.3 cm
Backstamp:	N-1
Introduced:	1995
Discontinued:	Current

Description	Can. $	U.S. $	U.K. £
Milestone Cottage	55.00	35.00	15.95

Photograph
not available
at press time

"MILK FOR MOM AND A COKE FOR ME"
Coca-Cola™ Country Collection

Inspired by a turn-of-the-century building in New Albany, Indiana, the Spring Street Market is representative of small town USA's neighbourhood grocery store. This model was designed by Ray Day.

Size:	3 ½", 8.9 cm
Backstamp:	Unknown
Introduced:	1998
Discontinued:	Current

Description	Can. $	U.S. $	U.K. £
Milk For Mom . . .	N.A.	95.00	N.A.

AMERICAN LANDMARKS COLLECTION

Afternoon Tea   The Birdsong   Harvest Mill

Holy Night   Lobster at the Pier   16.9 Cents per Gallon

COCA-COLA™ COUNTRY COLLECTION

"A Cherry Coke — Just The Prescription"   "Country Fresh Pickins"   'Fill 'Er Up and Check the Oil

Hazards of the Road   Hook, Line and Sinker   "We've Got It . . . (Or They Don't Make It!)"

CHRISTMAS COLLECTION

| Fir Tree Cottage | Ivy House | Plum Cottage | St. Joseph's School |

LAKELAND CHRISTMAS COLLECTION

| Langdale Cottage | Millbeck Cottage | Patterdale Cottage | Rydal Cottage |

Home For the Holidays (American Landmarks Collection)

Kerry Lodge (Christmas Lodge Collection)

ENGLISH COLLECTION — SOUTH-EAST

The Anchor   Birchwood Cottage   The Blue Boar

Calendar Cottage   Chalk Down   Cherry Blossom Cottage   Cradle Cottage

Crispin Cottage   Flowerpots   Gossip Gate

Honey Pot Cottage   John Barleycorn Cottage   Little Lupins   The Rustlings

Chipping Combe   The Cuddy   Double Cottage

Duckdown Cottage   Fuschia Cottage   Lazy Days

The Old Post Office   Pipit Toll   Purbeck Stores

Spring Gate   Stradling Priory   Sweet Pea Cottage

ENGLISH COLLECTION — MIDLANDS

| Button Down | Little Hay | Little Smithy | Milestone |

| Sulgrave Manor | Railway Cottage | Rosemary Cottage |

ENGLISH COLLECTION — NORTHERN

| Bluebell Farm | The Dalesman | Fry Days | Loxdale Cottage |

VILLAGE SHOPS

| The Baker's Shop | The China Shop | Penny Sweets | The Toy Shop |

ENGLISH TEA ROOM COLLECTION

Bargate Tea Rooms   Bo-Peep Tea Room   Grandma Batty's Tea Room

Kendal Tea House   New Forest Teas   Swaledale Teas

VICTORIAN SHOPS COLLECTION

Apothecary   Bookshop   Haberdashery

Horologist   Pawnbroker   Tailor

San Francisco House — Two Colourways

Danny — Style 2 (left), Style 1 (right)

Bermuda Cottage — 3 Colourways

Country Church — Variation 1 (left), Variation 2 (right)

The King's Arms

The Black Knight

The Merchant

The Dandy

Princess Nyneve

MILLBECK COTTAGE

Lakeland Christmas Collection

Millbeck Cottage is located in the village of Millbeck, close to Neswick in Cumbria.

Size:	2 ¾″, 9.5 cm
Backstamp:	O-1
Introduced:	1996
Discontinued:	Current

Description	Can. $	U.S. $	U.K. £
Millbeck Cottage	50.00	35.00	14.95

MILLERS

English Collection — South-East

This two-roomed cottage, with its shiplap weatherboard and brick quoins, is typical of the buildings to be found in Kent. As only soft stone was available for building, a large amount of wood was used for the external skin.

Introduced in February 1983, Millers was remodelled during the same year, when it was made smaller and the base became more pitted. The original version carried backstamp A-1 and has eight panes of glass in the upstairs windows. Just before the remodelling in late 1983 the backstamp was changed to C. In 1984 a new model was introduced and the panes in the upstairs window were reduced to six.

Version	Size	Backstamp	Intro.	Discon.	Can. $	U.S. $	U.K. £
1a - 8 panes	2 ½″, 6.5 cm	A-1	1983	1983	475.00	325.00	220.00
1b- 8 panes	2 ½″, 6.5 cm	C	1983	1984	375.00	275.00	175.00
2 - 6 panes	2 ½″, 6.5 cm	B	1984	1986	275.00	175.00	140.00

MINERS COTTAGE / MINERS

English Collection — Northern

Based on a typical terraced house in the north east of England, Miners was introduced in February 1983.

It was originally named "Miners Cottage" and was all grey in colour, with backstamp A-1. Renamed "Miners" in July 1983, it was remodelled and now carried backstamp B. It was made smaller and the colours from the previous mould were carried over (except the grey) onto the second mould. Another colour was now available and also carried the backstamp B.

Version	Size	Backstamp	Intro.	Discon.	Can. $	U.S. $	U.K. £
1a - Grey	2 ¾", 7 cm	A-1	1983	1983	1,125.00	750.00	450.00
1b - Sandy roof	2 ¾", 7 cm	A-1	1983	1983	900.00	600.00	325.00
1c - Black roof	2 ¾", 7 cm	A-1	1983	1983	750.00	500.00	275.00
2a - Sandy roof	2 ½", 6.7 cm	B	1983	1984	750.00	500.00	225.00
2b - Black roof	2 ½", 6.7 cm	B	1983	1985	675.00	450.00	200.00
2c - Olive roof	2 ½", 6.7 cm	B	1983	1985	600.00	400.00	175.00

MISTLETOE COTTAGE

Christmas Collection (1992 Annual Ornament)

Mistletoe Cottage was the first in the series of annual Christmas Ornaments. Based upon a small tile-hung cottage in Kent, the model was intended to be used as a Christmas decoration.

Size: 2 ½", 6.5 cm
Backstamp: K-1
Introduced: 1992
Discontinued: 1992

Description	Can. $	U.S. $	U.K. £
Mistletoe Cottage	75.00	50.00	55.00

"MMM . . . JUST LIKE HOME"

Coca-Cola™ Country Collection

This model is based on the the typical rural restaurant to be found in small American towns.

Designed by Ray Day under licence from the Coca-Cola™ company, this piece is manufactured in Ireland and cast in resin. Although not issued as a limited edition, all cottages in the series are hand-numbered on the base lablel. It is available in North America only.

Size:	3 ½", 8.9 cm
Backstamp:	O-2
Introduced:	1997
Discontinued:	Current

Description	Can. $	U.S. $	U.K. £
"Mmm . . . Just Like Home"	150.00	130.00	N.A.

MOONLIGHT COVE

English Collection — South-West

Situated on the estuary of the River Camel in Cornwall, this rugged fisherman's cottage still perpetuates the medieval arrangement of living quarters above, storage space below.

Size:	3 ¾", 9.5 cm
Backstamp:	J
Introduced:	1991
Discontinued:	1996

Description	Can. $	U.S. $	U.K. £
Moonlight Cove	90.00	60.00	35.00

MORETON MANOR

English Collection — Midlands

Built in the mid-1800s of local limestone, houses such as Moreton Manor can be found around the Cotswold villages of Lower and Upper Slaughter, Broadway and Moreton-in the-Marsh.

Size:	3 ½", 9.0 cm
Backstamp:	D
Introduced:	1985
Discontinued:	1989

Description	Can. $	U.S. $	U.K. £
Moreton Manor	225.00	150.00	85.00

MORNING HAS BROKEN

An American Journey

Babcock State Park, West Virginia, is home to this building created in 1976 from a variety of old mills.

Size:	3 ¾", 9.5 cm
Backstamp:	P-1
Introduced:	1998
Discontinued:	Current

Description	Can. $	U.S. $	U.K. £
Morning Has Broken	N.A.	85.00	49.95

MOSELHAUS

German Collection

Moselhaus is located in an area renowned for its wine, massive timber-framed houses and steeply terraced vineyards along the banks of the Moselle river.

Size:	5 ½", 14.0 cm
Backstamp:	F
Introduced:	1987
Discontinued:	1998

Description	Can. $	U.S. $	U.K. £
Moselhaus	185.00	150.00	70.00

MRS. PINKERTON'S POST OFFICE

English Collection — South-East

Based upon buildings to be found in Norfolk and Fiat Fenlands of East Anglia, Mrs. Pinkerton's Post Office is built of flint cobbles, gathered from the surrounding fields or from the local beaches, complemented by local brick at the corners. Built in the early 1800s just before Britain's Penny Post System was founded in 1840.

Initially this model was exclusively available from the UK Guild of Specialist China & Glass Retailers; however, after twelve months the model became generally available.

Size:	3 ¼", 8.0 cm
Backstamp:	H-1
Introduced:	1989
Discontinued:	1997

Description	Can. $	U.S. $	U.K. £
Mrs. Pinkerton's	100.00	70.00	40.00

NEW FOREST TEAS

English Tea Room Collection

Based on the "Thatched Cottage Hotel"(famous for it's cream teas) on Brooning Road in Brockenhurst, Hampshire, this model has a timber frame with red brick infills.

Size:	3 ¾", 9.5 cm
Backstamp:	N-1
Introduced:	1995
Discontinued:	Current

Description	Can. $	U.S. $	U.K. £
New Forest Teas	180.00	120.00	56.95

NIGHTINGALE

British Collection

The cottage on which this model was based was built near the end of the 17th century in Duddington, Northhamptonshire.

Size:	2 ¼", 5.5 cm
Backstamp:	Q-1
Introduced:	1998
Discontinued:	Current

Description	Can. $	U.S. $	U.K. £
Nightingale	35.00	25.00	9.95

NÜRNBERGER BÜRGERHAÜS

German Collection

Birthplace of the great painter and engraver Albrecht Dürer, Nüremberg is famed for its many historic buildings.

Nürnberger Bürgerhaus was sold in Central Europe during its first year of issue.

Size:	5", 13.0 cm
Backstamp:	B
Introduced:	1987
Discontinued:	1998

Description	Can. $	U.S. $	U.K. £
Nürnberger Bürgerhaus	185.00	150.00	70.00

THE NURSERY

Collectors Club

The Nursery is based on a building located in the village of Lamarsh, Suffolk.

It was introduced as a Collectors Club Much Valued Customer Programme (the first Lilliput Lane have offered). A pouch was issued to hold receipts to the value of £250 or $400 US in cottage purchases which the retailer filled in and sent off on the customers behalf.

Two varieties of The Nursery exist. The only difference between them is the backstamp. The earlier version's backstamp does not include the initials EEGG (which stand for Enesco European Giftware Group who purchased the company in 1996). After the purchase, EEGG was added to the new backstamps.

Variety	Size	Backstamp	Intro.	Discon.	Can. $	U.S. $	U.K. £
1 - Without EEGG	4", 7.3 cm	O-1	1996	1996	125.00	75.00	55.00
2 - With EEGG	4", 7.3 cm	O-2	1996	1997	500.00	375.00	250.00

THE NUTSHELL

English Collection — South-East

Mersea Island, south of Colchester in Essex, is famous among small-boat sailors, and in the old town of West Mersea some attractive old fishing cottages still survive. The Nutshell can be found on Mersea Island. Probably built in the mid-1800s, the timber-framed cottage has a half mansard roof to the front and weatherboarding on the walls.

Size:	2 ¾", 7.0 cm
Backstamp:	K-1
Introduced:	1992
Discontinued:	1995

Description	Can. $	U.S. $	U.K. £
The Nutshell	150.00	95.00	30.00

OAK COTTAGE

Style One
Blaise Hamlet Collection

Based on the Blaise Castle Estate in Henbury and designed in 1810, this is one of the nine cottages based upon buildings at Blaise Hamlet, near Bristol. Oak Cottage, Circular Cottage and Diamond Cottage were the first three to be launched. One of only three thatched cottages in the Hamlet, Oak Cottage is built of Cotswold stone and features mullion windows.

Size:	4 ½", 11.5 cm
Backstamp:	H-1
Introduced:	1989
Discontinued:	1993

Description	Can. $	U.S. $	U.K. £
Oak Cottage	225.00	150.00	80.00

OAK COTTAGE

Style Two
Classics Collection

One of the models in the miniature Classics Collection, Oak Cottage is a scaled down version of the cottage from the Blaise Hamlet Collection.

Size:	2 ½", 6.0 cm
Backstamp:	L
Introduced:	1993
Discontinued:	1995

Description	Can. $	U.S. $	U.K. £
Oak Cottage	150.00	95.00	40.00

OAK LODGE

Style One
English Collection — South-East

Oak Lodge is a typical example of a 16th-century Surrey farmhouse. Based upon a building to be found along the London-Portsmouth road, Oak Lodge has a timber frame infilled with brick (originally it would have been wattle and daub), and a clay tiled roof.

The model of Oak Lodge was remodelled in September 1983. On the second version the roof tiles on the right-hand side were reduced from seven rows to five rows; the roof overhang on the left-hand side was reduced; and the timber framing was straightened. There was also a noticeable change around the base. Version 2 has more foliage at the front and rear; the cobbles were more apparent; and the base was squared off.

Version	Size	Backstamp	Intro.	Discon.	Can. $	U.S. $	U.K. £
1 - 7 rows of roof tiles	3", 7.5 cm	None, A-1, A-2	1982	1983	1,500.00	1,000.00	400.00
2 - 5 rows of roof tiles	3", 7.5 cm	C	1983	1987	300.00	200.00	110.00

OAK LODGE

Style Two
Special Editions

This model is based on a 16th century Surrey farmhouse in the Village of Wrecclesham, near Farnham.

The Oak Lodge ten year award was created in 1993 and was given to employees with ten years of service. This cottage hardly resembled the Oak Lodge of 1982, with more of an emphasis on detail around the building and garden. As time passes more of these are likely to become available.

Front View

Rear View

Description	Size	Backstamp	Intro.	Discon.	Can. $	U.S. $	U.K. £
Oak Lodge	4 ½", 11.75 cm	L	1993	Ltd. Ed.	2,200.00	1,800.00	1,100.00

OAKWOOD SMITHY

English Collection — South-East

The horseshoe-shaped entrance tells prospective customers that Oakwood Smithy is the home of the local blacksmith.

Size:	4 ¾", 12.0 cm
Backstamp:	K-1
Introduced:	1992
Discontinued:	Current

Description	Can. $	U.S. $	U.K. £
Oakwood Smithy	420.00	300.00	135.00

OCTAGON TOWER

Studley Royal Collection

Limited to 5,000 pieces, this forms part of a 5 piece set. The other 'smaller' pieces in the set are Banqueting House, Temple of Piety and St Marys Church. The largest part of the set is Fountains Abbey the 'centre piece' of the collection, limited to 3,500 pieces. The 'Tower' along with the rest of the set are all exclusive to the USA only.

Size:	4 ¼", 10.8 cm
Backstamp:	M
Introduced:	1994 in a limited edition of 3,500
Discontinued:	Current

Description	Can. $	U.S. $	U.K. £
Octagon Tower	N.A.	85.00	N.A.

OH BY GOSH, BY GOLLY

Coca-Cola™ Country Collection

This model, designed by Ray Day, was only available in the United States.

Size:	Unknown
Backstamp:	Unknown
Introduced:	1997
Discontinued:	1997

Description	Can. $	U.S. $	U.K. £
Oh By Gosh, By Golly	N.A	85.00	N.A.

O'LACEY'S STORE

Irish Collection

In County Mayo the village store is the place to catch up on what's happening — and buy the groceries. Originally a single-storey dwelling, as business grew the second floor was added.

Size:	3", 7.5 cm
Backstamp:	H-1
Introduced:	1989
Discontinued:	1996

Description	Can. $	U.S. $	U.K. £
O'Lacey's Store	90.00	60.00	35.00

THE OLD CURIOSITY SHOP

English Collection — South-East

Situated in Portsmouth Street, in the famous 'Square Mile' of the City of London, The Old Curiosity Shop is a 16th-century antique shop which is reputed to have been the model for the book by Charles Dickens, who used to visit a friend near by.

The early variation of this piece had green windows whereas the second variation had tan windows.

Variation	Size	Backstamp	Intro.	Discon.	Can. $	U.S. $	U.K. £
1 - Green windows	3 ½", 9 cm	D	1985	1989	225.00	150.00	115.00
2 - Tan windows	3 ½", 9 cm	D	1985	1989	225.00	150.00	115.00

THE OLD FORGE

British Collection

This 18th century cruck-framed building in Queniborough, Leicestershire is thought to have been a forge at one time.

Size:	2 ¾", 7.0 cm
Backstamp:	P-1
Introduced:	1998
Discontinued:	Current

Description	Can. $	U.S. $	U.K. £
The Old Forge	90.00	55.00	24.95

OLD MILL

English Collection — South-West

Old Mill was the original version of Old Mine. Introduced in September 1982, it was soon realised that the model was a mine and not a mill; the model was quickly renamed Old Mine. It is believed that about 10 pieces were produced of Old Mill.

Size:	3 ½", 9.0 cm
Backstamp:	A-1
Introduced:	1982
Discontinued:	1982

Description	Can. $	U.S. $	U.K. £
Old Mill	9,000.00	6,000.00	2,500.00

OLD MINE

English Collection — South-West

Probably the most famous Lilliput Lane model, as well as also being rare. Introduced in September 1982, Old Mine was decorated in a very distinct shade. The model was only in production for 10 months before being retired. Only 200 pieces were produced, each with the original backstamp and the original label.

Size:	3 ½", 9.0 cm
Backstamp:	A-1
Introduced:	1982
Discontinued:	1983

Description	Can. $	U.S. $	U.K. £
Old Mine	6,750.00	4,500.00	1,650.00

OLD MOTHER HUBBARD'S

English Collection — South-West

Built around the 16th century, Mother Hubbard's Cottage can be found in Yealmpton, in Devon. Legend has it that in 1804, Sarah Martin (whilst on holiday at the Kitley estate near Plymouth), wrote a lengthy rhyme about the housekeeper of the estate and called it 'Old Mother Hubbard.' When the housekeeper retired, she went to live in a cottage owned by the estate at Yealmpton; hence the cottage became known as 'Mother Hubbard's Cottage.' Nearly demolished in 1960, work was carried out to try to save this house, it now runs and operates as a restaurant.

Size:	3 ½", 8.5 cm
Backstamp:	L
Introduced:	1993
Discontinued:	Current

Description	Can. $	U.S. $	U.K. £
Old Mother Hubbard's	175.00	120.00	56.95

Note: For the Dream Cottage Miniature model please see page 74.

THE OLD POST OFFICE

English Collection — South-West

Built around the 14th century, this building was originally a manor house. Shortly after the Penny Post System was set up in 1840, a room in the house was used as a receiving room. The manor house was sold in the late 19th century and the Post Office was relocated.

The Old Post Office was one of the early Lilliput Lane models which was painted to resemble the stone houses of Oxfordshire, with soft yellow limestone and imported clay tiles. Introduced in September 1982, there was a backstamp change in November 1982. The remodelled version, introduced in 1983 had more foliage added to the rear roof. The same mould was used in 1984 for Tintagel.

Version 3

Version	Size	Backstamp	Intro.	Discon.	Can. $	U.S. $	U.K. £
1a - Less foliage	2 ¾", 7 cm	A-1	1982	1982	1,125.00	750.00	400.00
1b - Less foliage	2 ¾", 7 cm	A-2	1982	1983	900.00	600.00	350.00
2 - More foliage	2 ¾", 7 cm	B, C	1983	1986	750.00	500.00	315.00

OLD SCHOOL HOUSE

English Collection — Northern

After Cliburn School was retired in February 1984, the mould was then used for Old School House. As well as changing the name, Old School House was also painted in different colours. After demolding breakages, the Bell Tower was remodelled. The depth of the tower and bell housing had more than doubled and now went back to the roof.

Version 2 — Larger Tower

Version	Size	Backstamp	Intro.	Discon.	Can. $	U.S. $	U.K. £
1 - Smaller tower	2 ½", 7 cm	A-1	1984	1985	2,250.00	1,500.00	500.00
2 - Larger tower	2 ½", 7 cm	D	1984	1985	1,875.00	1,250.00	410.00

OLD SHOP AT BIGNOR

English Collection — South-East

Close to the Weald and Downland Open Air Museum lies the village of Bignor, where the Old Shop is situated. A magnificent example of a 'Wealden' house, the Old Shop was built in the 15th century. Its oak frame is on a stone foundation, and the walls are made of wattle and daub with flint in-filling.

Size: 4 ½", 11.5 cm
Backstamp: J
Introduced: 1991
Discontinued: 1995

Description	Can. $	U.S. $	U.K. £
Old Shop at Bignor	350.00	225.00	65.00

THE OLD VICARAGE AT CHRISTMAS
Christmas Specials

Based on a 17th century vicars house, this fourth of the Christmas Specials depicts an enjoyable Christmas scene. Unlike it's predecessors, this cottage only ran from July to December 1991. This was also the last cottage to have had the snow incorporated into the mould. All cottages after this had snow added after completion.

Size:	4 ½″, 11.5 cm
Backstamp:	J
Introduced:	1991
Discontinued:	1991

Description	Can. $	U.S. $	U.K. £
The Old Vicarage	225.00	150.00	165.00

· OLDE YORK TOLL
Special Editions

Olde York Toll, located at one end of the Lendal Bridge which spans the River House in York, was first used as a Toll House in 1863 and was used until 1894. Generally available worldwide, in the UK Olde York Toll was only retailed through Peter Jones China.

Size:	4 ½″, 11.5 cm
Backstamp:	I-1
Introduced:	1989
Discontinued:	1991

Description	Can. $	U.S. $	U.K. £
Olde York Toll	225.00	150.00	170.00

Photograph
not available
at press time

ONE NATION UNDER GOD
Allegiance Collection

This model was inspired by a church from Thomaston, Maine.

Size:	4″, 10.0 cm
Backstamp:	P-1
Introduced:	1997
Discontinued:	Current

Description	Can. $	U.S. $	U.K. £
One Nation Under God	N.A.	75.00	34.95

ORCHARD FARM COTTAGE

English Collection — South-East

Located close to the village of Hever in Kent, Orchard Farm Cottage was built in the late 17th century. It is classic vernacular architecture which makes good use of local materials. Timber framed on a stone plinth, some of the panels are of brick infill whilst others are weatherboarded in timber.

Size:	3 ¼", 8.0 cm
Backstamp:	M
Introduced:	1994
Discontinued:	1998

Description	Can. $	U.S. $	U.K. £
Orchard Farm Cottage	160.00	110.00	50.00

OSTLERS KEEP

English Collection — South-West

Devon has the greatest concentration of earth-walled buildings, and the 'cob' cottage is characteristic of the area. Cob is a durable mixture of clay, straw and dung, which is usually laid on a stone foundation and then plastered with a clay and lime mixture. Ostlers Keep is based upon a 16th century farmhouse which is now a Public House.

Size:	2 ¾", 7.0 cm
Backstamp:	D
Introduced:	1985
Discontinued:	1991

Description	Can. $	U.S. $	U.K. £
Ostlers Keep	175.00	125.00	75.00

OTTER REACH

English Collection — South-West

Based in the Devon countryside near the Rover Otter, this is a cob cottage with a thick 'catslide' thatched roof.

Size:	2 ½", 6.0 cm
Backstamp:	I-2
Introduced:	1990
Discontinued:	1996

Description	Can. $	U.S. $	U.K. £
Otter Reach	45.00	30.00	25.00

OUT OF THE STORM

English Collection — South-West

Out of the Storm is based on Clovelly in North Devon.
The first models of this limited edition did not leave the factory until late March 1997. Possibly only 1,000 to 1,5000 models were available in the United Kingdom, with the rest of the edition being shipped abroad.

Size:	9 ¼", 23.5 cm
Backstamp:	P-1, with limited edition details below
Introduced:	1997 in a limited edition of 3,000
Discontinued:	1998

Description	Can. $	U.S. $	U.K. £
Out of the Storm	1,300.00	1,250.00	395.00

PAINSWICK POST OFFICE

Paint Your Own

Introduced in August, 1996 at the Annual Collectors Club Event in Chichestin and available at the Collectors Club, Visitors Centre at Penrith and Lilliput Lane Events featuring a Paint Your Own facility. Some "Paint Your Owns" are available for longer than a year, usually they are available until stocks run dry. "Paint Your Owns" are worth more left unpainted.

Size:	3 ¾", 9.5 cm
Backstamp:	O-2
Introduced:	1996
Discontinued:	Current

Description	Can. $	U.S. $	U.K. £
Painswick Post Office (unpainted)	N.A.	N.A.	18.00

PARADISE LODGE

English Collection — Midlands

Based upon a lodge house situated in the grounds of Hodnet Hall, in Shropshire, Paradise Lodge is named after the surrounding area of Paradise Valley, which is a haven for all manner of flora and fauna. Built in the 19th century using brick and stone, the lodge was originally occupied by the estate's gamekeeper.

Size:	4 ½", 11.5 cm
Backstamp:	J
Introduced:	1991
Discontinued:	1996

Description	Can. $	U.S. $	U.K. £
Paradise Lodge	150.00	95.00	50.00

Note: For the Dream Cottage Miniature model please see page 74.

PARGETTER'S RETREAT

English Collection — South-East

With its complex relief designs, this house could possibly be the home of a pargeter. Found mainly in the East Anglian region, pargeting was a method of creating relief plaster designs on the outside of a building, with each pargeter having his own recipe for the plaster.

Size:	4 ½", 11.5 cm
Backstamp:	G
Introduced:	1988
Discontinued:	1990

Description	Can. $	U.S. $	U.K. £
Pargetter's Retreat	200.00	125.00	80.00

PARSON'S RETREAT

British Collection

The building on which this model is based was once a priest's house in Clare, Suffolk. A striking feature of this house is the pargeting on the walls.

Size:	4 ¼", 11.0 cm
Backstamp:	P-2
Introduced:	1998
Discontinued:	Current

Description	Can. $	U.S. $	U.K. £
Parson's Retreat	160.00	90.00	44.95

PASTURES NEW

British Collection

This farmhouse, constructed from local limestone, is located in Duddington, Northamptonshire. The see-saw actually moves and the gate behind the farmer can be opened and shut.

Size:	5 1/8", 13.0 cm
Backstamp:	P-2
Introduced:	1998
Discontinued:	Current

Description	Can. $	U.S. $	U.K. £
Pastures New	480.00	350.00	135.00

PARTRIDGE COTTAGE
Christmas Collection

This model is based on a Cotswold stone cottage.

All of the miniature cottages in the Christmas Collection are intended to collectively set a lovely, wintery scene. Partridge Cottage conjures up thoughts of thick stone walls and roaring log fires.

Size:	2 ½", 6.0 cm
Backstamp:	L
Introduced:	1993
Discontinued:	1997

Description	Can. $	U.S. $	U.K. £
Partridge Cottage	50.00	35.00	20.00

PAT COHAN'S BAR
Irish Collection

This bar is located in County Mayo, Ireland. The atmosphere of an Irish bar cannot be described — it has to be experienced. The bar bustles with activity as drinks are dispensed, racing bets are exchanged and business deals are struck, whilst at the same time the regulars are catching up on the latest gossip. And all of this goes on to the accompaniment of the local musicians playing the uilleann pipes, tin whistle, accordion and fiddle.

Size:	3 ½", 9.0 cm
Backstamp:	H-1
Introduced:	1989
Discontinued:	1996

Description	Can. $	U.S. $	U.K. £
Pat Cohan's Bar	125.00	85.00	45.00

PATTERDALE COTTAGE
Lakeland Christmas Collection

This small snow-covered cottage, is typical of homes found in the Lake District.

Patterdale Cottage was introduced alongside Rydal Cottage and Langdale Cottage as part of the new Lakeland Christmas series.

Size:	2 ¾", 7.0 cm
Backstamp:	N-1
Introduced:	1995
Discontinued:	1998

Description	Can. $	U.S. $	U.K. £
Patterdale Cottage	60.00	35.00	15.95

PAWNBROKER
Victorian Shops Collection

Built at the turn of the century, this piece was based on part of the Eagle Parade in Buxton, Derbyshire.

Size:	5 ¼", 13.0 cm
Backstamp:	P-1
Introduced:	1997
Discontinued:	Current

Description	Can. $	U.S. $	U.K. £
Pawnbroker	100.00	75.00	29.95

PEAR TREE HOUSE
English Collection — Midlands

Based upon a building in Mansellacey, Herefordshire which is now used as the village post office, Pear Tree House was built in the 17th century of stone and timber and has an interesting dovecot gable.

Size:	3 ¼", 8.0 cm
Backstamp:	J
Introduced:	1991
Discontinued:	1995

Description	Can. $	U.S. $	U.K. £
Pear Tree House	125.00	80.00	35.00

PENKILL CASTLE
Historic Castles of Britain

South of the Isle of Arran in the Firth of Clyde sits Penkill Castle, ancestral seat of the Boyd family from the late 15th century. The Castle was visited many times by Gabriel and Christina Rossetti, who were friends with Alice Boyd.

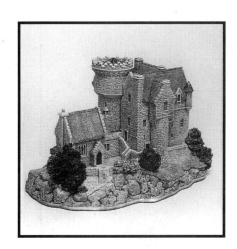

Size:	3 ¾", 9.5 cm
Backstamp:	N-2
Introduced:	1995
Discontinued:	Current

Description	Can. $	U.S. $	U.K. £
Penkill Castle	180.00	115.00	52.95

PENNY'S POST

English Collection — Midlands

Penny's Post, built in the 18th century, is based in Adlestrop, Gloucestershire.

Size:	2 ½", 6.0 cm
Backstamp:	N-1
Introduced:	1995
Discontinued:	Current

Description	Can. $	U.S. $	U.K. £
Penny's Post	70.00	50.00	19.95

PENNY SWEETS

Village Shops Collection

Based upon a building situated in a Cotswold market town in Gloucestershire, Penny Sweets continued the Village Shops Collection theme of the traditional Cotswold stores. Built around 1700 using Cotswold stone and long-straw thatch, the house was converted into a sweet shop in 1865.

In the UK, the model was initially exclusive to the UK Guild of Specialist China & Glass Retailers before general release.

Size:	3 ½", 9.0 cm
Backstamp:	K-1
Introduced:	1992
Discontinued:	1998

Description	Can. $	U.S. $	U.K. £
Penny Sweets	120.00	80.00	35.00

DE PEPERMOLEN

Netherlands Collection

Since the time of the Dutch East India Company spices have been a valuable commodity, and the cellars of De Pepermolen (The Peppermill) would probably have contained the aromas of the various spices to remind the spice merchant of his wealth.

Apart from the colouring, De Pepermolen is similar to Begijnhof. Begijnhof's roof is brown and De Pepermolen's is grey and white.

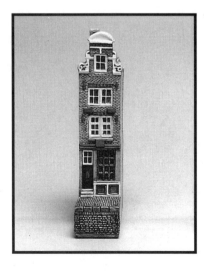

Size:	4 ¾", 12.0 cm
Backstamp:	J
Introduced:	1991
Discontinued:	1998
Variation:	Begijnhof

Description	Can. $	U.S. $	U.K. £
De Pepermolen	55.00	35.00	15.00

PEPSI COLA BARN

American Landmarks

This barn can be found along Highway 7, 2 miles north of Madison, Indiana.

After a relatively short production run, Pepsi Cola Barn was retired. This short production period has made it increasingly more difficult to acquire Pepsi Cola Barn on the secondary market.

Size:	3″, 7.5 cm
Backstamp:	I-2
Introduced:	1990
Discontinued:	1991

Description	Can. $	U.S. $	U.K. £
Pepsi Cola Barn	375.00	250.00	160.00

PERIWINKLE COTTAGE

English Collection — South-West

Selworthy, on the fringe of Exmoor, is a picturesque village of well-tended, white-washed cottages preserved by the National Trust as part of the Holnicote Estate. The cottages, which are grouped around a communal green with interconnecting paths, were built in 1810 by the 10th Holnicote baronet, Sir Thomas Acland, as retirement homes for faithful retainers from the estate workforce. Periwinkle Cottage is one of the most impressive cottages in the village.

Size:	4 ½″, 11.0 cm
Backstamp:	I-2
Introduced:	1990
Discontinued:	1996

Description	Can. $	U.S. $	U.K. £
Periwinkle Cottage	250.00	175.00	125.00

LE PETIT MONTMARTRE

French Collection

A favourite haunt of artists and writers, Le Petit Montmartre (Little Montmartre) is a colourful area which the majority of visitors to Paris want to visit. For the numerous bistros and cafes offering food and drink on the terrace, it means opening early in the morning and closing very late at night.

Size:	5″, 13.0 cm
Backstamp:	I-2
Introduced:	1990
Discontinued:	1997

Description	Can. $	U.S. $	U.K. £
Le Petit Montmartre	135.00	95.00	50.00

PETTICOAT COTTAGE
Collectors Club

Situated in Hampshire, on the edge of the New Forest, this cottage was built in the early 18th century. Using a stout timber frame within the brick walls, the cottage is topped with a decoratively gathered and swagged long-straw thatched roof.

When introduced, Petticoat Cottage was offered to members who joined the Collectors Club during the twelve months from March 1994 to February 1995.

Size:	2 ½", 6.5 cm
Backstamp:	M
Introduced:	1994
Discontinued:	1995

Description	Can. $	U.S. $	U.K. £
Petticoat Cottage	75.00	45.00	50.00

THE PINEAPPLE HOUSE
British Collection

This unusual model is based on the summer house found on the Earl of Dunmore's estate in Scotland.

The Pineapple House is exclusive to the Specialist Glass and China Retailiers in the United Kingdom for the first year of issue. It is available in general release in the rest of the world.

Size:	3 ¾", 9.5 cm
Backstamp:	Q-1
Introduced:	1998
Discontinued:	Current

Description	Can. $	U.S. $	U.K. £
The Pineapple House	70.00	60.00	19.95

PIONEER BARN
American Landmarks

The Pioneer Barn is located in southern Indiana about 25 miles north of the Ohio River.

As with Pepsi Cola Barn, Pioneer Barn (the smallest model in the American Landmarks collection) was only in production for a short time before being retired. Because of this, the model is difficult to find on the secondary market. It was sold only in the USA first year of issue before being released worldwide.

Size:	1 ¾", 4.5 cm
Backstamp:	I-1
Introduced:	1990
Discontinued:	1991

Description	Can. $	U.S. $	U.K. £
Pioneer Barn	150.00	100.00	90.00

PIPIT TOLL

English Collection — South-West

Pipit Toll was built around the 18th century and is located in Codford, Wiltshire.

Size:	3", 7.75 cm
Backstamp:	N-1
Introduced:	1995
Discontinued:	1998

Description	Can. $	U.S. $	U.K. £
Pipit Toll	80.00	50.00	20.00

PIXIE HOUSE

English Collection — South-West

At various locations throughout Cornwall unusual buildings can be found which bring back memories of the characters and dwellings described in *Grimms Fairy Tales* and other folklore. Pixie House conjures up visions of those green-clad, mischievous characters of Cornish folklore, the pixies.

Size:	2 ¼", 5.5 cm
Backstamp:	K-1
Introduced:	1992
Discontinued:	1995

Description	Can. $	U.S. $	U.K. £
Pixie House	90.00	60.00	25.00

PLOUGHMAN'S COTTAGE

Special Events

This 18th-century cottage in the village of Nobottle, is owned by the Althorp Estate, in Northamptonshire. Built from local stone and thatched with reed, the cottage was once the home of the estate manager.

Ploughman's Cottage was launched at the Annual Fair and was only available at Collectors Club events during the following twelve months. The cottage could be personalised with the flowers painted in the member's choice of colours.

Size:	3", 7.5 cm
Backstamp:	K-1
Introduced:	1992
Discontinued:	1993

Description	Can. $	U.S. $	U.K. £
Ploughman's Cottage	200.00	125.00	80.00

PLUM COTTAGE
Christmas Collection (1995 Annual Ornament)

Plum Cottage is located in the north of England.
It was introduced as the fourth Annual Christmas Ornament in February 1995.

Size:	2 ", 6.8 cm
Backstamp:	N-2
Introduced:	1995
Discontinued:	1995

Description	Can. $	U.S. $	U.K. £
Plum Cottage	75.00	50.00	35.00

THE POPPIES
British Collection

The Poppies can be found in the village of Pebworth in Worcestershire.

Size:	3", 7.6 cm
Backstamp:	P-1
Introduced:	1997
Discontinued:	Current

Description	Can. $	U.S. $	U.K. £
The Poppies	65.00	50.00	19.95

PORLOCK DOWN
Collectors Club

Porlock Down, located in Selworthy, Somerset, was part of the Holnicote Estate built by Sir Thomas Dyke Acland, 10th Baron Holnicote, in the 19th century. The village was built to house retired estate workers. Lorna Doone Cottage (Porlock Down) and the rest of the Holnicote Estate, was given to the National Trust in 1994 by Sir Richard Acland, the 15th Baronet.

Porlock Down was available to collectors club members only and had to be ordered through a retailer using a Redemption Certificate.

Size:	4 ", 10.5 cm
Backstamp:	N-1
Introduced:	1995
Discontinued:	1996

Description	Can. $	U.S. $	U.K. £
Porlock Down	175.00	125.00	80.00

LA PORTE SCHOENENBERG
French Collection

The Alsace region in France lies between the Vosges forest and Germany. An unusual region, to the tourist it appears to be more German than French. Based upon a gatehouse in the town of Riquewihr, which is famous for its excellent riesling, La Porte Schoenenberg (Schoenenberg Gatehouse) dates from the 16th century.

Size:	4", 10.0 cm
Backstamp:	I-2
Introduced:	1990
Discontinued:	Current

Description	Can. $	U.S. $	U.K. £
La Porte Schoenenberg	100.00	60.00	35.00

POTTER'S BECK
English Collection — Northern

Potter's Beck was constructed in the 17th century and is located in the Coverdale/Melmerby area of North Yorkshire.

Size:	2 ½ ", 6.0 cm
Backstamp:	O-2
Introduced:	1996
Discontinued:	Current

Description	Can. $	U.S. $	U.K. £
Potter's Beck	45.00	35.00	13.95

THE POTTERY
Collector's Club

When new members join the Collector's Club between March 1998 and February 1999 they are given a redemption certificate for The Pottery model which they can redeem at their local retailers. This model is not available through general release. The Pottery is a companion piece to Kiln Cottage (see page 128).

The Pottery is based on a 17th century house which features a classic Devon architectural style.

Size:	4", 10.0 cm
Backstamp:	R
Introduced:	1998
Discontinued:	1999

Description	Can. $	U.S. $	U.K. £
The Pottery	N.A.	N.A.	N.A.

PRESTON MILL

Scottish Collection

Now owned by the National Trust for Scotland, Preston Mill was based upon the oldest water-driven mill in East Linton near Dunbar, Scotland. Built in the 16th century, the pantiled roof shows the thriving trade that existed between Scotland and the Low Countries in the 16th and 17th centuries. The kiln portion of the building is thought to be 15th century. The rest was added 200 years later.

Introduced in February, 1985, the original version had stairs at the rear of the building, a barn door at the side and a short, pantiled roof. In December, 1986, it was extensively remodelled and the changes included: a water mill at the side of the building instead of the barn door; a tall, sectioned pantiled roof; foliage at the rear of the building instead of stairs; and new style outbuildings. Besides these major changes, there were other minor alterations to detail.

Version 1 — Short Roof

Version 2 — Tall Roof

Version	Size	Backstamp	Intro.	Discon.	Can. $	U.S. $	U.K. £
1 - Short roof	3 ½", 9 cm	D	1985	1986	275.00	175.00	140.00
2 - Tall roof	3 ½", 9 cm	F	1986	1992	200.00	125.00	90.00

THE PRIEST'S HOUSE

English Collection — Northern

After his church was closed in the 17th century, the local vicar used this house for his religious services. The balconey was used as a pulpit. Standing opposite the churchyard in Prestbury, in Cheshire, The Priest's House is a magnificent example of Tudor half-timbered architecture in the 'magpie' style. Built in 1580, it is thought that the heavy framing timbers were used to support the weight of the stone roof, but as well as being functional the timbers were also decorative. The building is now occupied by the National Westminster Bank.

Size:	5 ", 13.0 cm
Backstamp:	J
Introduced:	1991
Discontinued:	1995

Description	Can. $	U.S. $	U.K. £
The Priest's House	300.00	200.00	75.00

PRIMROSE HILL

English Collection — South-East

Typical of the 16th-century homes to be found in Chiddingstone, Kent, the hung tiles helped to protect the wattle and daub panels from the elements.

Size:	3″, 7.5 cm
Backstamp:	L
Introduced:	1991
Discontinued:	1996

Description	Can. $	U.S. $	U.K. £
Primrose Hill	75.00	45.00	25.00

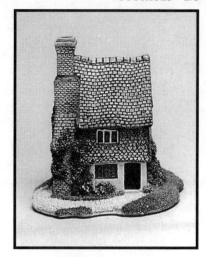

PUDDLEBROOK

Collectors Club

Based on a labourers cottage, made of stone, wood and thatch, Puddlebrook, a little thatched cottage, was offered as the free gift to members who joined the Lilliput Lane Collectors Club in the Club year beginning March, 1991. Whereas other joining gifts had been non-cottage subjects, this was the first cottage to be offered.

Size:	2 ½″, 6.5 cm
Backstamp:	J
Introduced:	1991
Discontinued:	1992

Description	Can. $	U.S. $	U.K. £
Puddlebrook	90.00	60.00	80.00

PUDDLE DUCK

British Collection

The original of this model can be found in Kersey, Suffolk.

Size:	3 ¾″, 9.5 cm
Backstamp:	P-2
Introduced:	1998
Discontinued:	Current

Description	Can. $	U.S. $	U.K. £
Puddle Duck	120.00	80.00	34.95

PUFFIN ROW

English Collection — South-West

Dating back nearly 400 years, on the north coast of Cornwall the only protected anchorage along a 40-mile stretch of inhospitable coastline is at Boscastle. Puffin Row is typical of the delightful white-washed cottages which greet the sailors when they enter Boscastle harbour.

Size:	3 ¼", 8.0 cm
Backstamp:	K-1
Introduced:	1992
Discontinued:	1997

Description	Can. $	U.S. $	U.K. £
Puffin Row	140.00	95.00	50.00

PURBECK STORES

English Collection — South-West

Nestling in the shadow of the ruins of Corfe Castle in Dorset, Purbeck Stores is a double bow-fronted cottage constructed from local stone. The roof, which also uses Purbeck stone, weighs around 1 ¼ tons per 100 square feet.

Size:	2 ½", 6.5 cm
Backstamp:	L
Introduced:	1993
Discontinued:	1997

Description	Can. $	U.S. $	U.K. £
Purbeck Stores	55.00	35.00	20.00

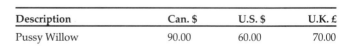

PUSSY WILLOW

Collectors Club

Based on a building from the Flat Fenlands of Northern Cambridgeshire, Pussy Willow was offered as the free gift to members who joined the Lilliput Lane Collectors Club during the Club year commencing March 1992. It was only offered for a twelve-month period.

Size:	2 ½", 6.0 cm
Backstamp:	K-1
Introduced:	1992
Discontinued:	1993

Description	Can. $	U.S. $	U.K. £
Pussy Willow	90.00	60.00	70.00

QUIET COTTAGE
Irish Collection

When film director John Ford made his well-known film *The Quiet Man*, starring John Wayne and Maureen O'Hara, County Galway was the location he chose to shoot the film. The cottage featured in the film was used by Lilliput Lane as the basis for Quiet Cottage.

Size:	2 ½", 6.0 cm
Backstamp:	H-1
Introduced:	1989
Discontinued:	1992

Description	Can. $	U.S. $	U.K. £
Quiet Cottage	190.00	125.00	70.00

RAILWAY COTTAGE
English Collection — Midlands

Railway Cottage is part of the Chatworth Estate and located in Edensor, Derbyshire. Dating back to 1838, it is thought to have inspired the 6th Duke of Devonshire to create his own small village for his estate workers.

Size:	3 ½", 9.2 cm
Backstamp:	O-2
Introduced:	1996
Discontinued:	Current

Description	Can. $	U.S. $	U.K. £
Railway Cottage	90.00	60.00	28.95

RAMBLING ROSE
American Landmarks

On the east coast of the USA, in the Massachusetts summer resort of Nantucket Island, the roses thrive in the blend of sunshine and fog that prevails on the island during the summer.

Size:	2 ½", 6.0 cm
Backstamp:	J
Introduced:	1991
Discontinued:	1995

Description	Can. $	U.S. $	U.K. £
Rambling Rose	125.00	75.00	45.00

DAS RATHAUS
German Collection

Serving as a centre for public meetings and elections and built in 1484, the town hall in Michelstadt is supported by stout oaken pillars. It is regarded as one of Germany's finest buildings.

Size: 5 ½", 14.0 cm
Backstamp: G
Introduced: 1988
Discontinued: 1998

Description	Can. $	U.S. $	U.K. £
Das Rathaus	200.00	150.00	70.00

READING COTTAGE
Paint Your Own

Reading Cottage was introduced in September, 1994 at the Lilliput Lane Event held at the Chiltern Open Air Museum and was only available at Lilliput Lane Events featuring "A Paint Your Own" facility, throught the Collectors Club and at the Visitors Centre. As with any of the "Paint Your Owns," they are more valuable unpainted.

Size: 3", 8.0 cm
Backstamp: M
Introduced: 1994
Discontinued: 1996

Description	Can. $	U.S. $	U.K. £
Reading Cottage	N.A.	N.A.	70.00

RED LION INN
English Collection — Northern

Red Lion Inn is based upon the architecture found in the city of York. Built from York stone, the roof uses pantiles (which originally came from Holland) and is part flagged at the rear of the building.

Size: 5 ¼", 13.5 cm
Backstamp: B
Introduced: 1983
Discontinued: 1987

Description	Can. $	U.S. $	U.K. £
Red Lion Inn	675.00	450.00	270.00

REFLECTIONS OF JADE

Garden Series

This is the third piece in the Garden Series (the predecessors being Tranquility and Leanoras Secret Garden) and limited to 3,950 pieces with priority given to members of the Collectors Club.

Size:	4", 10.5 cm
Backstamp:	Special Ltd. Ed.
Introduced:	1996 in a limited edition of 3,950
Discontinued:	1997

Description	Can. $	U.S. $	U.K. £
Reflections of Jade	600.00	400.00	200.00

REMBRANDT VAN RIJN

Netherlands Collection

The Dutch painter and graphic artist Rembrandt was the prodigious creator of over 600 paintings, about 300 etchings and nearly 2,000 drawings, many of which are regarded as masterpieces. The large house in Breestraat (now Jodenbreestraat), which he bought in 1639, and depicted in Rembrandt van Rijn (Rembrandt's House), is now a museum.

Size:	6", 15.0 cm
Backstamp:	J
Introduced:	1991
Discontinued:	1998

Description	Can. $	U.S. $	U.K. £
Rembrandt Van Rijn	125.00	90.00	40.00

RING O' BELLS

Christmas Collection

Another cottage in the miniature Christmas Collection, where the theme of the collection is a traditional village at Christmastime, Ring o' Bells shows the little country inn, built of Cotswold stone, which offers a warm welcome to locals and travellers alike.

Size:	2 ¾", 7.0 cm
Backstamp:	M
Introduced:	1994
Discontinued:	1997

Description	Can. $	U.S. $	U.K. £
Ring O' Bells	60.00	50.00	20.00

THE RISING SUN

English Collection — South-East

The Rising Sun, a small thatched public house, is situated in the village of Ickford, near Thame. The upper parts are timber framed which have then been infilled with wichert.

Size:	2 ¼", 6.0 cm
Backstamp:	G
Introduced:	1988
Discontinued:	1992

Description	Can. $	U.S. $	U.K. £
The Rising Sun	150.00	95.00	70.00

RIVERSIDE CHAPEL

American Landmarks

Riverside Chapel is located beside Blue River, 7 miles west of Corydon, Indiana. With the opening up of the American mid-west, the early settlers included European migrants who were searching for religious and political freedom. As religion was such an important part of the settlers life, a church or chapel was one of the first community buildings to be erected.

This model was sold exclusively in the USA the first year of issue before being released worldwide.

Size:	3 ½", 9.0 cm
Backstamp:	I-2
Introduced:	1990
Discontinued:	1993

Description	Can. $	U.S. $	U.K. £
Riverside Chapel	275.00	175.00	70.00

RIVERVIEW

English Collection — Midlands

This tiny cottage is situated just north of Welshpool on the border of England and Wales. Backing on to a tributary of the River Severn, the timber-framed cottage has retained its 'magpie' look on the southern front, but other than the addition of mains water and electricity the cottage is much the same as when it was originally built.

Riverview was introduced in July, 1987 and remodelled in approximately 1990. The roof on version 2 was finer in detail. On pieces produced before 1989 the rocks around the cottage were painted grey, whereas from 1989 onwards they were painted beige.

Version 1 — Plain Roof

Version	Size	Backstamp	Intro.	Discon.	Can. $	U.S. $	U.K. £
1 - Plain roof	2", 5 cm	F	1987	1990	125.00	75.00	60.00
2 - Finer roof	2", 5 cm	F	1990	1994	75.00	45.00	30.00

ROADSIDE COOLERS

American Landmarks

Built around 1890 in Huron, Indiana, Roadside Coolers is a typical gneral store. At the heart of every American small town was the General Store, and on hot, summer days the locals would come in search of refreshment. The store depicted in Roadside Coolers — with its stack of water melons outside — was ready and waiting.

It was sold exclusively in the USA the first year of issue before going into general release worldwide.

Size:	3", 7.5 cm
Backstamp:	I-2
Introduced:	1990
Discontinued:	1994

Description	Can. $	U.S. $	U.K. £
Roadside Coolers	200.00	125.00	65.00

ROBIN COTTAGE

Christmas Collection (1993 Annual Ornament)

The second in the series of Annual Ornaments intended for use as Christmas decorations, Robin Cottage was introduced in February 1993 and was only available during that year.

Size:	2 ½″, 6.0 cm
Backstamp:	L
Introduced:	1993
Discontinued:	1993

Description	Can. $	U.S. $	U.K. £
Robin Cottage	75.00	45.00	35.00

ROBINS GATE

English Collection — Midlands

This picturesque 19th century gatehouse is located in Staffordshire.

Size:	2 ½″, 6.0 cm
Backstamp:	I-2
Introduced:	1990
Discontinued:	1996

Description	Can. $	U.S. $	U.K. £
Robins Gate	45.00	30.00	20.00

RODING HEATH / HIGH RODING

Paint Your Own

Introduced at the Annual Fair held at the Chiltern Open Air Museum in September, 1994 and available only at the Visitors Centre in Penrith throughout the 12 months from introduction, Collectors Clubs and Lilliput Lane special events that featured a "Paint Your Own" activity, this cottage was also available at the 1995 Lilliput Lane Event but it was renamed High Roding. As with any of the "Paint Your Owns" it is more valuable unpainted.

Size:	3 ½″, 9.0 cm
Backstamp:	M
Introduced:	1994
Discontinued:	1996

Description	Can. $	U.S. $	U.K. £
Roding Heath (unpainted)	100.00	75.00	50.00

ROSE BOUQUET
British Collection

A fire in 1762 was responsible for the destruction of most of the thatched "Long Houses" from Wareham in Dorset, over 140 buildings were destroyed. Rose Bouquet is based on part of a "Long House."

Size:	2", 5.2 cm
Backstamp:	P-1
Introduced:	1997
Discontinued:	Current

Description	Can. $	U.S. $	U.K. £
Rose Bouquet	35.00	25.00	9.95

ROSE COTTAGE
Style One
English Collection — South-West

Situated in Blaise Hamlet (which has provided the subjects for a number of Lilliput Lane cottages), Rose Cottage was designed by the architects John Nash and George Repton. Built around 1810, the cottage featured a Cotswold split stone double roof, with brick-built chimney stacks. Nash and Repton used specially moulded materials for much of the brickwork.

Size:	4 ½", 11.5 cm
Backstamp:	J
Introduced:	1991
Discontinued:	1997

Description	Can. $	U.S. $	U.K. £
Rose Cottage	275.00	175.00	75.00

ROSE COTTAGE
Style Two
Classics Collection

As with the other models in this collection, Rose Cottage originates in Blaise Hamlet. Designed by John Nash and George Repton, Nash said that Blaise Hamlet imparted more pleasure than anything he had ever planned.

Size:	2 ½", 6.0 cm
Backstamp:	L
Introduced:	1993
Discontinued:	1995

Description	Can. $	U.S. $	U.K. £
Rose Cottage	150.00	95.00	40.00

Note: For the Dream Cottage Miniature of this model see page 74.

ROSE COTTAGE, SKIRSGILL
Special Editions

Built in 1760, Rose Cottage is within the Lilliput Lane Visitors Centre at Skirsgill, near Penrith, where the model of the cottage can be purchased by personal callers. Introduced in August 1991, after 200 pieces were produced the mould was changed in September 1991 and a dog added on the right-hand side. The cottage was later restyled to reflect the actual building itself, including the change of the right-hand chimney from render to brick mid-year 1994, plus added foliage now occupying 1/5 of the right side of the roof.

Version 1 — Without Dog, Version 2 — With Dog

Version 1 — Without Dog, Version 2 — With Dog

Version	Size	Backstamp	Intro.	Discon.	Can. $	U.S. $	U.K. £
1 - Without dog	3", 7.5 cm	J	1991	1991	900.00	650.00	500.00
2 - With dog	3", 7.5 cm	J	1991	1994	400.00	275.00	200.00
3 - Added foliage	3", 7.5 cm	M	1994	Current	N.A.	N.A.	120.00

ROSEMARY COTTAGE

English Collection — Midlands

This fine example of Victorian Gothic architecture is located near Northhampton.

Size:	3", 7.5 cm		
Backstamp:	O-2		
Introduced:	1996		
Discontinued:	Current		

Description	Can. $	U.S. $	U.K. £
Rosemary Cottage	100.00	70.00	29.95

ROSENGARTENHAUS

German Collection

Rosengarten is a suburb of Hamburg and Rosengartenhaus (Rosegarden House) is typical of the area. The timber-framed house, which has been converted from two barns, features an interesting piece of local legend. Homes in this area usually have two carved horses heads, either on the roof or on the gables. Believed to ward off bad luck, it is also said that if the heads point inwards then the daughter of the house is betrothed, if they point outwards, then she is still single.

Size:	2 ¾", 7.0 cm		
Backstamp:	K-1		
Introduced:	1992		
Discontinued:	1998		

Description	Can. $	U.S. $	U.K. £
Rosengartenhaus	130.00	90.00	40.00

ROSY RAFTERS

Paint Your Own

Introduced at the 10th Anniversary of the Collectors Club Event held at Lilliput Studios in Penrith on May 18th, 1996, this model was available only for 12 months from the Visitors Centre in Penrith, Collectors Clubs and Lilliput Lane Events featuring a "Paint Your Own" facility. As with any "Paint Your Owns" they are more valuable unpainted.

Size:	3 ¾", 9.5 cm		
Backstamp:	O-2		
Introduced:	1996		
Discontinued:	1997		

Description	Can. $	U.S. $	U.K. £
Rosy Rafters (unpainted)	25.00	20.00	15.00

ROWAN LODGE

Special Editions

Rowan Lodge is based on a derelict lodge on the edge of an estate close to Henley in Ardin.

The model was introduced in September, 1990 at the South Bend Show in the USA, when 350 pieces were produced each stamped "SOUTH BEND 90." It was given to people attending the Lilliput Lane dinner.

A second variation was then produced and made available at Collectors Club events. This version had the roof in a different colour, and it was possible for members to have the door painted in the colour of their choice. It was only available for one year after its introduction.

Variation	Size	Backstamp	Intro.	Discon.	Can. $	U.S. $	U.K. £
1 - South Bend	3 ½", 9 cm	I-2	1990	1990	750.00	500.00	350.00
2 - Collectors Club	3 ½", 9 cm	I-2	1990	1991	225.00	150.00	135.00

THE ROYAL OAK

English Collection — South-West

Based upon an inn to be found on Exmoor, this 12th-century building has smooth clay cob walls and Devon thatch.

Size:	4 ¼", 11.0 cm
Backstamp:	G
Introduced:	1988
Discontinued:	1991

Description	Can. $	U.S. $	U.K. £
The Royal Oak	275.00	175.00	125.00

ROZENGRACHT

Netherlands Collection

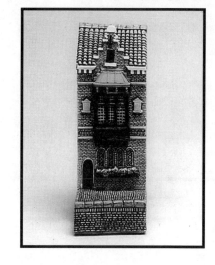

Built in the 17th century, Rozengracht (Rose Canal) can be found in the Jordaan area of Amsterdam. A modest but attractive house, its bow window and small stepped gable are typical of the district.

Unlike the majority of the models in the Netherlands Collection, this mould has not been used to produce another model with different colouring.

Size: 4 ¼", 11.0 cm
Backstamp: J
Introduced: 1991
Discontinued: 1998

Description	Can. $	U.S. $	U.K. £
Rozengracht	70.00	50.00	20.00

RUNSWICK HOUSE

English Collection —Northern

Runswick House typifies east Yorkshire vernacular architecture with its sturdy stone walls and pantile roof.

Size: 3 ¼", 8.0 cm
Backstamp: I-2
Introduced: 1990
Discontinued: 1998

Description	Can. $	U.S. $	U.K. £
Runswick House	80.00	55.00	25.00

RUSTIC ROOT HOUSE

English Collection — Midlands

Close to, but at the same time a discreet distance from, the main road leading to the Duke of Beaufort's estate at Badminton with its impressive Palladian mansion, is an 18th-century almshouse. Designed by Thomas Wright, Rustic Root House is a thatched cottage which looks somewhat like an upturned boat. It is situated in an attractive hamlet which predates Blaise Hamlet by about 60 years.

Size: 3 ¼", 8.0 cm
Backstamp: K-1
Introduced: 1992
Discontinued: 1997

Description	Can. $	U.S. $	U.K. £
Rustic Root House	125.00	95.00	55.00

THE RUSTLINGS

English Collection — South-East

This timber framed thatch cottage is located in Longstock, Hampshire.

Size:	3 ½", 9.0 cm
Backstamp:	N-1
Introduced:	1995
Discontinued:	1998

Description	Can. $	U.S. $	U.K. £
The Rustlings	130.00	95.00	45.00

RYDAL COTTAGE

Lakeland Christmas Collection

Based on a Cumbrian Cottage, Rydal Cottage was introduced with Langdale Cottage and Patterdale Cottage in February 1995 as part of the new Lakeland Christmas Collection.

Size:	2 ½", 6.7 cm
Backstamp:	N-1
Introduced:	1995
Discontinued:	Current

Description	Can. $	U.S. $	U.K. £
Rydal Cottage	55.00	35.00	14.95

RYDAL VIEW

English Collection — Northern

Rydal View is typical of the whitewashed houses which stand out against the green of the Lakeland countryside. Built around 300 years ago and using local grey/green slate with a split slate roof and round slate chimneys, the walls have been rendered with cement and then whitewashed.

Size:	5 ¼", 13.5 cm
Backstamp:	F
Introduced:	1987
Discontinued:	1989

Description	Can. $	U.S. $	U.K. £
Rydal View	450.00	300.00	150.00

SADDLER'S INN

English Collection — Midlands

Typical of the Staffordshire area because of the timber framing and the size of the panelling, this 17th century building was originally an inn. At one time it would have had a thatched roof, and there would have been some stables, but these have long since gone.

Size:	3", 7.5 cm
Backstamp:	F
Introduced:	1987
Discontinued:	1989

Description	Can. $	U.S. $	U.K. £
Saddler's Inn	150.00	95.00	70.00

SAFE HARBOR

An American Journey

This model is based upon the Old Boston Light on Brewster Island, Massachusetts.

Size:	4 ¼", 11.0 cm
Backstamp:	P-1
Introduced:	1997 in a limited edition of 1,783
Discontinued:	Current

Description	Can. $	U.S. $	U.K. £
Safe Harbor	N.A.	75.00	29.95

SAFFRON HOUSE

English Collection — South-East

Built in the late 1700s by the Gibson family, founders of Barclay's Bank, Saffron Walden in Essex is an unspoilt small town with superb medieval buildings. The town's wealth came from wool and from the saffron crop, which was a medicine as well as a dye.

Saffron House is based upon a Victorian hunting lodge which has some unusual features, particularly the ornate gables.

Size:	4 ¼", 11.0 cm
Backstamp:	M
Introduced:	1994
Discontinued:	1997

Description	Can. $	U.S. $	U.K. £
Saffron House	250.00	175.00	85.00

SAN FRANCISCO HOUSE

American Collection

This typical San Francisco House was introduced in October 1984. Produced in two colourways, the first (which is the rarer of the two) has pink walls, white windows and a brown door, whereas the second variation has yellow walls, white window frames, blue decoration above and below the first floor windows, and blue decoration over a blue door. When San Francisco House was retired, 400 pieces had been produced.

Variation	Size	Backstamp	Intro.	Discon.	Can. $	U.S. $	U.K. £
1 - Pink walls	4 ¼", 10.75 cm	C	1984	1985	1,125.00	750.00	525.00
2 - Yellow walls	4 ¼", 10 75 cm	C	1984	1985	1,000.00	700.00	425.00

SANTA'S CORNER

Coca Cola ™ Country Collection
(1996 Annual Ornament)

Made under license from the Coca Cola ™ Company and designed by Ray Day, this piece was introduced as a limited edition of 19,960. It is only available in North America.

Size:	3", 7.6 cm
Backstamp:	O-2
Introduced:	1996 in a limited edition of 19,960
Discontinued:	Current

Description	Can. $	U.S. $	U.K. £
Santa's Corner	50.00	37.50	N.A.

SATURDAY NIGHT JIVE

Coca-Cola™ Country Collection

Designed by Ray Day, and based on an old mill on Silver Creek in Southern Indiana, Saturday Night Jive is produced under license from the Coca-Cola™ company. This cottage is produced in resin and manufactured in Ireland. It is only available in North America. Although not issued as a limited edition, all cottages in this collection are hand-numbered on the base label.

Size: 3 ¾", 9.6 cm
Backstamp: O-2
Introduced: 1997
Discontinued: Current

Description	Can. $	U.S. $	U.K. £
Saturday Night Jive	120.00	100.00	N.A.

SAWREY GILL

English Collection — Northern

The writer Beatrix Potter lived at Hill Top Farm in Near Sawrey on the west side of Windermere. Her first book *The Tale of Peter Rabbit* was published in 1902, not long after she moved to Lakeland. When she died in 1943 she bequeathed her house and much of the surrounding land to the National Trust. Sawrey Gill was the Lilliput Lane interpretation of Beatrix Potter's house.

Size: 2 ½", 5.75 cm
Backstamp: D
Introduced: 1985
Discontinued: 1992

Description	Can. $	U.S. $	U.K. £
Sawrey Gill	150.00	100.00	55.00

SAXHAM ST. EDMUNDS

English Collection — South-East

Saxham St. Edmunds is an interpretation of a traditional Suffolk village. The name is derived from King Edmund, a canonized Saxon king. The distinctive thing about the village was the colour of the thatched cottages; the plaster was coloured, using elderberries or ox blood, to give the cottages a distinctive hue known as 'Suffolk Pink.'

Due to be produced in a limited edition of 4,500 pieces, priority was to be given for the first six months to Collectors Club members. Only 1,828 were produced.

Size: 6", 15.0 cm
Backstamp: Ltd. Ed.
Introduced: 1991
Discontinued: 1994

Description	Can. $	U.S. $	U.K. £
Saxham St. Edmunds	2,600.00	1,750.00	475.00

SAXON COTTAGE

English Collection — South-East

Saxon Cottage, in Steyning, East Sussex, was built in the 15th century and was once part of a much larger building. Oak framed with panels of split oak, laths and plaster, the cottage has a magnificent thatched catslide roof.

Size:	5 ½", 13.75 cm
Backstamp:	G
Introduced:	1988
Discontinued:	1989

Description	Can. $	U.S. $	U.K. £
Saxon Cottage	375.00	250.00	130.00

SCHOOL DAYS

American Landmarks

Based on school houses seen in Hartser and Fairplay, Colorado in 19th-century America, it was a simple one-roomed building. But however simple the building, it was still possible to teach the pupils the three Rs and basic discipline.

School Days was sold exclusively in the USA the first year of issue before being released worldwide.

Size:	2 ¾", 7.0 cm
Backstamp:	J
Introduced:	1991
Discontinued:	1997

Description	Can. $	U.S. $	U.K. £
School Days	75.00	60.00	40.00

SCHWARZWALDHAUS

German Collection

Based upon the buildings to be found in the Black Forest, the immediately noticeable feature of Schwarzwaldhaus is the roof. The large overhanging roof is designed to protect the windows, doors and verandah from the massive snowfalls which occur in this region in winter.

Schwarzwaldhaus was only available in Central Europe the first year of issue before going into worldwide release.

Size:	4 ¼", 11.0 cm
Backstamp:	F
Introduced:	1987
Discontinued:	1998

Description	Can. $	U.S. $	U.K. £
Schwarzwaldhaus	180.00	120.00	55.00

SCOTCH MIST
British Collection

This heather-clad cottage in Oban, Scotland was formerly an illicit distillery.

Size:	2 ¾", 7.0 cm
Backstamp:	P-2
Introduced:	1998
Discontinued:	Current

Description	Can. $	U.S. $	U.K. £
Scotch Mist	100.00	70.00	34.95

SCOTNEY CASTLE GARDEN
British Collection

The remains of this moated castle, located in a valley on the Kent/Sussex border, date back to The Hundred Years' War. The castle and grounds are now owned by The National Trust.

Scotney Castle Garden is due to be produced in a limited edition of 4,500.

Size:	4", 10.0 cm
Backstamp:	P-2
Introduced:	1997 in a limited edition of 4,500
Discontinued:	Current

Description	Can. $	U.S. $	U.K. £
Scotney Castle Garden	450.00	300.00	135.00

SECRET GARDEN
English Collection — Northern

From the way in which the garden paths and statuary have fallen into disrepair and the rampant growth of the plants been left unchecked, it seems that this Victorian Gothic house has been left unoccupied for a long time.

Size:	5 ½", 14.0 cm
Backstamp:	F
Introduced:	1987
Discontinued:	1994

Description	Can. $	U.S. $	U.K. £
Secret Garden	225.00	150.00	100.00

SEE ROCK CITY

American Landmarks

In an area of the Appalachian range on the Tennessee/Georgia state line, See Rock City can be found. Built around the turn of the century, this wooden building at the top of Lookout Mountain is a marvellous vantage point which, as well as giving you a good view of Rock City, also enables you to see seven of the American states on a clear day.

This model was available in the USA only for the first year of issue before being released worldwide.

Size:	2 ¾", 7.0 cm
Backstamp:	L
Introduced:	1993
Discontinued:	1997

Description	Can. $	U.S. $	U.K. £
See Rock City	55.00	37.50	30.00

SEEK AND FIND

American Landmarks

This model was inspired by a church that once stood in Welaka, Florida.

Size:	4 ¼", 11.0 cm
Backstamp:	P-1
Introduced:	1998
Discontinued:	Current

Description	Can. $	U.S. $	U.K. £
Seek And Find	N.A.	80.00	34.95

SETTLER'S SURPRISE

Exclusive

Settler's Surprise was based upon Sod Cottage, an early New Zealand settler's dwelling which has been rebuilt at Howick Colonial Village Museum near Auckland.

It is only available at the museum which is run by Howick & District's Historical Society in New Zealand and is open to the public. Settler's Surprise was produced exclusively for the New Zealand market.

Size:	2 ¼", 5.5 cm
Backstamp:	J
Introduced:	1991
Discontinued:	Current

Description	Can. $	U.S. $	U.K. £
Settler's Surprise	N.A.	N.A.	N.A.

SEVEN DWARFS COTTAGE
Exclusive

Sold exclusively at Disney World Lake Vista shops near Orlando,Florida for the 50th Anniversary of Mickey Mouse, the base label on this piece reads 1987 Copyright. David Tate requested this model be re-issued in 1989, this was obviously denied by Disney as it never went back into production. Only 470 pieces were produced.

Size:	5 ¼", 13.0 cm
Backstamp:	None
Introduced:	1986
Discontinued:	1986

Description	Can. $	U.S. $	U.K. £
Seven Dwarfs Cottage	1,500.00	1,000.00	875.00

7 ST. ANDREWS SQUARE
Scottish Collection

Culross, in Fife, is a town of 16th and 17th century red-tiled houses lining steep cobbled streets, which has been splendidly preserved by the National Trust for Scotland. 7 St. Andrews Square is a typical house from the region; built from yellow sandstone and roofed with tiles imported from the Low Countries, an interesting feature is the external stair.

Size:	2 ¼", 5.5 cm
Backstamp:	D
Introduced:	1985
Discontinued:	1986

Description	Can. $	U.S. $	U.K. £
7 St. Andrews Square	300.00	200.00	150.00

SHAVE AND A HAIRCUT
American Landmarks

Based on a 1900s Barber Shop in Wytopitloch, Maine, Shave and a Haircut takes you back to the days when, as well as being able to get a shave and a haircut, you could also be serenaded by the barber shop quartet.
Shave and a Haircut was available only in the USA the first year of issue before being released worldwide.

Size:	3", 7.5 cm
Backstamp:	L
Introduced:	1993
Discontinued:	1997

Description	Can. $	U.S. $	U.K. £
Shave and a Haircut	150.00	125.00	85.00

SHADES OF SUMMER

Anniversary Editions

Based on a cottage built in the early part of the 18th century, Shades of Summer can be seen in Patrixbourne, Kent.

Size:	4 ½", 11.5 cm
Backstamp:	Q-2
Introduced:	1998
Discontinued:	1998

Description	Can. $	U.S. $	U.K. £
Shades Of Summer	N.A.	170.00	85.00

SHIP INN

English Collection — Northern

Based upon the many similar buildings to be found in York, the Ship Inn has exposed timber framing, magnificent Tudor chimneys and pantiles (which were originally imported from Holland).

Size:	5 ¾", 14.5 cm
Backstamp:	G
Introduced:	1988
Discontinued:	1992

Description	Can. $	U.S. $	U.K. £
Ship Inn	450.00	300.00	165.00

SHROPSHIRE COTTAGE

Paint Your Own

Introduced in September 1993 at the Annual Collectors Fair held at Harewood House near Leeds, this piece was only available at the Fair, the Visitors Centre in Penrith and Lilliput Lane Special Events that featured a Paint Your Own facility, and from the Collectors Clubs.

Size:	3 1/8", 8.0 cm
Backstamp:	L
Introduced:	1993
Discontinued:	1994

Description	Can. $	U.S. $	U.K. £
Shropshire Cottage (unpainted)	125.00	75.00	60.00

SILVER BELLS

British Collection

This early 19th century Cotswold stone cottage is found in the village of Castle Combe, Wiltshire.

Size:	2″, 5.0 cm
Backstamp:	P-1
Introduced:	1997
Discontinued:	Current

Description	Can. $	U.S. $	U.K. £
Silver Bells	35.00	25.00	9.95

SIMPLY AMISH

American Landmarks

Simply Amish was built around the 1700s and is based in Harrison County, Indiana, 4 miles west of Corydon. A conservative Protestant sect which is well established in America, the Amish advocate strict community conformity. They are self-sufficient, so farming is of major importance to them. Simply Amish shows a typical barn used for storage.

The model was available exclusively in the USA during 1993 before going into worldwide release.

Size:	4″, 10.0 cm
Backstamp:	L
Introduced:	1993
Discontinued:	1998

Description	Can. $	U.S. $	U.K. £
Simply Amish	135.00	115.00	65.00

16.9 CENTS PER GALLON

American Landmarks

Based on Main St., New Russia, New York a combination of a General Store and Filling Station would have brought the owner up to the 20th century with the fuel needs for the occasional motorist and the groceries for the local people. With the advent of the motor car, many general stores began to sell fuel; in those early days a gallon was a lot cheaper than today! It is reported that Ray Day's father worked at this filling station in the early 1930s and at that time 16.9 cents per gallon was the price.

Size:	3″, 7.5 cm
Backstamp:	K-1
Introduced:	1992
Discontinued:	Current

Description	Can. $	U.S. $	U.K. £
16.9 Cents per Gallon	150.00	100.00	59.95

SMALL TOWN LIBRARY

American Landmarks

Small Town Library is located in Rugby, Tennessee and was constructed in the late 1800s. Together with the church and chapel, the library was erected for the benefit of the community.

Available only in the USA the first year of issue before being released worldwide.

Size:	4", 10.0 cm
Backstamp:	K-1
Introduced:	1992
Discontinued:	1995

Description	Can. $	U.S. $	U.K. £
Small Town Library	225.00	150.00	75.00

THE SMALLEST INN

English Collection — South-West

There are a number of public houses in England which lay claim to be the smallest in the country, and the one upon which this Lilliput Lane model is based can be found in Dorset. Built in the 15th century, this thatched inn is reputed to have been a blacksmith's shop until King Charles II stopped to have his horse shod and asked for a drink. When the blacksmith told the King that he had no licence to serve drink, the King granted him one there and then.

Size:	2 ¼", 6.0 cm
Backstamp:	G
Introduced:	1988
Discontinued:	1991

Description	Can. $	U.S. $	U.K. £
The Smallest Inn	200.00	150.00	100.00

SNOWDON LODGE

Christmas Lodge Collection

The third in the series of four Christmas lodges, Snowdon Lodge was based upon the granite lodge at the entrance to the estate of the Sir Clough Williams-Ellis family at Garreg, near Portmeirion in Wales.

Size:	4 ¼", 11.0 cm
Backstamp:	M
Introduced:	1994
Discontinued:	1994

Description	Can. $	U.S. $	U.K. £
Snowdon Lodge	275.00	175.00	90.00

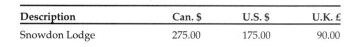

SORE PAWS

English Collection — Northern

This veterinary surgery is located in the Village of Yorkshire in Middleham. This area is renowned for its training of race horses.

Size:	3 ¾", 9.5 cm
Backstamp:	O-2
Introduced:	1996
Discontinued:	Current

Description	Can. $	U.S. $	U.K. £
Sore Paws	100.00	70.00	34.95

THE SPINDLES

English Collection — Northern

The inspiration for The Spindles is a 16th century cottage in the Village of Kilburn. It is one of the few timber framed buildings still in existence in Yorkshire.

Size:	3", 9.35 cm
Backstamp:	O-2
Introduced:	1996
Discontinued:	Current

Description	Can. $	U.S. $	U.K. £
The Spindles	80.00	65.00	34.95

THE SPINNEY

Collectors Club

This 18th century farmworker's cottage, with later Victorian additions, is located in Cambridgeshire Fens.

The Spinney was offered as the free gift to members who joined the Lilliput Lane Collectors Club in the Club year beginning March 1993.

Size:	2 ½", 6 5 cm
Backstamp:	L
Introduced:	1993
Discontinued:	1994

Description	Can. $	U.S. $	U.K. £
The Spinney	100.00	75.00	55.00

SPRING BANK

English Collection — South-West

Many timber-framed thatched cottages are to be found around the Lyme Regis area of Dorset, and most of them date back many centuries.

Size:	2 ½", 6.5 cm
Backstamp:	E
Introduced:	1986
Discontinued:	1991

Description	Can. $	U.S. $	U.K. £
Spring Bank	125.00	85.00	70.00

SPRING GATE COTTAGE

English Collection — South-West

The picturesque village of Luccombe, in Somerset, is part of the Holnicote Estate and is owned by the National Trust. Spring Gate Cottage, which can be found in the village, was built in the early 17th century and shows a wide diversity of style and material used in the design and construction.

Size:	4", 10.0 cm
Backstamp:	M
Introduced:	1994
Discontinued:	1997

Description	Can. $	U.S. $	U.K. £
Spring Gate Cottage	150.00	100.00	50.00

SPRING GLORY

A Year in an English Garden

Located in a village in Wiltshire, Spring Glory is one of the four cottages in the series which shows how each season affects the appearance of a cottage. The seasonal portrayals are: spring (Spring Glory), summer (Summer Impressions), autumn (Autumn Hues) and winter (Winter's Wonder).

Size:	3 ½", 8.5 cm
Backstamp:	N-1
Introduced:	1995
Discontinued:	1997

Description	Can. $	U.S. $	U.K. £
Spring Glory	125.00	85.00	45.00

SPRING VICTORIAN

American Landmarks

This distinctive house was constructed in the late 19th century in Georgetown, Colorado.

This model was only available in the USA the first 6 months of production and then available worldwide.

Size: 3 ¾", 9.5 cm
Backstamp: M
Introduced: 1994
Discontinued: Current

Description	Can. $	U.S. $	U.K. £
Spring Victorian	250.00	180.00	145.00

Photograph
not available
at press time

STARS AND STRIPES FOREVER

Allegiance Collection

Stars And Stripes Forever is based on the home of Betsy Ross in Philadelphia, Pennsylvania.

Size: 3 ¾", 9.5 cm
Backstamp: Unknown
Introduced: 1998
Discontinued: Current

Description	Can. $	U.S. $	U.K. £
Stars And Stripes Forever	N.A.	75.00	34.95

ST. COLUMBA'S SCHOOL

Irish Collection

Located in Coony, Donegal, St. Columba's School is typical of the small Irish school where the local people would have received their early education, some of them possibly going on to become scholars, writers and poets.

Size: 2 ½", 6.0 cm
Backstamp: H-1
Introduced: 1989
Discontinued: 1996

Description	Can. $	U.S. $	U.K. £
St. Columba's School	65.00	45.00	25.00

ST. GOVAN'S CHAPEL

Welsh Collection

Situated at St. Govan's Head in Pembrokeshire, St. Govan's Chapel measures only 20ft by 12ft (6m by 3 ½ m), and is perched halfway down the cliffs and approached by a steep flight of steps. The chapel dates from the 13th century, but the altar and seat were cut into the stone much earlier. Some parts of this chapel date back to the 5th century.

Size:	2 ½", 6.0 cm
Backstamp:	K-1
Introduced:	1992
Discontinued:	Current

Description	Can. $	U.S. $	U.K. £
St. Govan's Chapel	70.00	50.00	19.95

ST. JOHN THE BAPTIST

English Collection — Northern

Located in the North Yorkshire dales of Blubberhouse near the Forest of Knaresborough, this traditional church is made from stone and slate found locally.

Size:	4", 10.0 cm
Backstamp:	O-2
Introduced:	1996
Discontinued:	Current

Description	Can. $	U.S. $	U.K. £
St. John the Baptist	100.00	75.00	29.95

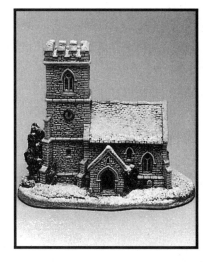

ST. JOSEPH'S CHURCH

Christmas Collection

The Christmas Collection is a series of miniature cottages and buildings. With the theme of a traditional wintery village scene at Christmastime, St. Joseph's Church prepares for the villagers attending midnight Mass.

Size:	3 ½", 9.0 cm
Backstamp:	L
Introduced:	1993
Discontinued:	1997

Description	Can. $	U.S. $	U.K. £
St. Joseph's Church	80.00	40.00	25.00

ST. JOSEPH'S SCHOOL

Christmas Collection

Another building in the miniature Christmas Collection, St. Joseph's School is based upon a similar building at Eastcombe, near Stroud in Gloucestershire. This Victorian school-house, which was built in 1878, has separate entrances for boys and girls.

Size:	2 ¾", 7.0 cm
Backstamp:	M
Introduced:	1994
Discontinued:	1997

Description	Can. $	U.S. $	U.K. £
St. Joseph's School	55.00	40.00	25.00

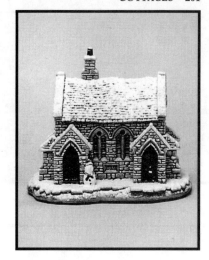

ST. KEVIN'S CHURCH

Irish Collection

Situated in Glen Dalough Valley, County Wicklow, St. Kevin's Church is one of the most important ancient ecclesiastical buildings in Ireland. The church is named after St. Kevin, who was a 7th century hermit who lived in a tiny cell near by and devoted his time and energy to a simple religious life. He was a Christian monk who became the Abbot of Glen Dallough in Sloan. St. Kevin's Church was built around the $11^{th}/12^{th}$ century.

Size:	4", 10.0 cm
Backstamp:	H-1
Introduced:	1989
Discontinued:	1996

Description	Can. $	U.S. $	U.K. £
St. Kevin's Church	75.00	50.00	35.00

ST. LAWRENCE CHURCH

English Collection — Northern

The Church of St. Lawrence can be found in Crosby Ravensworth, Cumbria. The oldest existing part of the present church dates back to the 12th century, but most of the structure dates back to the 19th century. It is encircled by old trees and is one of the finest churches in east Cumbria and is like a miniature cathedral in appearance.

Size:	5", 12.5 cm
Backstamp:	H-1
Introduced:	1989
Discontinued:	Current

Description	Can. $	U.S. $	U.K. £
St. Lawrence Church	120.00	85.00	39.95

ST. MARKS

English Collection — Midlands

Based upon Kington Church which is in Hereford and Worcester, St. Marks depicts a timber-framed church which was built in the 15th/16th century, but does have features which suggest that it could be as old as the 14th century.

Size:	3 ¾", 9.5 cm
Backstamp:	G
Introduced:	1988
Discontinued:	1991

Description	Can. $	U.S. $	U.K. £
St. Marks	225.00	150.00	125.00

ST. MARY'S CHURCH

Style One
English Collection — Midlands

St. Mary's Church depicts the classic English church which is to be found in so many towns and villages, and has been built from a variety of stone and slate.

Size:	3 ¾", 9.5 cm
Backstamp:	D
Introduced:	1985
Discontinued:	1988

Description	Can. $	U.S. $	U.K. £
St. Mary's Church	275.00	175.00	130.00

ST. MARY'S CHURCH

Style Two
Studley Royal Collection

Designed in 1859 and built by the Marchioness of Ripon in 1871-78, St. Mary's Church was designed by William Burges. Situated at the west end of the main avenue at Studley Royal in Yorkshire, the Church is owned by the Church of England and maintained by the Historic Buildings and Monuments Commission, but shown by the National Trust.

5,000 limited edition pieces were produced in 1994 exclusively for the USA. It is only available in that country.

Size:	6", 15 cm
Backstamp:	M
Introduced:	1994 in a limited edition of 5,000
Discontinued:	Ltd.Ed.

Description	Can. $	U.S. $	U.K. £
St. Mary's Church	200.00	150.00	95.00

ST. NICHOLAS CHURCH

Christmas Specials

Based upon a church in southern Lakeland not far from Penrith, St. Nicholas Church was the second model in the Christmas Specials. As with all the early Christmas pieces the snow was incorporated into the mould.

Size:	4", 10.0 cm
Backstamp:	H-1
Introduced:	1989
Discontinued:	1990

Description	Can. $	U.S. $	U.K. £
St. Nicholas Church	375.00	250.00	160.00

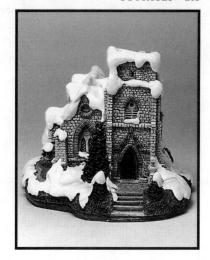

ST. PATRICK'S CHURCH

Irish Collection

St. Patrick's Church is located in County Donegal. In Ireland the Roman Catholic Church plays a significant role in the lives of the people and also in the country, and churches such as St. Patrick's (together with the parish priest or minister) are vital to the well-being of the community.

Size:	6", 16.0 cm
Backstamp:	H-1
Introduced:	1989
Discontinued:	1993

Description	Can. $	U.S. $	U.K. £
St. Patrick's Church	350.00	225.00	110.00

ST. PETER'S COVE

English Collection — South-East

St. Peter's Cove was the Lilliput Lane interpretation of a Southern England village. The dwellings depicted in the sculpture were based upon buildings to be found in the Isle of Wight at Godshill and Ventnor, together with other buildings from the Meon Valley in Hampshire and the New Forest around Christchurch in Dorset. There were nine individual buildings on the sculpture including a church, thatched and brick-built cottages.

Size:	8", 20.0 cm
Backstamp:	Special Ltd. Ed.
Introduced:	1989 in a limited edition of 3,000
Discontinued:	1991

Description	Can. $	U.S. $	U.K. £
St. Peter's Cove	3,375.00	2,250.00	1,075.00

ST. STEPHEN'S CHURCH

Christmas Specials

St. Stephen, who was stoned to death, dedicated his life to the orphaned, widowed, poor and the sick. St. Stephen's Church was built in 1861 at Higham, Suffolk.

This is the last in the series of the annual Christmas Cottages.

Size:	5 ½", 14.0 cm
Backstamp:	O-2
Introduced:	1996
Discontinued:	1996

Description	Can. $	U.S. $	U.K. £
St. Stephen's Church	150.00	95.00	55.00

STOCKLEBECK MILL

English Collection — Northern

Stocklebeck Mill depicts a 19th century watermill in Cumbria and features the typical building materials of that time. Although some parts probably constructed during the saxon times. The sculpture was created by Lilliput Lane from descriptions and old drawings.

When introduced there were more orders than supplies and Stocklebeck Mill was not available for the first 6 months of production.

Size:	4 ¾", 12.0 cm
Backstamp:	L
Introduced:	1993
Discontinued:	Current

Description	Can. $	U.S. $	U.K. £
Stocklebeck Mill	275.00	195.00	92.95

STOCKWELL TENEMENT

Scottish Collection

Stockwell Tenement dates back to the 1800s. When Stockwell Tenement was built, the word 'tenement' was used to refer to a room or set of rooms within a house, whereas today people associate it more with blocks of high-rise flats.

Size:	4 ¼", 11.0 cm
Backstamp:	H-1
Introduced:	1989
Discontinued:	1996

Description	Can. $	U.S. $	U.K. £
Stockwell Tenement	100.00	70.00	40.00

STOKESAY

Historic Castles of Britain

Stokesay, south of Craven Arms in Shropshire, is a perfectly preserved 13th century fortified stone manor, which consists of two sturdy stone towers joined by a great gabled banqueting hall with tall Gothic windows. The 'black-and-white' Elizabethan gatehouse has a stone roof and an overhanging upper storey. The Ludlows sold Stokesay in 1570 and after three consecutive owners, it was bought by Dame Elizabeth Craven in 1620. After the civil war in 1645 the walls were badly damaged. The moat, 30 feet across in some parts, dried up. Two hundred years later J.D. Allcroft took on the task of saving the castle from slow decay.

Size:	3 ½", 8.5 cm
Backstamp:	M
Introduced:	1994
Discontinued:	Current

Description	Can. $	U.S. $	U.K. £
Stokesay	120.00	85.00	39.95

STONE COTTAGE
English Collection — South-East

Version 1, introduced in September 1982, had 10 roof peak tiles and a very straight roof. This Stone Cottage lacks a backstamp which could have been removed through fettering. It also lacks a single lintel above the main window. Stone Cottage was remodelled approximately a month after its introduction. The single lintel was added and it carried either no backstamp or an A-1 backstamp. It still had 10 peak roof tiles and the roof was straight. By the end of 1982, a double lintel was apparent above the main window, creating Version 3. The roof peak tiles decreased to just over 5 and the cottage carried either backstamp A-1 or A-2, the roof was still very straight. Introduced in September, 1983, Version 4 had a visably sagging roof, the lintel reverted back to a single and the base lacking the 'cut look.' Unlike it's predecessor, this base is also larger and has 4 roof peak tiles. Version 5 is now hard to find. The base is slightly smaller than version 4, but more obvious is the height of the chimney pots which were raised. This version had 4 peak roof tiles.

Version 2 (left), Version 5 (right)

Version	Size	Backstamp	Intro.	Discon.	Can. $	U.S. $	U.K. £
1 - 10 tiles, no lintel	3 ¾", 9.5 cm	None	1982	1982	1,800.00	1,200.00	900.00
2 - 10 tiles, single lintel	3 ¾", 9.5 cm	A-1, None	1982	1982	1,100.00	750.00	525.00
3 - 5 tiles, double lintel	3 ½", 8.9 cm	A-1, A-2	1982	1983	900.00	600.00	450.00
4 - 4 tiles, single lintel	3 ¾", 9.5 cm	C	1983	1986	625.00	450.00	265.00
5 - 4 roof tiles	4", 10.1 cm	C	1986	1986	950.00	650.00	425.00

STONEYBECK

English Collection — Northern

Built over 200 years ago of local stone with a split slate roof, Stoneybeck is a typical Cumbrian whitewashed cottage, and examples can be seen dotted all over the Lake District.

Early Stoneybeck models have light blue windows and rocks. The later variation has buff windows and rocks.

Variation	Size	Backstamp	Intro.	Discon.	Can. $	U.S. $	U.K. £
1 - Light blue	2 ¾", 7 cm	F	1987	1992	125.00	75.00	60.00
2 - Buff	2 ¾", 7 cm	F	1987	1992	125.00	75.00	60.00

THE STONEMASON

British Collection

This mason's cottage with its half-hipped roof can be found in Sandy Lane, Wiltshire.

Size: 3 ¾", 9.5 cm
Backstamp: Q-2
Introduced: 1998
Discontinued: Current

Description	Can. $	U.S. $	U.K. £
The Stonemason	180.00	120.00	49.95

STRADLING PRIORY

English Collection — South-West

Stradling Priory was built in 1836 by William Stradling, supposedly on the site of a Benedictine monastery near Glastonbury, Somerset. His intention was to create a museum of artefacts and curiosities from the area. Over the years a variety of objects were accumulated, but in 1938 many of them were taken and never returned. The building is now a private property.

Size: 4 ¼", 11.0 cm
Backstamp: L
Introduced: 1993
Discontinued: 1997

Description	Can. $	U.S. $	U.K. £
Stradling Priory	120.00	95.00	45.00

STRANDVOGTHAUS

German Collection

Strandvogthaus (Beach Warden's House) originates from the Frisian island of Sylt in northern Germany. Originally built in 1699 by a sea captain called Lorens Petersen de Hahn, the house has now been moved and rebuilt at the Schleswig-Holstein Open Air Museum near Kiel.

Size: 2 ¾", 7.0 cm
Backstamp: I-1
Introduced: 1992
Discontinued: 1998

Description	Can. $	U.S. $	U.K. £
Strandvogthaus	130.00	90.00	40.00

STRAWBERRY COTTAGE

English Collection — South-East

Strawberry Cottage, in Steyning, East Sussex, was built in the 15th century. Originally the home of a tinker, the cottage is half-timbered with oak beams and wattle and daub infill. Thatched with reed from the nearby Romney Marsh, the roof has a catslide on one side.

Size:	2 ½", 6.5 cm
Backstamp:	I-1
Introduced:	1990
Discontinued:	1998

Description	Can. $	U.S. $	U.K. £
Strawberry Cottage	55.00	35.00	15.00

STRAWBERRY TEAS

English Tea Room Collection

This model is based upon Dunnose Cottage Tea Rooms, a 16th century cottage in Dunnose on the Isle of Wight.

Size:	3 ¾", 9.5 cm
Backstamp:	P-2
Introduced:	1998
Discontinued:	Current

Description	Can. $	U.S. $	U.K. £
Strawberry Teas	180.00	100.00	49.95

STREET SCENE COLLECTION

The ten models which make up the Street Scene collection were introduced in February 1987. Each model had the company name impressed on the rear, together with a number (from 1 to 10), but other than this there was no other means of identification. It has been reported that ten street scenes a year were to be produced, but this was put on hold because of poor sales. The collection was only produced for ten months.

Street Scene Models 1 through 5 (left to right)

Street Scene Models 6 through 10 (left to right)

Description	Size	Backstamp	Intro.	Discon.	Can. $	U.S. $	U.K. £
Street Scene 1	6-7", 15-17.5 cm	F	1987	1987	275.00	175.00	75.00
Street Scene 2	6-7", 15-17.5 cm	F	1987	1987	275.00	175.00	75.00
Street Scene 3	6-7", 15-17.5 cm	F	1987	1987	300.00	200.00	75.00
Street Scene 4	6-7", 15-17.5 cm	F	1987	1987	225.00	150.00	55.00
Street Scene 5	6-7", 15-17.5 cm	F	1987	1987	225.00	125.00	55.00
Street Scene 6	6-7", 15-17.5 cm	F	1987	1987	225.00	125.00	55.00
Street Scene 7	6-7", 15-17.5 cm	F	1987	1987	225.00	125.00	55.00
Street Scene 8	6-7", 15-17.5 cm	F	1987	1987	225.00	125.00	55.00
Street Scene 9	6-7", 15-17.5 cm	F	1987	1987	225.00	125.00	55.00
Street Scene 10	6-7", 15-17.5 cm	F	1987	1987	225.00	125.00	55.00
Set					2,250.00	1,500.00	700.00

SUFFOLK COTTAGE
Paint Your Own

Introduced in September 1995 at the Lilliput Annual Event held at Grimsthorpe Castle, Suffolk Castle was only available for a year through the Collectors Clubs mail order department, Visitors Centre in Penrith and Lilliput Lane Events that featured a Paint Your Own facility.

Size: 3", 7.6 cm
Backstamp: N-1
Introduced: 1995
Discontinued: Current

Description	Can. $	U.S. $	U.K. £
Suffolk Cottage (unpainted)	N.A.	N.A.	15.00

SULGRAVE MANOR
English Collection — Midlands

Built in 1560 by Lawrence Washington, an ancestor of George Washington, Sulgrave Manor is located in Northhamptonshire. George Washington never visited this manor but many items he once owned are displayed there. This house was bought by British and American subscribers in the 1920s. They restored and refurbished Sulgrave and opened the place as a public monument in memory of the George Washington family on June 21st, 1921. The manor house is now a museum.

Size: 3 ¾", 9 5 cm
Backstamp: H-1
Introduced: 1990
Discontinued: 1992

Description	Can. $	U.S. $	U.K. £
Sulgrave Manor	300.00	200.00	160.00

SUMMER DAYS
Anniversary Editions

Summer Days is based on a 17th century old cottage from the Village of Cuddington in Buckinghamshire.

Size: 4", 10.2 cm
Backstamp: P-1
Introduced: 1997
Discontinued: 1997

Description	Can. $	U.S. $	U.K. £
Summer Days	200.00	165.00	59.95

SUMMER HAZE

English Collection — Midlands

Built almost 400 years ago, this small, cruck-framed, thatched cottage can be found in Oxfordshire.

Size:	4″, 10.0 cm
Backstamp:	F
Introduced:	1987
Discontinued:	1993

Description	Can. $	U.S. $	U.K. £
Summer Haze	275.00	175.00	70.00

SUMMER IMPRESSIONS

A Year in an English Garden

Summer Impressions is one of the four cottages in the series which shows how each season affects the appearance of a cottage. The seasonal portrayals are: spring (Spring Glory), summer (Summer Impressions), autumn (Autumn Hues) and winter (Winter's Wonder). Autumn Hues and Winter's Wonder were released in 1994, with the remaining two cottages being released in 1995.

Size:	3 ½″, 8.5 cm
Backstamp:	N-1
Introduced:	1995
Discontinued:	1997

Description	Can. $	U.S. $	U.K. £
Summer Impressions	125.00	90.00	45.00

SUNNYSIDE

English Collection — South-East

Sunnyside is situated in Hampshire not far from the village of Selborne, the birthplace and home of Gilbert White the naturalist. This small thatched house has walls built from flattened stone cobbles, while the wall edges are of dressed stone.

Size:	2 ½″, 6.5 cm
Backstamp:	M
Introduced:	1994
Discontinued:	1997

Description	Can. $	U.S. $	U.K. £
Sunnyside	55.00	35.00	20.00

SUSSEX MILL

English Collection — South-East

Based upon a building to be found south of the Sussex Weald, Sussex Mill is a small mill with an undershot wheel. The use of clay tiles and hipped roof show its vernacular origins, and the walls would have been a mixture of soft stone, bricks and flint.

One of the early Lilliput Lane models, Sussex Mill was introduced in September, 1982 and carried backstamps A-1 and A-2. However, in July, 1984 it was remodelled and the following changes made: the rear wall now had five windows (previously seven); the side wall now had one window (previously there were two); there was more foliage on the side wall and around the window; the windows in the roof were positioned higher up; the window in the roof on the left side was removed; and the base became more circular without a cutaway. The windows were now reduced from twenty-eight to fourteen.

Front: Version 1 (left), Version 2 (right)

Rear: Version 1 (left), Version 2 (right)

Side: Version 1 (left), Version 2 (right)

Version	Size	Backstamp	Intro.	Discon.	Can. $	U.S. $	U.K. £
1 - 28 windows	2 ¼", 5.7 cm	A-1, A-2	1982	1984	1,350.00	900.00	400.00
2 - 14 windows	2 ½", 6.7 cm	C	1984	1986	675.00	450.00	250.00

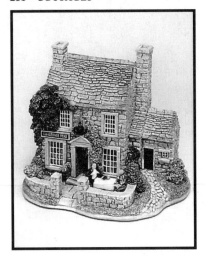

SWALEDALE TEAS

English Tea Room Collection

Built in 1680 as a vicarage, the building has since been a Post Office, sweet shop, and a guest house. Located in the Swaledale Village of Muker in North Yorkshire, it is now a teashop.

Size:	3 ½", 9 cm
Backstamp:	O-2
Introduced:	1996
Discontinued:	Current

Description	Can. $	U.S. $	U.K. £
Swaledale Teas	120.00	85.00	34.95

THE SWAN INN

English Collection — South-East

Located in Midhurst, Sussex, The Swan Inn is a 15th century timber-framed building. Whilst some repair work was being carried out a portion of a 15th century mural was found; it is now displayed in the Inn's Restaurant.

Size:	5", 12.5 cm
Backstamp:	G
Introduced:	1988
Discontinued:	1992

Description	Can. $	U.S. $	U.K. £
The Swan Inn	275.00	175.00	110.00

SWEET BRIAR COTTAGE

Style One
English Collection — South-West

Originally designed and built around 1810 by John Nash and George Repton, Sweet Briar Cottage is the smallest of the cottages in Blaise Hamlet near Bristol.

Introduced in February 1990, Sweet Briar Cottage was initially in the Blaise Hamlet Collection but in 1994 was transferred to the English Collection — South-West.

Size:	4 ½", 11.5 cm
Backstamp:	I-2
Introduced:	1990
Discontinued:	1995

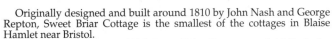

Description	Can. $	U.S. $	U.K. £
Sweet Briar Cottage	225.00	150.00	75.00

SWEET BRIAR COTTAGE

Style Two
Classics Collection

Based upon the building in Blaise Hamlet, near Bristol, Sweet Briar Cottage is built from Cotswold stone and roofed with split stone.

Size:	2 ½", 6.0 cm
Backstamp:	L
Introduced:	1993
Discontinued:	1995

Description	Can. $	U.S. $	U.K. £
Sweet Briar Cottage	150.00	95.00	40.00

SWEET PEA COT

English Collection — South-West

Sweet Pea Cot, built around 1800, is based upon a similar cottage at Selworthy in Somerset. This stone-built thatched gate-lodge provided housing for retired workers from the Holnicote estate. Selworthy, which is renowned for its picturesque cottages, is owned by the National Trust.

Size:	2 ½", 6.0 cm
Backstamp:	M
Introduced:	1994
Discontinued:	1997

Description	Can. $	U.S. $	U.K. £
Sweet Pea Cot	55.00	35.00	20.00

SWEET WILLIAM

British Collection

Based on the thatched brown stone cottages from the Village of Stagsden in Bedfordshire.

Size:	2 ¼", 5.5 cm
Backstamp:	P-1
Introduced:	1997
Discontinued:	1998

Description	Can. $	U.S. $	U.K. £
Sweet William	35.00	25.00	10.00

SWIFT HOLLOW

English Collection — South-East

To be found in Hampshire, this timber-framed house was built in the 17th century. Over the years some loss has occurred where panels have decayed and been replaced by brick, some of the deep thatch has been replaced by tiles and in some sections oak weatherboarding protects the timber framing.

Size: 3 ¼", 8 cm
Backstamp: G
Introduced: 1988
Discontinued: 1990

Description	Can. $	U.S. $	U.K. £
Swift Hollow	150.00	95.00	110.00

THE TAILOR

Victorian Shops Collection

This piece is based on an 1888 building in Cumbria.

Size: 4", 10.5 cm
Backstamp: P-1
Introduced: 1997
Discontinued: Current

Description	Can. $	U.S. $	U.K. £
The Tailor	125.00	90.00	37.95

TANGLEWOOD LODGE

English Collection — South-East

The eastern Cotswolds bordering the Wychwood Forest and the Evenlode Valley became a fashionable area — both as a place to visit and as a place to live — during the reign of Queen Victoria. Buildings such as Tanglewood Lodge were constructed in response to the fashion.

Size: 4 ½", 11.25 cm
Backstamp: H-1
Introduced: 1989
Discontinued: 1992

Description	Can. $	U.S. $	U.K. £
Tanglewood Lodge	200.00	125.00	110.00

TANNERS COTTAGE

English Collection — Midlands

Tanners Cottage can be found close to Bedford, in an area where many of the battles were fought in the Civil War. The cottage, which is built of Cotswold stone with a thatched roof, has its own distinctive style.

Introduced in 1987, Tanners Cottage underwent a colour change in 1990. Apart from the colour changes there was no change in the mould. In variation 1, the door and the foliage is dark. In variation 2, the door is light brown and there is a difference in the foliage colour (brighter)

Variation	Size	Backstamp	Intro.	Discon.	Can. $	U.S. $	U.K. £
1 - Dark brown	2", 5 cm	F	1987	1990	100.00	75.00	60.00
2 - Light brown	2", 5 cm	F	1990	1992	75.00	45.00	35.00

TEA CADDY COTTAGE

English Collection — South-East

Tea Caddy Cottage is situated in Constable country on the Suffolk-Essex border just north of Higham. An unusual oval-shaped cottage with its Gothic-type design, the excellent brickwork is topped by a red clay tiled roof.

Size: 3 ½", 9.0 cm
Backstamp: M
Introduced: 1994
Discontinued: Current

Description	Can. $	U.S. $	U.K. £
Tea Caddy Cottage	90.00	60.00	28.95

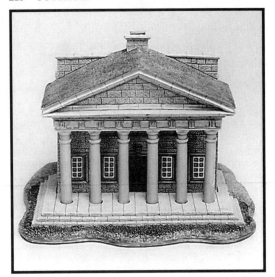

TEMPLE OF PIETY

Studley Royal Collection

Studley Royal, near Ripon in Yorkshire, was created by John Aislabie and his son William between 1716 and 1781. The building of the Temple of Piety began in 1740, and was originally dedicated to Hercules. However, William rededicated the Greek Doric temple after his father's death in 1742 as a symbol of filial piety. The interior was finished in 1748 and decorated by Guiseppe Cortese, a York plasterer.

Temple of Piety is one of 5 pieces in the Studley Royal Collection. 5,000 pieces of this model were produced. This piece is only available in the USA.

Size:	3″, 8.0 cm
Backstamp:	M
Introduced:	1994 in a limited edition of 5,000
Discontinued:	Current

Description	Can. $	U.S. $	U.K. £
Temple of Piety	N.A.	95.00	N.A.

THATCHER'S REST

English Collection — South-East

The Meon Valley in south Hampshire is where houses such as Thatcher's Rest can be found. Built in the early 17th century with oak timber framing, the roof has a catslide thatch.

Size:	3 ½″, 9.0 cm
Backstamp:	B
Introduced:	1983
Discontinued:	1988

Description	Can. $	U.S. $	U.K. £
Thatcher's Rest	600.00	400.00	200.00

"THEY DON'T MAKE'EM LIKE THEY USED TO"
Coca-Cola™ Country Collection

An old Federal style brick structure in New England inspired this antique shop. This model is available only in North America.

Size:	3 ¼", 8.3 cm
Backstamp:	Unknown
Introduced:	1998
Discontinued:	Current

Description	Can. $	U.S. $	U.K. £
They Don't Make'em...	N.A.	70.00	N.A.

Photograph not available at press time

THIMBLE COTTAGE
Collectors Club

Thimble Cottage is based on cottages found around the Veryan area of Cornwall.

This model was introduced in March 1995 and given free to newly joined members of the Collectors Club.

Size:	2 ½", 6.3 cm
Backstamp:	N-1
Introduced:	1995
Discontinued:	1996

Description	Can. $	U.S. $	U.K. £
Thimble Cottage	75.00	50.00	40.00

THOOR BALLYLEE
Irish Collection

Located in the county of Galway, Ireland, Thoor Ballylee was built around the 12th century with the thatched cottage added later. William Butler Yeats, the Irish poet and dramatist, was attracted to the tower houses of Ireland, and subsequently bought a small ruined Norman tower. Yeats restored the tower and lived there for eleven years. The tower was of significance to him, and from 1919 there are references to the tower in many of his poems.

Size:	4", 10.5 cm
Backstamp:	H-1
Introduced:	1989
Discontinued:	1992

Description	Can. $	U.S. $	U.K. £
Thoor Ballylee	450.00	300.00	90.00

Version 2 — Black Metal Sign

THREE FEATHERS

English Collection — South-East

Three Feathers is the Lilliput Lane interpretation of a public house in Cambridgeshire, and is based upon the many medieval inns that exist in the area. Oak framed and with Tudor chimneys, the building is strong and solid.

Introduced in February 1986, the original version had a long white inn sign (which was plastic) and was in production for only 3 months. In April 1986, the sign was changed to black and was made of metal.

Version	Size	Backstamp	Intro.	Discon.	Can. $	U.S. $	U.K. £
1 - White sign	4 ¾", 12 cm	E	1986	1989	500.00	325.00	300.00
2 - Black sign	4 ¾", 12 cm	E	1986	1989	300.00	200.00	150.00

TILLERS GREEN

English Collection — Midlands

Situated in the heart of Gloucestershire, this cottage is built from Cotswold stone and features stone window mullions and a flagged roof.

Size:	2 ¾", 7.0 cm
Backstamp:	J
Introduced:	1991
Discontinued:	1995

Description	Can. $	U.S. $	U.K. £
Tillers Green	100.00	65.00	30.00

TINTAGEL

English Collection — South-West

Tintagel, on the north coast of Cornwall, is famous for its association with King Arthur. Originally built as a manor house in the 14th century and used as a receiving room for the Post Office from 1840-1892 (see Old Post Office)., it is built from local granite and roofed with split stone tiles; it is now preserved by the National Trust.

Introduced in September 1984, Tintagel used the same mould as The Old Post Office (which was retired in 1986), but was painted in different colours.

Size:	2 ¾", 7.0 cm
Backstamp:	C
Introduced:	1984
Discontinued:	1988
Variation:	Old Post Office

Description	Can. $	U.S. $	U.K. £
Tintagel	375.00	250.00	170.00

TIRED TIMBERS

English Collection — Midlands

Tired Timbers is situated at Preston-on Stour, Warwickshire. Known fondly as the 'Priest House' because it was built as a priest lodgings in the early 1500s, it is currently available as a holiday rental. It is timber framed on a brick-built plinth and features an impressive brick chimney stack.

Size:	3", 7.5 cm
Backstamp:	M
Introduced:	1994
Discontinued:	1997

Description	Can. $	U.S. $	U.K. £
Tired Timbers	90.00	60.00	35.00

TITMOUSE COTTAGE

English Collection — South-West

In the vernacular style of Dorset, Titmouse Cottage is built of local stone with umbrella thatch.

Size:	4", 10 cm	
Backstamp:	H-1	
Introduced:	1989	
Discontinued:	1995	

Description	Can. $	U.S. $	U.K. £
Titmouse Cottage	200.00	125.00	50.00

TITWILLOW COTTAGE

English Collection — Midlands

Located in Eardisley, Herefordshire, this 'cruck' house is the oldest in the area. It was built around the 14th century.

Size:	2 ½", 6.5 cm
Backstamp:	L
Introduced:	1993
Discontinued:	1997

Description	Can. $	U.S. $	U.K. £
Titwillow Cottage	60.00	45.00	25.00

TO GRANDMOTHER'S HOUSE WE GO

Christmas in America

Designed by Ray Day, this model is based on a Queen Anne style home located in Corydon, Indiana.

Size:	4 ½", 11.5 cm
Backstamp:	P-1
Introduced:	1997
Discontinued:	1997

Description	Can. $	U.S. $	U.K. £
To Grandmother's . . .	N.A.	158.00	59.95

TOLL HOUSE

English Collection — South-East

Toll House is typical of the cottages to be found in Hertfordshire because of its oak beams and short straw thatch. At one time this cottage would have been at the beginning of a road for which travellers had to pay a toll. Although toll roads have virtually disappeared, the toll houses can still be found. Introduced in February 1983, Toll House was remodelled that same year when it became smaller. The versions can be distinguished by the backstamp. Version 2 was only produced with backstamp B, whereas version 1 carried either backstamp A-1 or backstamp A-2.

Front: Version 1 — Narrow, Version 2 — Wide

Side: Version 1 — Narrow, Version 2 — Wide

Version	Size	Backstamp	Intro.	Discon.	Can. $	U.S. $	U.K. £
1 —Narrow	2 ¼", 5.5 cm	A-1, A-2	1983	1983	525.00	350.00	200.00
2 — Wide	2 ¼", 5.5 cm	B	1983	1987	350.00	225.00	140.00

THE TOY SHOP

Village Shops Collection

The Toy Shop was only available through the Guild of Specialist China and Glass Retailers in the UK for the first 6 months of production before general UK release.

Size: 4", 9.85 cm
Backstamp: M
Introduced: 1994
Discontinued: Current

Description	Can. $	U.S. $	U.K. £
The Toy Shop	120.00	80.00	34.95

TRANQUILITY

Garden Series

Priority was given to Collectors Club member for this second piece in the Garden Series. Issued in a limited edition of 2,500, this piece was fully subscribed in 2 months.

Size: 5 ½", 14.3 cm
Backstamp: N-1
Introduced: 1995 in a limited edition of 2,500
Discontinued: 1995

Description	Can. $	U.S. $	U.K. £
Tranquility	1,200.00	750.00	300.00

TROUTBECK FARM

English Collection — Northern

Troutbeck is one of the oldest villages in the Lake District and so it has many farm buildings which date back to the 16th century. Troutbeck Farm was based on such a farm.

The model of Troutbeck Farm was made from a form of crystacal. This early version was very light in weight and the grey almost blended into the building. In 1985 the medium was changed to amorphite. It was heavier in weight and had a greenish grey roof. The other noticeable differences between the two versions are that version 2 has white chimney pots and the sheep were brighter in colour and it carries the backstamp B and C. Troutbeck Farm was also produced using resin, although to date only one piece is known to exist.

Version	Size	Backstamp	Intro.	Discon.	Can. $	U.S. $	U.K. £
1 - Resin	3 ½", 9 cm	Unknown	Unknown	Unknown		Very Rare	
2 - Crystacal	3 ½", 9 cm	B	1983	1985	1,250.00	850.00	300.00
3 - Amorphite	3 ½", 9 cm	B, C	1985	1987	900.00	600.00	225.00

TUCK SHOP

English Collection — Northern

Lake Windermere has many gift shops which, although vernacular in style, were built by the Victorians at the time when travelling to the Lake District became popular. Tuck Shop was based upon these buildings.

Introduced in February 1983, Tuck Shop was remodelled during that same year. The first version, which carried either backstamp A-1 or B, was light in colour, whereas on version 2 the timber frame, bay window and the roof were dark in colour. Also the centre panel of the bay window was increased from ten panes of glass to twenty panes.

Version	Size	Backstamp	Intro.	Discon.	Can. $	U.S. $	U.K. £
1 - 10 panes	3 ½", 8 cm	A-1, B	1983	1983	1,275.00	850.00	425.00
2 - 20 panes	3 ½", 8 cm	C	1983	1986	900.00	600.00	290.00

TUDOR COURT

English Collection — Midlands

Based upon buildings to be seen in the ancient part of Shrewsbury, around Bear Steps, Tudor House portrays a 16th century shopping area.

There are three versions of Tudor Court. The first version, introduced in 1986, has a grey chimney, brown fencing, and no retaining wall at the rear of the building where the cart horse-wheel is resting. Introduced circa 1989, version 2 has a black chimney, white fence posts, and also lacks the retaining wall. Version 3, introduced in 1990 (approximately), has a black chimney, white fence posts and has a retaining wall where the wheel is standing. This was put there to add support to the bush to the right of the building, as demoulding and transportation caused this bush to break.

Version 1 — Grey Chimney

Version 2 — Black Chimney

Version 3 — Black Chimney

Version 1 — Without Wall

Version 2 — Without Wall

Version 3 — With Wall

Version	Size	Backstamp	Intro.	Discon.	Can. $	U.S. $	U.K. £
1 - Grey chimney without retaining wall	5 ½", 13.5 cm	E	1986	1989	675.00	450.00	225.00
2 - Black chimney without retaining wall	5 ½", 13.5 cm	E	1989	1990	600.00	400.00	200.00
3 - Black chimney with retaining wall	5 ½", 13.5 cm	E	1990	1992	500.00	375.00	180.00

TUDOR MERCHANT

Welsh Collection

Located near the harbour in Tenby, this 15th-century Tudor merchant's house, which is now owned by the National Trust, is a reminder of the town's prosperous trading days.

Size:	4 ½", 11.5 cm
Backstamp:	I-2
Introduced:	1991
Discontinued:	1997

Description	Can. $	U.S. $	U.K. £
Tudor Merchant	100.00	60.00	40.00

TUPPENNY BUN

British Collection

Cottage's with the architectural style of Tuppenny Bun can be seen in Brigstock, Northamptonshire.

Size:	2 ½", 6.0 cm
Backstamp:	P-1
Introduced:	1998
Discontinued:	Current

Description	Can. $	U.S. $	U.K. £
Tuppenny Bun	60.00	35.00	16.95

TWO HOOTS

English Collection — South-East

In the 16th and 17th centuries the use of bricks became more and more popular in vernacular building, spreading rapidly through areas where timber frame construction was the main building method. Such an area was Alresford in Hampshire, and Two Hoots is an example of a brick-built cottage with a thatched roof that can be found there.

Size:	3", 7.5 cm
Backstamp:	M
Introduced:	1994
Discontinued:	1997

Description	Can. $	U.S. $	U.K. £
Two Hoots	80.00	45.00	30.00

UGLY HOUSE

Welsh Collection

Ty Hyl (Ugly House) can be found near Betws-y-Coed in the Conwy Valley. Built by two outlaw brothers in 1475, the house was a hideout for thieves until the early 19th century. Used by the Snowdonia National Park Society for its headquarters, the house was recently restored, upon completion of which it won a conservation award. Its name — Ugly House — comes from the huge ungainly boulders used in its walls.

Size:	2 ½", 6.5 cm
Backstamp:	I-2
Introduced:	1991
Discontinued:	Current

Description	Can. $	U.S. $	U.K. £
Ugly House	80.00	50.00	19.95

VANBRUGH LODGE

Special Editions

Located in the grounds of the Grimsthorpe Castle Estate near Bourne, Lincolnshire, home of the 1995 Lilliput Lane Event, this model was available throughout the year at Lilliput Lane Events. The door was uncoloured and could be painted to the choice of the collector by any of the painters.

Size:	3", 7.6 cm
Backstamp:	N-1
Introduced:	1995
Discontinued:	1996

Description	Can. $	U.S. $	U.K. £
Vanbrugh Lodge	125.00	90.00	65.00

THE VICARAGE

Christmas Collection

Built from Cotswold stone and with a stone roof, the model is based upon a 19th century building near Littleworth in Oxfordshire.

The Vicarage is an essential building in the traditional village which is depicted in the Christmas Collection. The backstamp is hard to find because of the snow.

Size:	2 ¾", 7.0 cm
Backstamp:	M
Introduced:	1994
Discontinued:	1997

Description	Can. $	U.S. $	U.K. £
The Vicarage	55.00	35.00	20.00

VICTORIA COTTAGE

English Collection — Northern

Victoria Cottage is typical of those first private houses which were built around 1880 when, because of Great Britain's dominance in world trade, new classes of society began to emerge and move away from rented accommodation.

Version 2 has a deeper base and is heavier than the earlier model.

Version	Size	Backstamp	Intro.	Discon.	Can. $	U.S. $	U.K. £
1 - Thinner base	3 ½", 8.5 cm	H-1	1989	1990	125.00	75.00	60.00
2 - Thicker base	3 ½", 8.5 cm	H-1	1990	1993	100.00	65.00	50.00

VICTORIANA
American Landmarks

   Inspired by houses in the coastal Town of Rockport, Maine this model was based on a 19th century house.
   Victoriana was introduced in June 1991 and was limited to 2,500 pieces. Only available in the USA, Victoriana was fully subscribed inside a year.

Size:	6″, 15.0 cm
Backstamp:	J
Introduced:	1991
Discontinued:	1992

Description	Can. $	U.S. $	U.K. £
Victoriana	650.00	450.00	450.00

VICTORIAN ELEGANCE
An American Journey

This model is inspired by a house in San Francisco, California.

Size:	4 ¾″, 12.0 cm
Backstamp:	P-1
Introduced:	1997
Discontinued:	Current

Description	Can. $	U.S. $	U.K. £
Victorian Elegance	N.A.	130.00	64.95

VILLAGE SCHOOL
English Collection — Northern

   Built around 1876, this model of a Victorian school is located in Sawley, Lancashire.

Size:	3 ¼″, 8.0 cm
Backstamp:	J
Introduced:	1991
Discontinued:	1996

Description	Can. $	U.S. $	U.K. £
Village School	125.00	85.00	50.00

VINE COTTAGE

Style One
English Collection — South-West

Built around 1810 by the architects John Nash and George Repton as one of the cottages at Blaise Hamlet, Vine Cottage is built from stone and slate. Like Double Cottage, Vine Cottage has a gable which features a pigeon loft.

Introduced in February 1990, Vine Cottage was initially in the Blaise Hamlet Collection, but in 1994 was transferred to the English Collection — South-West.

Size:	4 ½", 11.5 cm
Backstamp:	I-2
Introduced:	1990
Discontinued:	1995

Description	Can. $	U.S. $	U.K. £
Vine Cottage	225.00	125.00	75.00

VINE COTTAGE

Style Two
Classics Collection

From the miniature range of sculptures based upon buildings at Blaise Hamlet near Bristol, Vine Cottage is one of the cottages most frequently seen illustrated in calendars. Built by the architects John Nash and George Repton around 1810, Blaise Hamlet provided homes for the retired employees from the Blaise Hamlet estate.

Size:	2 ½", 6.0 cm
Backstamp:	L
Introduced:	1993
Discontinued:	1995

Description	Can. $	U.S. $	U.K. £
Vine Cottage	150.00	95.00	40.00

WALLACE STATION
American Collection

In the 1800s, "Whistle Stations" were a common sight along the Union and Pacific Railway Lines.

Wallace Station was based on one of these stations. Only 150 pieces were produced.

Size:	2 ½", 6.5 cm
Backstamp:	C
Introduced:	1984
Discontinued:	1985

Description	Can. $	U.S. $	U.K. £
Wallace Station	1,875.00	1,250.00	600.00

WALTON LODGE
British Collection

This gatehouse to Chestnut Park Estate, Hertfordshire, was built in 1795 by Richard Cromwell's great-grandson.

Size:	3 ¾", 8.6 cm
Backstamp:	P-1
Introduced:	1997
Discontinued:	Current

Description	Can. $	U.S. $	U.K. £
Walton Lodge	90.00	65.00	27.95

WARWICK HALL

English Collection — Northern

Warwick Hall is based on an Elizabethan manor at Alderley Edge, Cheshire.

When it was first introduced in February 1983, Warwick Hall had its name filled with paint on the front of the base; however, towards the middle of that year it was remodelled and the name removed. Both versions had a three window section to the right of the tree. Remodelled again in September 1983, version 3 now had a two window section to the right of the tree.

Version	Size	Backstamp	Intro.	Discon.	Can. $	U.S. $	U.K. £
1 - With name 3 windows	5 ½", 14 cm	A-1	1983	1983	4,500.00	3,000.00	1,600.00
2 - Without name 3 windows	5 ½", 14 cm	B	1983	1983	3,750.00	2,500.00	1,050.00
3 - 2 windows	5 ½", 14 cm	C	1983	1985	3,000.00	2,000.00	800.00

WASH DAY

Collectors Club

Washday was introduced in March 1996 and given free to new members of the Collectors Club. It is reported that membership of the Collectors Club was exceeding 75,000 when this cottage was produced. It has the largest production run of any of the cottages to date.

Size: 2 ½", 5.9 cm
Backstamp: O-2
Introduced: 1996
Discontinued: 1997

Description	Can. $	U.S. $	U.K. £
Wash Day	60.00	45.00	30.00

WATERMEADOWS

Anniversary Editions

Watermeadows is one of the two oldest houses in the village of Osmaston near Ashbourne in Derbyshire. The cottage, which in parts is almost 400 years old, is part of the estate of the Walker-Okeover family, and was originally two homes.

Introduced in February 1994, Watermeadows was only available in that year.

Size:	3 ¾", 9.5 cm
Backstamp:	M
Introduced:	1994
Discontinued:	1994

Description	Can. $	U.S. $	U.K. £
Watermeadows	275.00	175.00	80.00

WATERMILL

English Collection — South-West

Built in the 17th century, this small overshot mill, which would have been found in Dorset, is attached to a cruck-framed thatched cottage. Many cottages such as this still survive today.

Introduced in July 1985, the early pieces were quite dark in colour especially around the watermill itself, and lacked any shine; later pieces were lighter and shinier

Variation	Size	Backstamp	Intro.	Discon.	Can. $	U.S. $	U.K. £
1 - Dark colour	2 ¼", 5.75 cm	D	1985	1990	100.00	65.00	50.00
2 - Light colour	2 ¼", 5.75 cm	D	1990	1993	90.00	60.00	40.00

WATERSIDE MILL

English Collection — Midlands

Based upon old drawings and etchings of various Shropshire mills, Waterside Mill depicts a 17th century undershot mill, which combines both living accommodation (which is of stone and thatch) and working area (which is of stone and slate).

Size: 2 ½", 6.0 cm
Backstamp: M
Introduced: 1994
Discontinued: Current

Description	Can. $	U.S. $	U.K. £
Waterside Mill	75.00	50.00	19.95

WEALDEN HOUSE

English Collection — South-East

Typical of the houses found on the Sussex Weald, with the forward projecting jettied upper storeys at each end, Wealden House was built in the 15th century. There has been some repair work on the ground floor and the chimneys are a later addition. The wattle and daub panelling has been hung with tiles to provide added weather protection, and the hipped roof may once have been thatched.

Size: 4 ½", 11.5 cm
Backstamp: F
Introduced: 1987
Discontinued: 1990

Description	Can. $	U.S. $	U.K. £
Wealden House	275.00	175.00	130.00

WEDDING BELLS

English Collection — Northern

Based on a 12th century church at Upleatham in Cleveland (believed to be the smallest in England). Built from local stone with a pantile roof, measuring 17 ¾ ft by 13 ft (5 ½ m by 4 m) . In 1836 the church was closed when another was built locally. In 1967 the doors re-opened for the wedding of Jennifer Sutcliffe and Douglas Kyle. In 1992, Lilliput Lane invited them back to the Leatham Church and David Tate presented them with a silver plate version of 'Wedding Bells' as a 25th anniversary gift.

Size: 3 ¼", 8.0 cm
Backstamp: K-1
Introduced: 1992
Discontinued: Current

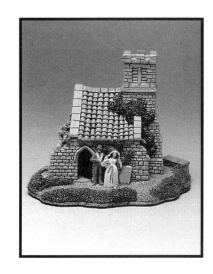

Description	Can. $	U.S. $	U.K. £
Wedding Bells	80.00	50.00	19.95

WELLINGTON LODGE

English Collection — Midlands

Wellington Lodge, located near Cheltenham, was constructed in 1827 with a Greek influence visible in the architecture. All of the bridges on the Gloucester and Sharpness canal have opening spans, so it was necessary to have the bridges manned. Wellington Lodge was originally a bridgeman's cottage and would have been built in readiness for the canal being opened.

Size: 2 ½", 6.0 cm
Backstamp: J
Introduced: 1991
Discontinued: 1995

Description	Can. $	U.S. $	U.K. £
Wellington Lodge	90.00	60.00	30.00

WENLOCK RISE

Collectors Club

Offa's Dyke, which runs from the mouth of the River Dee in Clwyd to Chepstow in Gwent, is believed to have been built by Offa, King of Mercia, to mark the border between Mercia and Wales, and also to reduce raiding by the Welsh tribes. Today it is the setting for Wenlock Rise, a magnificent timber-framed house.

Wenlock Rise was only available to members of the Lilliput Lane Collectors Club for a twelve-month period and was never available to the general public.

Size: 6", 15.0 cm
Backstamp: G
Introduced: 1988
Discontinued: 1989

Description	Can. $	U.S. $	U.K. £
Wenlock Rise	450.00	300.00	250.00

"WET YOUR WHISTLE"

Coca-Cola™ Country Collection

Based on a hundred-year-old water tower, this model was designed by Ray Day and produced under license from the Coca Cola™ Company. Although not a limited edition, each piece is individually hand numbered. This collection was produced in Ireland and are all made of resin. Only available in North America.

Size: 3 ½", 8.9 cm
Backstamp: O-2
Introduced: 1997
Discontinued: Current

Description	Can. $	U.S. $	U.K. £
"Wet Your Whistle"	60.00	42.00	N.A.

"WE'VE GOT IT....(OR THEY DON'T MAKE IT!)"

Coca-Cola ™ Country Collection

This model was Inspired by country stores near White Springs, Missouri and Jamestown, California built in the late 1920s.

Designed by Ray Day and produced under license from the Coca-Cola™ Company. Only available in North America.

Size:	3 ¼", 8.2 cm
Backstamp:	O-2
Introduced:	1996
Discontinued:	Current

Description	Can. $	U.S. $	U.K. £
"We've Got It . . ."	130.00	100.00	N.A.

WHEYSIDE COTTAGE

English Collection — South-West

Built around the 1850s, Wheyside Cottage is situated on the border of Somerset and Devon. Using local stone and thatch, the cottage features arched Gothic leaded windows.

Size:	2 ¾", 7.0 cm
Backstamp:	K-1
Introduced:	1992
Discontinued:	1998

Description	Can. $	U.S. $	U.K. £
Wheyside Cottage	55.00	35.00	16.00

Version 2 — Larger Windows

WIGHT COTTAGE

English Collection — South-East

The Isle of Wight is a very popular holiday resort, and as the many visitors tour around the island they see a number of very delightful and attractive cottages such as Wight Cottage.

Around 1990, the cottage was remodelled slightly and the windows of the building were increased in size from 6.26 mm to 7.29 mm.

Version	Size	Backstamp	Intro.	Discon.	Can. $	U.S. $	U.K. £
1 - Smaller windows	2 ¾", 7 cm	H-1	1989	1990	100.00	65.00	30.00
2 - Larger windows	2 ¾", 7 cm	H-1	1990	1994	100.00	65.00	30.00

WILLIAM SHAKESPEARE'S BIRTHPLACE 1989

English Collection — Midlands

Shakespeare was born in 1564 in this house in Henley Street, Stratford-upon-Avon. In Shakespeare's lifetime it was two separate buildings. Built in the 16th century it is a typical middle-class dwelling of the period, and like many other buildings in the town dating from that time, it is half-timbered infilled with wattle and daub.

This new model of Shakespeare's birthplace had more foliage and garden around the house than its predecessor. The foliage is brown green, and it has dark chimneys and grey lattice windows. Varition 2 had bright green foliage and the lattice windows had a hint of blue.

Variation	Size	Backstamp	Intro.	Discon.	Can. $	U.S. $	U.K. £
1 - Grey windows	3", 7.5 cm	H-1	1989	1989	300.00	200.00	105.00
2 - Blue windows	3", 7.5 cm	H-1	1989	1992	250.00	150.00	80.00

WILLIAM SHAKESPEARE'S BIRTHPLACE

English Collection — Midlands

Stratford-upon-Avon has become one of the world's most famous tourist centres due to its association with William Shakespeare. This is one of the best preserved Tudor houses in England. The model was an almost perfect scale replica of Shakespeare's home.

The original version had the wording 'Shakespeare's Cottage' embossed across the front of the base. When the cottage was restyled, the wording across the front was removed. Versions 1 and 2 had similar colouring, with the timbers and chimneys almost charcoal and the base a dark green. The cottage was restyled again (1984), with the base being more finely detailed and coloured light green, and the roof lighter in colour.

Version 1 — With Wording *Version 2 —Without Wording* *Version 3 — Without Wording*

Version	Size	Backstamp	Intro.	Discon.	Can. $	U.S. $	U.K. £
1 - With wording, Dark green base	3", 7.5 cm	A-1	1983	1983	2,250.00	1,500.00	700.00
2 - Without wording Dark green base	3", 7.5 cm	B	1983	1984	450.00	300.00	250.00
3 - Without wording Light green base	3", 7.5 cm	C	1984	1989	225.00	150.00	90.00

WINDY RIDGE

English Collection — Northern

This model is based on a 17th century cottage located in the village of Middleham, North Yorkshire.

Size:	3 ¾", 8.0 cm
Backstamp:	O-2
Introduced:	1996
Discontinued:	Current

Description	Can. $	U.S. $	U.K. £
Windy Ridge	65.00	50.00	19.95

WINNIE'S PLACE

American Landmarks

Winnie's Place was built in 1881 in the Romantic Italianate style, and is the home of Winnie Watson Sweet, the owner of a collectables and gift shop in Indiana. Winnie is well-known for her connections with the South Bend Show. She is also the organizer of the South Bend International Plate and Collectables Exposition. Her house is an open house during the show each year for tours.

Winnie's Place was limited to 2,000 pieces and was only available in the USA.

Size:	6", 15.0 cm
Backstamp:	K-1, Ltd. Ed.
Introduced:	1992 in a limited edition of 2,000
Discontinued:	1993

Description	Can. $	U.S. $	U.K. £
Winnie's Place	900.00	600.00	550.00

THE WINNOWS

Collectors Club

The Winnows was built in the 16th century in Castle Combe, Wiltshire.

This piece was given to collectors who enrolled another member in the Collectors Club. In past experience, these pieces (only two previous cottages have been made) have proved very popular and became hard to find within a short length of time.

Size:	2 ½", 6.4 cm
Backstamp:	N-1
Introduced:	1996
Discontinued:	1997

Description	Can. $	U.S. $	U.K. £
The Winnows	100.00	75.00	55.00

WINTER AT HIGH GHYLL

English Collection — Northern

Apart from the snow effect and the white limewashing now a distinctive cream, there is no model change from the original High Ghyll Farm. Only available in the UK, with retailers being restricted to a maximum of six pieces each. This piece was only available for one month and 2,000 pieces were produced.

Size:	5", 12.5 cm
Backstamp:	K-1
Introduced:	1995
Discontinued:	1995

Description	Can. $	U.S. $	U.K. £
Winter at High Ghyll	525.00	350.00	150.00

WINTER'S WONDER

A Year in an English Garden

Winter's Wonder is one of four cottages portraying the seasonal changes. The seasonal portrayals are: spring (Spring Glory), summer (Summer Impressions), autumn (Autumn Hues) and winter (Winter's Wonder).

Size:	3 ½", 8.5 cm
Backstamp:	M
Introduced:	1994
Discontinued:	1997

Description	Can. $	U.S. $	U.K. £
Winter's Wonder	125.00	85.00	45.00

WISHING WELL

Collectors Club

Wishing Well, which showed a traditional well-head, was introduced in March, 1988 and was offered as a free gift to members joining the Collectors Club during the twelve months from March 1988 to February 1989, at which time it was retired. During the period that Wishing Well was being offered, membership of the Club increased to just over 12,500.

Size:	2 ½", 6.5 cm
Backstamp:	None
Introduced:	1988
Discontinued:	1989

Description	Can. $	U.S. $	U.K. £
Wishing Well	275.00	175.00	115.00

WITHAM DELPH

English Collection — Midlands

To be found alongside a Lincolnshire dyke, Witham Delph is built from hand-made bricks and features a pantiled roof, which shows the influence of the trading with the Low Countries.

Size:	3 ½″, 8.5 cm
Backstamp:	J
Introduced:	1991
Discontinued:	1994

Description	Can. $	U.S. $	U.K. £
Witham Delph	200.00	125.00	45.00

DE WOLHANDELAAR

Netherlands Collection

De Wolhandelaar (The Wool Merchant) shows a typical workshop which was used for turning wool from England into cloth. Some of these workshops were established almost 600 years ago. The straight-sided bell gable became a particularly popular feature in the 18th century.

De Wolhandelaar is similar in appearance to De Branderij apart from the colouring. De Branderij's roof is white while De Wolhandelaar's is grey.

Size:	5 ¼″, 13.5 cm
Backstamp:	J
Introduced:	1991
Discontinued:	1998
Variations:	De Branderij

Description	Can. $	U.S. $	U.K. £
De Wolhandelaar	80.00	55.00	25.00

WOODCUTTERS

English Collection — South-West

Situated in Devon, Woodcutters is a clay cob cottage with a thatched roof. In previous times the walls would have been painted with lime wash to provide waterproofing.

Introduced in February 1983, Woodcutters was restyled late in 1983 when it was made smaller.

Version	Size	Backstamp	Intro.	Discon.	Can. $	U.S. $	U.K. £
1 — Large	2 ½ ", 5.5 cm	A-1, B	1983	1983	450.00	300.00	210.00
2 — Small	2 ¼", 5.4 cm	B	1983	1987	350.00	225.00	150.00

WOODMAN'S RETREAT

Collectors Club

Situated on the edge of woodland near Faringdon in Oxfordshire, Woodman's Retreat is a small thatched cottage which was built in the 18th century. Timber framed with brick infill, the cottage reflects the cult of the 'picturesque' with its varying roof heights jutting out at all angles.

Introduced in March 1994, Woodman's Retreat was only available to members of the Lilliput Lane Collectors Club during the Club year from March 1994 to February 1995.

Size: 4", 10.5 cm
Backstamp: M
Introduced: 1994
Discontinued: 1995

Description	Can. $	U.S. $	U.K. £
Woodman's Retreat	225.00	150.00	90.00

WREN COTTAGE
Collectors Club

Introduced in 1991, Wren Cottage was offered at a preferential price to existing Club members who enrolled a new member. The cottage was not available for general purchase through the Club, nor was it generally available.

Size:	2 ¼″, 5.75 cm
Backstamp:	J
Introduced:	1991
Discontinued:	1993

Description	Can. $	U.S. $	U.K. £
Wren Cottage	225.00	150.00	190.00

WYCOMBE TOLL HOUSE
Special Editions

The sixth Lilliput Lane Annual Fair was held at the Chiltern Open Air Museum near Amersham, in Buckinghamshire, on September 3rd and 4th, 1994. The Museum is dedicated to rescuing and rebuilding local condemned buildings. Wycombe Toll House was based upon a cottage in the Museum grounds that was constructed in 1826 to replace an older toll house.

Only 3,834 of Wycombe Toll House were produced. They were only available to those members attending the two day Fair.

Size:	2 ¾″, 7.0 cm
Backstamp:	M
Introduced:	1994
Discontinued:	1994

Description	Can. $	U.S. $	U.K. £
Wycombe Toll House	425.00	275.00	165.00

YEW TREE FARM
Collectors Club

Based upon the Cumbrian Farm House which was the home of David Tate founder of Lilliput Lane, Yew Tree Farm can be found in Cumbria and dates from the late 1600s. Built from rubble it was originally a single-roomed thatched house, but in 1737 when it was renovated the upstairs was added. Adjoining the main house are barns and associated buildings, also built of rubble and roofed with Lakeland slate.

This was the second cottage available to current members of the Collectors Club.

Size:	3 ¼″, 8.0 cm
Backstamp:	F
Introduced:	1987
Discontinued:	1988

Description	Can. $	U.S. $	U.K. £
Yew Tree Farm	600.00	400.00	250.00

YORKVALE COTTAGE
British Collection

Close to the River Derwent, Yorkvale Cottage nestles into a hillside on the edge of the North Yorkshire Moors.

Size: 3", 8.0 cm
Backstamp: P-1
Introduced: 1997
Discontinued: Current

Description	Can. $	U.S. $	U.K. £
Yorkvale Cottage	65.00	50.00	19.95

YULETIDE INN
Christmas Specials

Yuletide Inn, a timber framed and jettied building which dates from the 16th century, can be found on the Pilgrim's Way in Kent.
Introduced in September 1990, this was the third of the Christmas Specials and as with the others in the Collection was retired in February of the following year.

Size: 5 ¼", 13.0 cm
Backstamp: I-2
Introduced: 1990
Discontinued: 1991

Description	Can. $	U.S. $	U.K. £
Yuletide Inn	300.00	200.00	160.00

DE ZIJDEWEVER
Netherlands Collection

The cluster of mulberries adorning the top of the spout gable identified the owner of De Zijdewever (The Silk Weaver). It was a fine home which would have had fine furnishings and silk wallhangings.
Apart from the colouring, De Zijdewever is similar to Bloemenmarkt. The basement door on De Zijdewever is red while it is brown on Bloemenmarkt.

Size: 6 ¼", 15.5 cm
Backstamp: J
Introduced: 1991
Discontinued: 1998
Variations: Bloemenmarkt

Description	Can. $	U.S. $	U.K. £
De Zijdewever	80.00	60.00	27.00

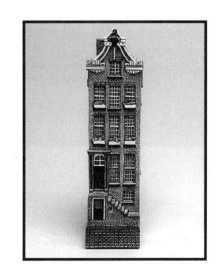

A YEAR IN AN ENGLISH GARDEN COLLECTION

Autumn Hues

Spring Glory

Summer Impressions

Winter's Wonder

COLLECTING BY SERIES

A YEAR IN AN ENGLISH GARDEN
Autumn Hues
Spring Glory
Summer Impressions
Winter's Wonder

ALLEGIANCE COLLECTION
By Dawn's Early Light
Fourth of July, The
I'll Be Home For Christmas
In Remembrance
I Pledge Allegiance
One Nation Under God
Stars and Stripes Forever

AMERICAN COLLECTION
Adobe Church
Adobe Village
Cape Cod Cottage
Country Church
Covered Bridge
Forge Barn
Fresh Bread
General Store
Grist Mill
Lighthouse
Log Cabin
Midwest Barn
San Francisco House
Wallace Station

AMERICAN LANDMARKS
Afternoon Tea
The Birdsong
Country Church
Countryside Barn
Covered Memories
Falls Mill
Fire House 1
Gold Miner's Claim
Great Point Light
Harvest Mill
Holy Night
Home of the Brave
Home Sweet Home
Hometown Depot
Lobster at the Pier
Mail Pouch Barn
Pepsi Cola Barn
Pioneer Barn
Rambling Rose
Riverside Chapel
Roadside Coolers
School Days
See Rock City
Seek and Find
Shave and a Haircut
Simply Amish
16.9 Cents per Gallon
Small Town Library
Spring Victorian
Victoriana
Winnie's Place

AN AMERICAN JOURNEY
Daydreams
Dog Days of Summer
Lace House
Morning Has Broken
Safe Harbour
Victorian Elegance

ANNIVERSARY EDITIONS
Cotman Cottage
Cruck End
Gertrude's Garden
Honeysuckle Cottage 1992
Shades of Summer
Summer Days
Watermeadows

BLAISE HAMLET COLLECTION
Circular Cottage
Dial Cottage
Diamond Cottage
Oak Cottage

BRITISH COLLECTION
Appleby East
Best Friends
Bowbeams
Bumble Bee Cottage
Buttermilk Farm
Bwthyn Bach Gwyn
Canterbury Bells
Catkin Cottage
Coach and Horses, The
Cockleshells
Cowslip Cottage
Crathie Church
Devon Leigh
First Snow at Bluebell
George Inn, The
Golden Memories
Golden Years
Green Gables
Granny's Bonnet
Halcyon Days
Harvest Home
Hubble-Bubble
Lilac Lodge
Mangerton Mill
Medway Manor
Nightingale
Old Forge, The
Parson's Retreat
Pastures New
Pineapple House, The
Poppies, The
Puddle Duck
Rose Bouquet
Scotch Mist
Scotney Castle Garden
Silver Bells
Stonemason, The
Sweet William
Tuppenny Bun
Walton Lodge
Yorkvale Cottage

CHRISTMAS COLLECTION
Chestnut Cottage
Cranberry Cottage
Evergreens
Fir Tree Cottage
Frosty Morning
Gingerbread Shop
Great Expectations
Hollytree House
Ivy House
Lady Jane's Cottage
Mistletoe Cottage
Partridge Cottage
Plum Cottage
Ring O'Bells
Robin Cottage
St. Joseph's Church
St. Joseph's School
The Vicarage

CHRISTMAS IN AMERICA
Home For the Holidays
Let Heaven and Nature Sing
To Grandmother's House We Go

CHRISTMAS LODGE COLLECTION
Eamont Lodge
Highland Lodge
Kerry Lodge
Snowdon Lodge

CHRISTMAS SPECIALS
Christmas Party
Deer Park Hall
The Old Vicarage at Christmas
St. Nicholas Church
St. Stephen's Church
Yuletide Inn

CLASSICS COLLECTION
Circular Cottage
Dial Cottage
Diamond Cottage
Double Cottage
Jasmine Cottage
Oak Cottage
Rose Cottage
Sweet Briar Cottage
Vine Cottage

COCA-COLA ™ COUNTRY COLLECTION
"A Cherry Coke-Just The Prescription"
"Country Fresh Pickins"
'Fill'Er Up & Check the Oil
Hazards of the Road
Hook, Line and Sinker
Lunch Line, The
"Milk For Mom and a Coke For Me"
"Mmm . . . Just Like Home"
Oh By Gosh, By Golly
Santas Corner
Saturday Night Jive

COCA-COLA ™ COUNTRY COLLECTION con't . . .

"They Don't Make'Em Like They Used To"
"Wet Your Whistle"
"We've Got It... (Or They Don't Make It!)"

COLLECTORS CLUB

Bridle Way
Cider Apple Cottage
Cosy Corner
Counting House Corner
Crendon Manor
Curlew Cottage
Dovecot
Forget-Me-Not
Gardener's Cottage
Hampton Manor
Hampton Moat
Heaven Lea Cottage
Kiln Cottage
Lavender Cottage
Meadowsweet Cottage
Nursery, The
Petticoat Cottage
Porlock Down
Pottery, The
Puddlebrook
Pussy Willow
The Spinney
Thimble Cottage
Wash Day
Wenlock Rise
The Winnows
Wishing Well
Woodman's Retreat
Wren Cottage
Yew Tree Farm

DREAM COTTAGE MINIATURES COLLECTION

Bridge House
The Chocolate House
Cotman Cottage
Honeysuckle Cottage
Old Mother Hubbard's
Paradise Lodge
Rose Cottage
St. Lawrence Church
Summer Haze
Titmouse Cottage
The Toy Shop
Vine Cottage

ENGLISH COLLECTION — MIDLANDS

Anne Hathaway's Cottage
Anne Hathaway's Cottage 1989
Armada House
Beehive Cottage
Birdlip Bottom
Bow Cottage
Bramble Cottage
Bredon House
Buttercup Cottage

Button Down
Chiltern Mill
Cobblers Cottage
Drapers
Elm Cottage
Farriers
Farthing Lodge
Fiddler's Folly
Fiveways
Four Seasons
Foxglove Fields
Granny Smiths
Izaak Walton's Cottage
Junk and Disorderly
Lace Lane
Ladybird Cottage
Lapworth Lock
Larkrise
Little Hay
Little Smithy
Magpie Cottage
Milestone Cottage
Moreton Manor
Paradise Lodge
Pear Tree House
Penny's Post
Railway Cottage
Riverview
Robins Gate
Rosemary Cottage
Rustic Root House
Saddler's Inn
St. Marks
St. Mary's Church
Sulgrave Manor
Summer Haze
Tanners Cottage
Tillers Green
Tired Timbers
Titwillow Cottage
Tudor Court
Waterside Mill
Wellington Lodge
William Shakespeare's Birthplace 1989
William Shakespeare's Birthplace
Witham Delph

ENGLISH COLLECTION — NORTHERN

Beacon Heights
Bluebell Farm
Bridge House
Bridge House 1991
Bridge House in Winter
Brontë Parsonage
Burnside
Castle Street
Chatsworth View
The Chocolate House
Dale Farm
Dale Head
Dale House
The Dalesman
Derwent-Le-Dale
Dove Cottage
Dovetails
Fry Days
Helmere Cottage

High Ghyll Farm
Holly Cottage
Holme Dyke
Inglewood
Keeper's Lodge
Lakeside House
Loxdale Cottage
Micklegate Antiques
Miners
Old School House
Potter's Beck
The Priest's House
Red Lion Inn
Runswick House
Rydal View
Sawrey Gill
Secret Garden
Ship Inn
Sore Paws
The Spindles
St. John the Baptist
St. Lawrence Church
Stocklebeck Mill
Stoneybeck
Troutbeck Farm
Tuck Shop
Victoria Cottage
Village School
Warwick Hall
Wedding Bells
Windy Ridge
Winter at High Ghyll

ENGLISH COLLECTION — SOUTH EAST

Acorn Cottage
The Anchor
Anne of Cleves
April Cottage
Ash Nook
Bay View
Birchwood Cottage
The Blue Boar
Boxwood Cottage
Brockbank
Calendar Cottage
Camomile Lawn
Chalk Down
Cherry Blossom Cottage
Cherry Cottage
Chine Cot
Clare Cottage
Cley-Next-The-Sea
Coach House
Coopers
Cradle Cottage
Crispin Cottage
Crown Inn
Daisy Cottage
Finchingfield
Flowerpots
Flower Sellers
The Gables
Gossip Gate
Grantchester Meadows
Greensted Church
Honey Pot Cottage
Honeysuckle Cottage

Hopcroft Cottage
John Barleycorn Cottage
Kentish Oast House
The King's Arms
Little Lupins
Marigold Meadow
Millers
Mrs Pinkerton's Post Office
The Nutshell
Oak Lodge
Oakwood Smithy
The Old Curiosity Shop
Old Shop at Bignor
Orchard Farm Cottage
Pargetter's Retreat
Primrose Hill
The Rising Sun
The Rustlings
Saffron House
Saxham St. Edmunds
Saxon Cottage
St. Peter's Cove
Stone Cottage
Strawberry Cottage
Sunnyside
Sussex Mill
The Swan Inn
Swift Hollow
Tanglewood Lodge
Tea Caddy Cottage
Thatcher's Rest
Three Feathers
Toll House
Two Hoots
Wealden House
Wight Cottage

ENGLISH COLLECTION — SOUTH WEST

Applejack Cottage
The Briary
Butterwick
Cats Coombe Cottage
Chipping Coombe
Clover Cottage
Convent in the Woods
Creel Cottage
The Cuddy
Dial Cottage
Double Cottage
Duckdown Cottage
Fisherman's Cottage
Fuchsia Cottage
Harriet's Cottage
Jasmine Cottage
Lazy Days
Moonlight Cove
Old Mill
Old Mine
Old Mother Hubbard
The Old Post Office
Ostlers Keep
Otter Reach
Periwinkle Cottage
Pipit Toll
Pixie House
Puffin Row

Purbeck Stores
Rose Cottage
The Royal Oak
The Smallest Inns
Spring Bank
Spring Gate Cottage
Stradling Priory
Sweet Briar Cottage
Sweet Pea Cot
Tintagel
Titmouse Cottage
Vine Cottage
Watermill
Wheyside Cottage
Woodcutters

ENGLISH TEA ROOM COLLECTION

Bargate Tea Rooms
Bo-Peep Tea Room
Grandma Batty's Tea Room
Kendal Tea House
New Forest Teas
Strawberry Teas
Swaledale Teas

EXCLUSIVE

Bermuda Cottage
Chantry Chapel
Clockmaker's Cottage
Fire Station 105
Guildhall
Hall of Presidents, The
Haunted House, The
Settler's Surprise
Seven Dwarfs Cottage

FOUNDER'S CHOICE COLLECTION

The Almonry

FRENCH COLLECTION

L'Auberge D'Armorique
La Bergerie du Perigord
La Cabane du Gardian
La Chaumiere du Verger
Locmaria
Le Manoir de Champfleuri
Le Mas du Vigneron
La Maselle de Nadaillac
Le Petit Montmartre
La Porte Schoenenberg

GARDEN SERIES

Hestercombe Gardens
Leonora's Secret Garden
Reflections of Jade
Tranquility

GERMAN COLLECTION

Alte Schmiede
Der Bücherwurm
Der Familienschrein
Das Gebirgskirchlein
Haus Im Rheinland
Jagdhütte
Die Kleine Backerei
Meersburger Weinstube

Moselhaus
Nürnberger Bürgerhaus
Das Rathaus
Rosengartenhaus
Schwarzwaldhaus
Strandvogthaus

HISTORIC CASTLES OF BRITAIN

Bodiam
Castell Coch
Penkill Castle
Stokesay

IRISH COLLECTION

Ballykerne Croft
Donegal Cottage
Hegarty's Home
Kennedy Homestead
Kilmore Quays
Limerick House
Magilligan's
O'Lacey's Store
Pat Cohan's Bar
Quiet Cottage
St. Columba's School
St. Kevin's Church
St. Patrick's Church
Thoor Ballylee

LAKELAND CHRISTMAS COLLECTION

All Saints Watermillock
Borrowdale School
Langdale Cottage
Millbeck Cottage
Patterdale Cottage
Rydal Cottage

MINIATURE TOWN BUILDINGS

Penny Lanes

NETHERLANDS COLLECTION

Aan de Amstel
Begijnhof
Bloemenmarkt
De Branderij
De Diamantair
De Pepermolen
Rembrandt Van Rijn
Rozengracht
De Wolhandelaar
De Zijdewever

PAINT YOUR OWN

Ashleigh Down
Essex Cottage
Flaxton Beck
Kentish Cottage
Little Birch
Marche House
Painswick Post Office
Reading Cottage
Roding Heath / High Roding
Rosy Rafters
Shropshire Cottage
Suffolk Cottage

SCOTTISH COLLECTION

Amisfield Tower
Blair Atholl
Burns Cottage, Alloway
Carrick House
Cawdor Castle
Claypotts Castle
Craigievar Castle
The Croft / Crofter's Cottage
Culloden Cottage
Culross House
Duart Castle
East Neuk
Edzell Summer-House
Eilean Donnan Castle
Eriskay Croft
Fisherman's Bothy
Glenlochie Lodge
Hebridean Hame
Inverlochie Hame
John Knox House
Kenmore Cottage
Kinlochness
Kirkbrae Cottage
Ladybank Lodge
Mair Haven
Preston Mill
7 St. Andrews Square
Stockwell Tenement

SPECIAL EDITIONS

Aberford Gate
Amberley Rose
Arbury Lodge
Ashberry 92
Cliburn School
Comfort Cottage
Cornflower Cottage
Cotman Dream Cottage
Dormouse Cottage
Gamekeeper's Cottage
Guildhall
Honeysuckle Dream Cottage
Honeysuckle III
Leagrave Cottage
Mayflower House
Oak Lodge
Olde York Toll
Ploughman's Cottage
Rose Cottage, Skirsgill
Rowan Lodge
Vanbrugh Lodge
Wycombe Toll House

STUDLEY ROYAL COLLECTION

Banqueting House
Fountains Abbey
Octagon Tower
St. Mary's Church
Temple of Piety

VICTORIAN SHOPS COLLECTION

Apothecary
Bookshop
Haberdashery
Horologist
Jeweller
Pawnbroker
The Tailor

VILLAGE SHOPS COLLECTION

The Baker's Shop
The China Shop
The Greengrocer's
Jones the Butcher
Penny Sweets
The Toy Shop

WELSH COLLECTION

Brecon Bach
Bro Dawel
Hermitage
St. Govan's Chapel
Tudor Merchant
Ugly House

CLOWNS

ALPHONSE

Little is known about the set of five clowns which were produced between 1983 and 1984. Alphonse has recorded sales of less than 100 pieces.

Colour: Red jacket, dark brown trousers, mustard shoes
Size: 5 ½", 14.0 cm
Backstamp: A-1
Introduced: 1983
Discontinued: 1984

Description	Can. $	U.S. $	U.K. £
Alphonse	2,250.00	1,500.00	425.00

BUSTER

Buster has recorded sales of less than 100 pieces.

Colour: Black hat, light brown trousers, brown jacket
Size: 4 ½", 11.0 cm
Backstamp: A-1
Introduced: 1983
Discontinued: 1984

Description	Can. $	U.S. $	U.K. £
Buster	2,250.00	1,500.00	425.00

CLARENCE

As with Alphonse, Buster, Danny and Emile, little is known about Clarence. Sales are believed to have been very low, with possibly less than 100 pieces being sold.

Colour: Black jacket, light brown trousers, black shoes
Size: 4 ½", 11.0 cm
Backstamp: A-1
Introduced: 1983
Discontinued: 1984

Description	Can. $	U.S. $	U.K. £
Clarence	2,250.00	1,500.00	425.00

DANNY

Originally wearing a red jacket and leaning forwards with his hands on his stomach, Danny was remodelled with a beige jacket, a large yellow and blue tie, and leaning backwards with his hands on his stomach. Recorded sales of the original version are less than 100 pieces, and even though more pieces were made of the restyled version, it is still rare.

Style 1

Style 2

EMILE

Originally, Emile was alone and the base of the model was larger. In the remodelled version, Emile has a dog with him and the base is smaller. Emile is dressed all in white with black trim. Recorded sales of the original version are less than 100 pieces, and even though more pieces were made of the restyled version, it is still rare.

Style 1

Style 2

Description	Size	Backstamp	Intro.	Discon.	Can. $	U.S. $	U.K. £
Danny Style 1	5 ½", 13 cm	A-1	1983	1983	3,750.00	2,500.00	425.00
Danny Style 2	5 ½", 13 cm	C	1983	1984	2,250.00	1,500.00	375.00
Emile Style 1	6", 15 cm	A-1	1983	1983	3,750.00	2,500.00	475.00
Emile Style 2	5", 12.5 cm	C	1983	1984	2,250.00	1,500.00	375.00

DOMINIQUE GAULT

A range of flat-back houses were introduced in 1995, designed by Dominique Gault. There are two main series available: the London series and the Provence series. The main pieces are all made of resin. Complementing the series are a range of miniature characters, furniture, trees, wells and display bases which are made of metal and hand-painted.

THE LONDON COLLECTION

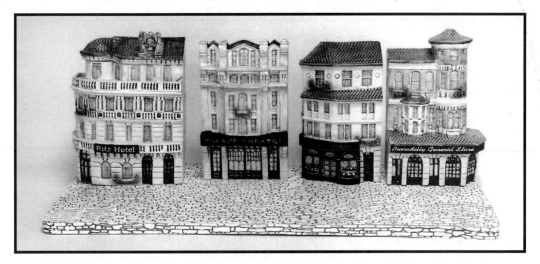

Left to right: Ritz Hotel, Palace Theatre, Bond Street Jewellers, Picadilly General Store

Description	Can. $	U.S. $	U.K. £
Bond Street Jewellers	N.A.	N.A.	19.95
Burlington Bakery	N.A.	N.A.	24.95
Florist	N.A.	N.A.	16.50
Grocery	N.A.	N.A.	14.95
Grosvenor Antiques	N.A.	N.A.	19.95
Kings Arms, The	N.A.	N.A.	19.95
London Tavern, The	N.A.	N.A.	16.50
Palace Theatre	N.A.	N.A.	24.95
Piccadilly General Store	N.A.	N.A.	24.95
Porch	N.A.	N.A.	14.95
Post Office	N.A.	N.A.	24.95
Red Lion, The	N.A.	N.A.	16.50
Regent Pharmacy	N.A.	N.A.	19.95
Ritz Hotel	N.A.	N.A.	29.95
Savoy, The	N.A.	N.A.	16.50
Scottish House	N.A.	N.A.	29.95
Sherlock Holmes, The	N.A.	N.A.	16.50
St. Paul's Bookshop	N.A.	N.A.	19.95
Tea Shop	N.A.	N.A.	19.95
Trafalgar Terrace Gift Set	N.A.	N.A.	99.95

THE PROVENCE COLLECTION

Left to right: Epicerie, The Bell Tower, Hotel d'Azur

Description	Can. $	U.S. $	U.K. £
Antiquites	N.A.	N.A.	16.95
Auberge	N.A.	N.A.	12.95
Bar des amis	N.A.	N.A.	7.95
Bell Tower, The	N.A.	N.A.	12.95
Bistrot des Artistes	N.A.	N.A.	19.95
Blanchisserie	N.A.	N.A.	16.95
Boulangerie	N.A.	N.A.	16.95
Double House with Porch	N.A.	N.A.	12.95
Ecole	N.A.	N.A.	16.95
Epicerie	N.A.	N.A.	16.95
Fleuriste	N.A.	N.A.	12.95
Hotel d'Azur	N.A.	N.A.	19.95
Hotel	N.A.	N.A.	19.95
House with Bench	N.A.	N.A.	7.95
House with climbing vine	N.A.	N.A.	12.95
House with Porch	N.A.	N.A.	16.95
La Poste	N.A.	N.A.	16.95
La Provence	N.A.	N.A.	16.95
Librairie	N.A.	N.A.	19.95
Mairie	N.A.	N.A.	12.95
Patisserie	N.A.	N.A.	19.95
Pharmacie	N.A.	N.A.	19.95
Pigeon House	N.A.	N.A.	7.95
Poterie	N.A.	N.A.	16.95
Salon de the	N.A.	N.A.	12.95
Small House	N.A.	N.A.	7.95
Small Porch, The	N.A.	N.A.	7.95
La Place Cezanne Gift Set	N.A.	N.A.	84.95

LAND OF LEGENDS

Lilliput Lane introduced the following Land of Legend ranges in the late 1980s: Bears Like Us; Castles; Dream Dragons; Ethelred Flametail; Genies; Jesters, Wizards and Dragons; Swan Princess; and Under the Hedge (Folk). The partnership between David Tate and Bill Dodd desolved in the early 1990s. Bill Dodd then opened up a separate company, known as The Land of Legend Studios, which continued some of the above ranges. The company is now known as Collectable World Studios. Early Land of Legend pieces carry a trademark of 5 Ls (Lilliput Lane Land of Legend Limited) and have been collected by Lilliput Lane collectors because of this. Land of Legend pieces carry only 2 Ls (Land of Legend). The following pages contain listings of the pieces produced under the Land of Legend name as well as photographic examples of the range if we have any available. Since the castles are of particular interest to Lilliput Lane cottage collectors, we have included pricing tables for this section. We ask that collectors having further information on the Land of Legend pieces to forward it to our Toronto editorial offices (see front of book for address).

Schloss Rheinjungfrau

BEARS LIKE US

This series was introduced in the late 1980s and discontinued in the early 1990s.

Name	Size	Name	Size
Bear With A Sore Head	3 ¾", 10.0 cm	Safe and Sound	4 ¼",11.0 cm
Christening	4 ¼", 11.0 cm	See You Soon	4 ¾", 12.5 cm
Easter Teddy	4 ¾", 12.0 cm	Sporting Teddies	3 ½", 10.0 cm
First Kiss	3 ½", 10.5 cm	Teddy Bear Band	5 ½", 14.0 cm
Get Well Soon	3 ½", 10.0 cm	Teddy Occupations	Unknown
Major League	3 ½", 10.0 cm	Welcome Home	Unknown
Message Bears	Unknown	You're a Star	3 ½", 10.0 cm

CASTLES

These castles were produced from the mid 1980s until 1988-89.

From left to right: The Golden Chalice, The Ransomed King, Schloss Rheinjungfrau,
The Sleeping Princess

Description	Introduced	Discontinued	Can. $	U.S. $	U.K. £
Exiled Prince	Mid-1980s	1988	350.00	225.00	160.00
Golden Chalice	Mid-1980s	1988	300.00	200.00	140.00
Ransomed King	Mid-1980s	1988	400.00	250.00	180.00
Red Knight	Mid-1980s	1988	350.00	225.00	150.00
Schloss Neuschwanstein	1988	1989	1,100.00	850.00	550.00
Schloss Rheinjungfrau	1988	1990	875.00	575.00	375.00
Sleeping Princess	Mid-1980s	1988	350.00	225.00	150.00
Sorcerer's Retreat	Mid-1980s	1988	350.00	225.00	140.00
Wizard's Tower	1988	1989	400.00	250.00	170.00

DREAM DRAGONS

Introduced in the 1980s, the Dream Dragons Series was retired on September 30th, 1991.

From left to right: Bathtime, Especially For You, Hazy Daze, Love Letter

Name	Size	Name	Size
Bathtime	1 ¾", 4.5 cm	Lipstick and Lashes	2 ¾", 7.0 cm
Breakout	2 1/3", 6.0 cm	Little Sister	3 ½", 9.0 cm
Double Trouble	2 ¼", 5.5 cm	Love Letters	1 ¾", 4.5 cm
Dream Baby	1 ½", 4.0 cm	Off to School	2 ¾", 7.0 cm
Especially For You	2 ½", 6.5 cm	Party Time	3 ½", 9.0 cm
Hazy Daze	1 ¾", 4.5 cm	She Loves Me	2 1/3", 6.0 cm
Help	2 ½", 6.5 cm	Stay Cool	2 1/3", 6.0 cm
Hi There	2 ½", 6.5 cm	Strike One	4 ½", 11.5 cm
Kiss, The	3 1/3", 8.5 cm	Wild Wheels	3 ¼", 8.0 cm

ETHELRED FLAMETAIL

The Ethelred Flametail range is a series of figurines from Ethelred's birth through all of his adventures. The series also includes various dwarfs and goblins he encounters along the way. The entire range is sculpted by Tom Raine.

From left to right: The Black Knight, The Dandy, The Merchant, Mr. Bonzer, Princess Nyneve

Name	Size	Name	Size
Black Knight,The	4", 10.0 cm	Princess Nyneve	4 ½", 11.5 cm
Early Days	3 ½", 8.75 cm	Ranol	2 ½", 6.5 cm
Eureka	4", 10.0 cm	School Days	5", 12.5 cm
Flying Lesson, The	4 ½", 11.5 cm	Swamp Bird, The	3", 7.5 cm
Hello World	2 ½", 6.5 cm	Tender Loving Care	4 ½", 11.5 cm
Jeremy the Dandy	5", 12.5 cm	Three Cheers	7", 17.5 cm
Lift Off	7", 17.5 cm	Tree Topper	3 ½", 8.75 cm
Magic Water	4 ½", 11.5 cm	Troll, The	4", 10.0 cm
Merchant, The	4", 10.0 cm	Wily Wizard, The	5", 12.5 cm
Mr. Bonzer	4", 10.0 cm	Young Inventor, The	4", 10.0 cm
On the Runway	3", 7.5 cm		

WIZARDS, JESTERS, DRAGONS

Designed by Hap Henriksen, this series is inspired by classical mythology and legends.

Wizards	*Jesters*	*Dragons*
Balance of Truth	His Majestic, Majesty Baldrick the	Dragon of the Golden Hoard
Dragon Master	Incredibly Simple	Guardian of the Keep
Foreshadow The Seer	Jockomo	Hatched
Howland The Wise	Jollies Pitchbelly	Let Sleeping Dragons Lie
Lackey the Apprentice	La Di Da Too Goode	Leviathan
Merlyn Wizard Watcher	Merry Andrew	Wyvern
Merryweather Sunlighter	Puck	
Moriah	Smack Thickwit	
Mydwyntee	Twit Coxcombe	
Ponder The Quest	Ursala	
Repository of Magic		
Rimbaugh		
Thorbauld		

SWAN PRINCESS

This series is comprised of five castles and five keepers. It was retired at the end of 1989.

Castles	*Keepers*
Castle of the Masters of the Forest	Alarch Silver Beard
Castle of the Swan Princess	Aspard
Dragon's Lair, The	Kobold Walter
Judges Retreat, The	Palace of the Emperor Child, The
(Castle of the Lord Protector)	Rotundo the Tuscan
	Salix the Bold

UNDER THE HEDGE

This collection is designed by Hap Henrikson and Real Musgrave. The entire range was discontinued at the end of 1991.

A Winter's Friend	Father Christmas	Sparkling Clean
Artful Bowler, The	Favourite Uncle	Spotting Strays
Artist, The	Jelly Sandwiches	Stemms and Bowles Ltd.
Aunt Violet & Pudgy	Junius Bug	Sunday Afternoon
Baskets of Love	Just Guarding the Hamper	Sword in the Stone
Carefully Wrapped	Keep Your Tail Warm	Tea Table, The
Counter Sign	Mighty Percy at the Bat	Trapped on the Summit
Cousin Bertie's Revenge	Miss Amelia's Turn	Waiting for a Light
Cousin Reggie	Out of Town Guest, The	Watching the Herd
Deck the Halls	Slow and Steady	Wicket Keeper, The
Fashion Plate, The	Snowballs & Top Hats	

Paint Kit

COMMEMORATIVE MEDALLION

This medallion was issued to diners at the 1989 South Bend collectors dinner. This was the first gift given to collectors and guests. The following year saw the start of the cottage giveaways. The medallion is shown here in it's original case.

Description	Height	Intro.	Discon.	Can. $	U.S. $	U.K. £
Medallion	2", 5.1 cm	1989	1989	300.00	200.00	130.00

FOSSIL

Introduced at the September 1995 Annual Fair at Grimsthorpe Castle, this fossil was given to children aged three to seven who successfully answered how many fossils were shown in the gypsum cave exhibit. Many collectors and dealers are unaware this item exists as very few were made.

Description	Height	Intro.	Discon.	Can. $	U.S. $	U.K. £
Fossil	3", 7.6 cm	1995	1995	650.00	450.00	300.00

GULLIVER 1986

Gulliver's Travels was written by Jonathan Swift in 1726 as a satire on contemporary politics. Lemuel Gulliver, the hero of the tale, was shipwrecked on the island of Lilliput, the inhabitants of which were 6 inches high. Introduced in February 1986, the model shows Gulliver tied to the ground by the Lilliputians. Initial production pieces had the backstamp positioned on the front, although at some point the backstamp was repositioned on the rear (it is thought that collectors were unhappy with the positioning of the backstamp on the front). Version 1 was available in two colourways —Gulliver's coat is either red or black.

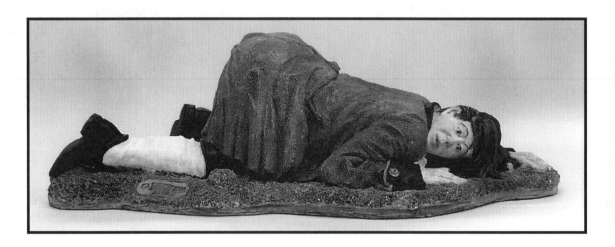

Description	Size	Backstamp	Intro	Discon.	Can. $	U.S. $	U.K. £
BS Front (red)	3", 7.5 cm	F	1986	1986	900.00	600.00	375.00
BS Front (black)	3", 7.5 cm	F	1986	1986 Sold at Lilliput Lane Auction (1996) £450.00			
BS Rear	3", 7.5 cm	F	1986	1986	750.00	500.00	350.00

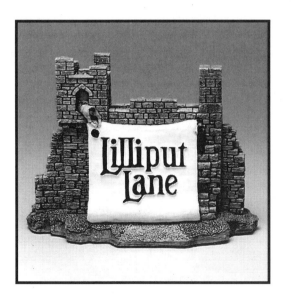

GULLIVER'S GATE

Miscellaneous

Gulliver's Gate is based upon crenellated stone walls at Kirkoswald near Penrith, Cumbria. Gulliver's Gate could be regarded as a point-of-sale item, but it has proved popular with collectors as did Scroll on the Wall.

Size:	3 ¼", 8.0 cm
Backstamp:	O
Introduced:	1994
Discontinued:	1997

Description	Can. $	U.S. $	U.K. £
Gulliver's Gate	40.00	30.00	20.00

HONEYSUCKLE TRINKET BOX

Based on the newly built visitor's centre, this piece was only available at the Penrith visitor's centre from January 1997 onwards. The roof detaches to reveal a square hollow area which contains a title deed rolled up with a thin red ribbon.

Size: 3 ½", 9cm
Backstamp: V
Introduced: 1997
Discontinued: Current

Description	Can. $	U.S. $	U.K. £
Honeysuckle Trinket	N.A.	N.A.	N.A.

LITTLE LOST DOG

Collectors Club

Little Lost Dog shows a sheepdog standing beside a signpost indicating the way to London and the way to Penrith (the home of Lilliput Lane). The model was offered as a free gift to members who joined the Collectors Club from March, 1987 to February, 1988. Two versions were produced. Originally, the hole in the circle at the top of the post was smaller and the direction pointers closer to the top of the post. The second version had a larger hole in the centre of the circle, and the lettering appeared grey in comparison to the original. The pointers are lower down on the post. The pointers were welded/soldered onto the post on version 1 and some versions of this are very crude. It is vastly improved on version 2 (the join is not as noticable). Just under 7,000 pieces of Little Lost Dog were produced and given to members during its production life. Some (but not all) of the pieces distributed contained a verse inside the box:

Little Lost Dog
Our little dog sat by the post
The words he couldn't unravel,
He unfortunately took the London Road
And far he had to travel.
But now he's safely found his home
I'm very glad to say,
And never more will search or roam,
Now he's with you, we're sure he'll stay.

Version	Size	Backstamp	Intro.	Discon.	Can. $	U.S. $	U.K. £
1 - Small hole	2 ½", 6.5 cm	None	1987	1988	600.00	400.00	275.00
2 - Large hole	2 ½", 6.5 cm	None	1987	1988	450.00	300.00	225.00

LILLIPUT LANE MARKET STALL

Limited Edition by Cardew Design Teapots

Lilliput Lane and Cardew Design joined forces in 1996 to produce a limited edition teapot. The minature cottages are made of resin, the teapot of fine clay china. Mostly used for decorative purposes, this is no doubt a collectors item of the future. Cardew Design with a strong work force of 200 plus, are proving to be a strong competitor in the collectable market, with a collectors club rapidly growing throughout the world.

Description	Size	Backstamp	Intro	Discon.	Can. $	U.S. $	U.K. £
Teapot	8", 23.0 cm	N.A.	1996	1996	450.00	300.00	160.00

PENNY LANES

Miniature Town Buildings

Penny Lanes is a set of miniature models of town buildings, such as houses and shops. These models were never released into the retail market, hence there is very little information available about them. The models are not scaled down versions of the Street Scenes buildings which were produced in the same year. Due to the rarity of Penny Lanes, should any of them come onto the secondary market they would certainly command a high premium.

Description	Size	Backstamp	Can. $	U.S. $	U.K. £
Penny Lanes	(approx.) 2 - 2 ½", 5 - 6.5 cm	Unknown	1,5000.00	1,000.00	700.00

Note: Price listed is per piece. Collectors having any information on this set is asked to please contact our editorial offices in Toronto.

MUGS

Lilliput Lane introduced its first series of mugs in 1995. The three mugs in this series are: Periwinkle, Puffin Row and Waterside Mill. The second series of mugs, which includes Cotman Cottage, Old Mother Hubbards, Tea Caddy and a second version of Waterside Mill, were introduced in 1996.

Series One

Description	Size	Intro.	Discon.	Can. $	U.S. $	U.K. £
Periwinkle	Unknown	1995	Current	N.A.	N.A.	5.95
Puffin Row	Unknown	1995	Current	N.A.	N.A.	5.95
Waterside Mill	Unknown	1995	Current	N.A.	N.A.	5.95

Series Two

Description	Size	Intro.	Discon.	Can. $	U.S. $	U.K. £
Cotman Cottage	Unknown	1996	Current	N.A.	N.A.	5.95
Old Mother Hubbards	Unknown	1996	Current	N.A.	N.A.	5.95
Tea Caddy	Unknown	1996	Current	N.A.	N.A.	5.95
Waterside Mill	Unknown	1996	Current	N.A.	N.A.	5.95

UNTITLED KIT MODELS 1991

Paint Your Own

Introduced in September, 1991 at the Lilliput Lane Event at Ragley Hall. The kit is comprised of a box of fifteen paints. This model was available through the Collectors Club and at the Visitors Centre in Penrith until its retirement at the 1992 Event held at Althorpe Estate. This "Paint Your Own" is the hardest one to find. The value of this piece is considerably more if found unpainted.

Size:	Unknown
Backstamp:	L
Introduced:	1991
Discontinued:	1992

Description	Can. $	U.S. $	U.K. £
1991	400.00	300.00	200.00

UNTITLED KIT MODEL 1992

Paint Your Own

Introduced at the Lilliput Lane Event held at Althorpe Estate in September 1992. It was available with fifteen paints. This piece was obtainable through selected events held throughout the following year, also at the Visitors Centre in Penrith. Retired at the Lilliput Annual Event in 1993 held at Harewood House near Leeds. "Paint Your Owns" are worth more unpainted.

Size:	2 ½", 6.7 cm
Backstamp:	M-2
Introduced:	1992
Discontinued:	1993

Description	Can. $	U.S. $	U.K. £
1992	325.00	250.00	120.00

UNTITLED KIT MODEL 1993

Paint Your Own

Introduced at the Annual Fair held at Harewood House near Leeds in September 1993. After a year and up until 1995 it has been available at events held throughout the years at the Collectors Club and the Visitors Centre in Penrith. "Paint Your Owns" are worth more unpainted.

Size:	2 ½", 6.0 cm
Backstamp:	N
Introduced:	1993
Discontinued:	Current

Description	Can. $	U.S. $	U.K. £
1993	225.00	150.00	75.00

PLAQUES AND PLATES

In the late 1980s Lilliput Lane produced a range of wall plaques. More than forty-five plaques were produced covering a variety of subjects, some of them were framed, others were unframed. The unframed plaques were produced in varying sizes, with some being small, some medium and some large; the framed plaques had a frame size of 7 ½ in. by 9 in. (19 cm by 23 cm). All of the plaques were withdrawn between 1992 and 1993. They do not seem to have been particularly popular and some can still be obtained at retail outlets.

Lilliput Lane has made several ventures into the plate market. American landscape artist Ray Day, designed a series of plates to complement the American Landmarks collection of cottages. These plates were commissioned by Gift Link of Maryland. In conjunction with The Franklin Mint, Lilliput Lane produced a series of six collectors plates. Through the Hamilton Mint, Lilliput Lane marketed a series of 3-D plates made of resin, as well as two Calendar Cottage plates made of resin.

PLAQUES

Seven series of plaques were produced in total. The series are listed below and those we have photographs for are pictured on the following pages. We ask that collectors having any information on these plaques contact us at our editorial office in Toronto.

COUNTRYSIDE SCENE COLLECTION

Bottle Kiln
Cornish Tin Mine
Country Inn
Cumbrian Farmhouse
Lighthouse
Norfolk Windmill
Oast House
Old Smithy
Parish Church
Post Office
Village School
Watermill

ENGLISH COLLECTION (framed)

Ashdown Hall (illustrated)
Battle View
Catslide Cottage
Coombe Cot (illustrated)
Fell View
Flintfields
Huntingdon House
Jubilee Lodge
Stourside
Treven Cove

IRISH COLLECTION (framed)

Ballyteeg House
Crockuna Croft
Pearse's Cottage
Shannons Bank

LAKELAND BRIDGE COLLECTION

Aira Force
Ashness Bridge
Birks Bridge
Bridge House
Hartsop Packhorse
Stockley Bridge

LONDON COLLECTION

Big Ben
Buckingham Palace
Houses of Parliament
Piccadilly Circus
St. Paul's Cathedral
Tower Bridge
Tower of London
Trafalgar Square

PAINT YOUR OWN NURSERY PLAQUES

Gingerbread House
Hansel and Gretal
Hey Diddle Diddle
Old Woman Who Lived In a Shoe
Owl and the Pussycat
Three Bears
Three Little Pigs

SCOTTISH COLLECTION (framed)

Barra Blackhouse
Fife Ness
Kyle Point
Preston Oat Mill

SCOTTISH COLLECTION (Unframed)

Cobble Combe Cottage (medium) (illustrated)
Lower Brockhampton (large) (illustrated)
Somerset Springtime (large)
Stoneywell Lea (small)
Wishing Well Cottage (medium) (illustrated)
Woodside Farm (small)

ASHDOWN HALL
English Collection (framed)

Size:	7 ½″ x 9″, 19.0 cm x 23.0 cm
Backstamp:	H-1
Introduced:	ca. 1989
Discontinued:	ca. 1992-1993

Description	Can. $	U.S. $	U.K. £
Ashdown Hall	200.00	150.00	100.00

COBBLE COMBE COTTAGE
Scottish Collection (unframed)

Size:	Medium
Backstamp:	H-1
Introduced:	ca. 1989
Discontinued:	ca. 1992-1993

Description	Can. $	U.S. $	U.K. £
Cobble Combe	150.00	100.00	75.00

COMBE COT
English Collection (framed)

Size:	7 ½″ x 9″, 19.0 cm x 23.0 cm
Backstamp:	H-1
Introduced:	ca. 1989
Discontinued:	ca. 1992-1993

Description	Can. $	U.S. $	U.K. £
Combe Cot	200.00	150.00	100.00

HONEYSUCKLE PLAQUES

Honeysuckle Cottage is located in Oakhanger, Hampshire. There are two variations of the Honeysuckle plaque. On May 18th, 1996, Lilliput had an open day at their studios in Penrith to celebrate the 10th anniversary of the Collectors Club. 1,500 Honeysuckle plaques with "Open Day Special" stamped on the back were available on that day only. There are doves flying from the dovecot in the garden. The other Honeysuckle plaque was available to personal callers to the Lilliput Visitor Centre in Penrith. This piece is stamped "Collectors Club 10th Anniversary Special," and was available until February 1997. Unlike the One Day Special, this plaque lacks the doves.

Open Day Special (left), 10th Anniversary Special (right)

Open Day Special (left), 10th Anniversary Special (right)

Description	Size	Backstamp	Intro.	Discon.	Can. $	U.S. $	U.K. £
Open Day	5 ½" x 8 ½"	O-2	1996	1996	350.00	225.00	150.00
10th Anniversary	5 ½" x 8 ½"	O-2	1996	1997	300.00	200.00	95.00

LOWER BROCKHAMPTON
Scottish Collection (unframed)

Size: Large
Backstamp: H-1
Introduced: c.1989
Discontinued: c.1992-1993

Description	Can. $	U.S. $	U.K. £
Lower Brockhampton	300.00	200.00	140.00

WISHING WELL COTTAGE
Scottish Collection (unframed)

Size: 7 ½" x 9", 19.0 cm x 23.0 cm
Backstamp: H-1
Introduced: ca. 1989
Discontinued: ca. 1992-1993

Description	Can. $	U.S. $	U.K. £
Wishing Well	125.00	75.00	65.00

LONDON COLLECTION PLAQUES

There are seven plates which comprise the London Series: Big Ben, Buckingham Palace, Houses of Parliament, St. Paul's Cathedral, Tower Bridge, Tower of London and Trafalgar Square. These items will be phased out during 1997.

Buckingham Palace (left), Houses of Parliament (right)

St. Paul's Cathederal (left), Tower Bridge (right)

Description	Intro.	Discon.	Can. $	U.S. $	U.K. £
Big Ben	1995	1997	50.00	35.00	25.00
Buckingham Palace	1995	1997	50.00	35.00	25.00
Houses of Parliament	1995	1997	50.00	35.00	25.00
Picadilly Circus	1995	1997	50.00	35.00	25.00
St. Paul's Cathederal	1995	1997	50.00	35.00	25.00
Tower Bridge	1995	1997	50.00	35.00	25.00
Tower of London	1995	1997	50.00	35.00	25.00
Trafalagar Square	1995	1997	50.00	35.00	25.00

PAINT YOUR OWN NURSERY PLAQUES

There are seven plaques available in the Nursery Paint Your Own series: Gingerbread House, Hansel and Gretal, Hey Diddle Diddle, Old Woman Who Lived In a Shoe, Owl and the Pussycat, the Three Bears and the Three Little Pigs. All of these pieces came unpainted. Also available is a painting kit, comprised of an artists palette, brushes and paint. They are available through the Collectors Clubs and the Lilliput Lane Visitors Centre in Penrith. It is not known when these plaques were discontinued, as most of the plaques seem to remain in production until stocks "sell-out" and the new plaque(s) are introduced. As with all "paint your owns," they are worth more if left unpainted.

Left to Right: Gingerbread House, Hansel and Gretal, Owl & the Pussycat, Three Little Pigs

Description	Size	Backstamp	Intro.	Discon.	Can. $	U.S. $	U.K. £
Gingerbread House	6 ½", 16.2 cm	L	1993	Unknown	200.00	150.00	100.00
Hansel & Gretal	4 ¾", 12.0 cm	L	1993	1997	40.00	30.00	20.00
Hey Diddle Diddle	4 ½" 11.5 cm	Unknown	1997	Current	N.A.	N.A.	8.50
Old Woman . . .	5", 12.6 cm	M	1994	Unknown	120.00	90.00	60.00
Owl & the Pussycat	4 ½, 11.4 cm	0-2	1996	Current	N.A.	N.A.	15.00
Three Bears	5 ¼", 13.2 cm	K-2	1992	Unknown	350.00	225.00	175.00
Three Little Pigs	5 ½", 13.3 cm	K-2	1992	1997	30.00	20.00	15.00

PLATES
AMERICAN LANDMARK SERIES PLATES

Following on from his work on the American Landmarks collection, in 1990 Ray Day designed plates related to the American Landmarks. The plates were commissioned by Gift Link Inc., from Columbia, Maryland, and were limited editions of 5,000 pieces. The five subjects were: Country Church, Meramic Caverns, Perennial Favourites, Riverside Chapel and Rock City. The plates were not available in the UK, and only two (Country Church and Riverside Chapel) are still available in the USA, the others being fully subscribed.

Country Church

Country Church backstamp

Riverside Chapel

Riverside Chapel backstamp

Description	Diameter	Intro.	Discon.	Can. $	U.S.$	U.K.£
Country Church	3 ½", 8.6 cm	1992	Ltd. Ed.	150.00	100.00	50.00
Meramic Caverns	3 ½", 8.6 cm	1992	Ltd. Ed.	200.00	150.00	75.00
Perennial Favourites	3 ½", 8.6 cm	1992	Ltd. Ed.	200.00	150.00	75.00
Riverside Chapel	3 ½", 8.6 cm	1992	Ltd. Ed.	150.00	100.00	50.00
Rock City	3 ½", 8.6 cm	1992	Ltd. Ed.	200.00	150.00	75.00

THE CALENDAR COTTAGES OF ENGLAND

Introduced in 1996 through the Hamilton Gallery (Lilliput's own mail order company and test market), this pair of plates are cast in resin. It is anticipated that if sales are good these will become part of the general range. The Hamilton Gallery has now formed a partnership with the Bradford Exchange.

Welford-on-Avon, front

Welford-on-Avon, back

Wherwell Green, front

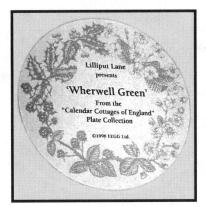

Wherwell Green, back

Description	Diameter	Intro.	Discon.	Can. $	U.S. $	U.K. £
Welford-On-Avon	6", 15.5 cm	1996	Current	80.00	60.00	40.00
Wherwell Green	6", 15.5 cm	1996	Current	80.00	60.00	40.00

COCA-COLA™ COUNTRY FOUR SEASONS SERIES

These plates were designed by Ray Day and are companion pieces to the Coca-Cola™ series of cottages.

Catch of the Day

Ice Cold Coke

Spring Has Sprung

When I Was Your Age

Description	Diameter	Intro.	Discon.	Can. $	U.S. $	U.K. £
Catch of the Day	8", 20.3 cm	1998	Current	45.00	40.00	N.A.
Ice Cold Coke	8", 20.3 cm	1998	Current	45.00	40.00	N.A.
Spring Has Sprung	8", 20.3 cm	1998	Current	45.00	40.00	N.A.
When I Was Your Age	8", 20.3 cm	1998	Current	45.00	40.00	N.A.

COLLECTORS PLATES

In 1994, Lilliput Lane produced their first-ever collectors plate for Franklin Mint. Entitled Wishing Well Cottage, the 8-in. (20 ¼ cm) diameter plate was limited to the number of orders received by the closing date of October 15th, 1994. Two years later, five further plates were produced to complete the set, which comprises of: Convent in the Woods, The Gables, Granny Smiths, Paradise Lodge, Titmouse Cottage and Wishing Well Cottage. The plates were limited to 45 firing days, and therefore production and editions depend on orders received. These plates are produced in fine porcelain.

Convent in the Woods

The Gables

Granny Smiths

Paradise Lodge

Titmouse Cottage

Wishing Well Cottage

Description	Size	Intro.	Discon.	Can. $	U.S. $	U.K. £
Convent in the Woods	8", 20.5 cm	1996	1996	50.00	35.00	25.00
The Gables	8", 20.5 cm	1996	1996	50.00	35.00	25.00
Granny Smiths	8", 20.5 cm	1996	1996	50.00	35.00	25.00
Paradise Lodge	8", 20.5 cm	1996	1996	50.00	35.00	25.00
Titmouse Cottage	8", 20.5 cm	1996	1996	50.00	35.00	25.00
Wishing Well Cottage	8", 20.5 cm	1994	1995	90.00	60.00	45.00

3-D PLATES

Made of resin, these plates could be obtained through the Hamilton Mint, UK division at the end of 1995 through newspaper advertisements. It was not offered to retailers until the beginning of 1996. Shortly after production the plates were discontinued. It is likely that poor sales figures caused their early retirement, although production problems could also be the reason. All plates measure 8 inches (20.5 cm) in diameter.

Cotman Cottage

Description	Backstamp	Intro.	Discon.	Can. $	U.S. $	U.K. £
Cotman Cottage	N-2	1996	1996	280.00	200.00	140.00
Paradise Lodge	N-2	1996	1996	325.00	250.00	160.00
Rose Cottage	N-2	1996	1996	400.00	300.00	200.00

SIGNS

COUNTRY CANVAS
Coca-Cola™ Country Collection

This traditional style "billboard," found in most rural midwestern towns, was designed by Ray Day. Cast in resin and manufactured in Ireland, this piece is only available in North America.

Size:	2 ½", 5.7 cm
Backstamp:	O-2
Introduced:	1997
Discontinued:	Current

Description	Can. $	U.S. $	U.K. £
Country Canvas	N.A.	15.50	N.A.

PACKHORSE BRIDGE
Collectors Club

When the Lilliput Lane Collectors Club was launched in March 1986, Packhorse Bridge was offered as the free gift to all members joining in that Club year, a tradition that still continues today. Based upon a Lake District structure, this version of Packhorse Bridge differed from the North American dealer sign inasmuch as the shield carried the wording "Official Collector Lilliput Lane," and the scroll design and wording underneath was omitted. In that first year, 5,000 people joined the Club.

Size:	1 ½", 3.5 cm
Backstamp:	E
Introduced:	1986
Discontinued:	1987

Description	Can. $	U.S. $	U.K. £
Packhorse Bridge	1,500.00	1,000.00	375.00

PACKHORSE BRIDGE
Dealer Sign

An accurate copy of a Lake District structure, Packhorse Bridge was originally produced as a dealer sign for use in the North American market. The shield carried the wording 'Lilliput Lane Ltd,' and in a scroll design underneath, the wording 'Parvus est Bellus' (which loosely translated means 'Small things are beautiful'). Retired in December 1985 for use as a dealer sign, Packhorse Bridge was then produced as a Collectors Club model in 1986.

Size:	1 3/8", 3.5 cm
Backstamp:	None
Introduced:	1985
Discontinued:	1985

Description	Can. $	U.S. $	U.K. £
Packhorse Bridge	900.00	600.00	475.00

SCROLL ON THE WALL

Scroll on the Wall shows the Lilliputians unfurling a banner which has the wording 'Lilliput Lane' upon it.

Size:	3 ¼", 8.0 cm
Backstamp:	E
Introduced:	1986
Discontinued:	1987

Description	Can. $	U.S. $	U.K. £
Scroll on the Wall	450.00	300.00	225.00

SIGN OF THE TIMES

American Landmarks

Sign of the Times recalls the early days of motoring in America when billboards were positioned alongside the two-lane roads, long before the advent of highways and interstates. When it was pointed out by Ray Day that the grass was too yellow, this was changed early in 1990. Approximately 200 pieces were produced with this yellow grass. Sold exclusively in the USA in first year of issue.

Variation	Size	Backstamp	Intro.	Discon.	Can. $	U.S. $	U.K. £
1 - Yellow grass	2 ¼", 5.5 cm	I-1	1990	1990	160.00	120.00	80.00
2 - Green grass	2 ¼", 5.5 cm	I-1	1990	1996	60.00	45.00	30.00

VANS

Lilliput Lane has produced a total of eight vans. Six of these belong to the Village Shop Collection — The Baker Shop, The China Shop, Greengrocers, Jones the Butcher, Penny Sweets and The Toy Shop. These vans were released shortly after their respective shop models. Lilliput Lane also produced a limited edition van for NALED (National Association of Limited Edition Dealers) and one to celebrate their own ten year anniversary in 1992.

Description	Colour	Intro.	Discon.	Can. $	U.S. $	U.K. £
10th Anniversary Van	Red and cream	1992	1992	150.00	100.00	75.00
Baker Shop Van	Green and white	1996	Current	N.A.	N.A.	12.00
China Shop Van	Blue	1996	Current	N.A.	N.A.	12.00
Greengrocers Van	Unknown	1994	1995	80.00	60.00	40.00
Jones the Butcher Van	Red and cream	1994	Current	N.A.	N.A.	12.00
NALED Van	Black	1992	Unknown	150.00	100.00	70.00
Penny Sweets Van	Unknown	1995	1995	80.00	60.00	40.00
Toy Shop Van	Red and yellow	1995	Current	N.A.	N.A.	12.00